HUMAN
POTENTIALITIES

HUMAN POTENTIALITIES

BY *Gardner Murphy*

Basic Books, Inc.

NEW YORK

To our grandchildren

I think it probable that civilization somehow will last as long as I care to look ahead—perhaps with smaller numbers, but perhaps also bred to greatness and splendor by science. I think it not improbable that man, like the grub that prepares a chamber for the winged thing it never has seen but is to be— that man may have cosmic destinies that he does not understand. And so beyond the vision of battling races and an impoverished earth I catch a dreaming glimpse of peace.

—Justice Oliver Wendell Holmes

Preface

This may seem to be an odd time in which to undertake long-range weather-forecasting for humanity. It seems uncertain whether we shall get through the next storm. There seems some reason, however, to believe that storms make a good basis for long-range thinking about human weather. If I can claim the companionship of Sir Thomas More in looking far ahead while in the midst of crisis, I shall ask no more.

There is, however, a new fund of knowledge about mankind, so amazing and breathtaking by virtue of the unprecedented acceleration of all the sciences in recent years that one may actually lay before one's readers some of the possibilities among which humanity must and will soon choose. It is an age of new knowledge and an age of many possible kinds of Utopias, and the urgency of the task is plain.

I believe that in this century and the next there is a serious possibility that thoughtful men and women may define the various kinds of future societies and the various kinds of individual lives which are realistically possible, and make conscious and voluntary choices.

"We do not live," said Groddeck; "we are lived." But we can learn to live, to study the latent potentialities of mankind, discover which ones are feasible and satisfying, and utilize science, education, and government to achieve them. I shall try to show why, under the conditions now coming into existence, it is improbable that knowledge or power can be kept in the hands of a few. When a few have made a beginning in asking about human potentialities, more and more of humanity will become interested and begin to participate in the choices.

There is no dearth of literature, from Utopias to science fiction, to tell mankind that life can be explosively new. My aim is a little different. I will let the physical scientists, biological scientists, and engineers describe man's future *environment*. My own hope here is to show what kind of things we shall need to know if we are to realize our potentialities *as human beings*. For this reason the future environment of man is considered only insofar as it is "foreseeable" (Sir George Thomson's word); and only insofar as its repercussions upon human nature are guessable. Indeed, even much that is human and is foreseeable is left out as being beyond our scope. This book is about the changing qualities of human individuals and their societies. Others can write a great deal better about the architecture of the future, atomic energy and its uses, automation, Basic English, city planning, cybernetics, diplomacy, the increasing life span, interplanetary travel, the managerial revolution, Marxism, the new pharmacology, psychoanalysis, world government, and a thousand other valuable themes. It is the human stuff that concerns me.

But I have believed for a long time that human nature is a reciprocity of what is inside the skin and what is outside; that it is definitely not "rolled up inside us" but our way of being one with our fellows and our world. I call this field theory, and have elsewhere spelled it out as well as I could.

I cannot, however, get away from it. In 1953 the Society for the Psychological Study of Social Issues asked me to give the Kurt Lewin Memorial lecture and I chose the topic, "Human Potentialities." When Arthur Rosenthal read that paper in 1954, he asked me if I would make these ideas into a book. This volume is the result.

My gratitude to him is great; likewise to the generous policy of the Menninger Foundation in encouraging me to escape for long periods into my half-formed thoughts; Dorothy Diehl did a superb job in preparing the manuscript. Lois Barclay Murphy is, as always, the chief sustainer of my efforts.

GARDNER MURPHY

Birchlea
Ashland, New Hampshire
August 1957

Contents

PART I

The First Human Nature

Chapter I

Our Twentieth-century Vantage Point

In the rollicking melodrama *The Skin of Our Teeth,* human history from Dawn Man to Manhattan Islander is conceived as a series of crises; magical hairbreadth escapes lead around one booby trap after another, and mankind muddles through to an awareness, an explicit confrontation, of his predicament. Man, if he is to be man at all, must somehow create and somehow escape his engines of destruction. He is the kind of animal that lives from one crisis to another, and it is his nature to surmount them. He will surmount those of the present century because he continues to be man.

A case could, indeed, be made for the view that man achieves some measure of understanding of himself only in facing crises; or we could adopt Toynbee's view that only by meeting challenges can he raise himself to a new level of creativeness. One might say that the time in which to think most productively about the future of mankind and what mankind can become is the period of direst threat to his existence, not the period of the opening plain with its vistas of expanding self-realization. Indeed, one would have much of history on one's side. Did not Plato's *Republic* emerge to the tune of the death rattle of the Greek city state? Did not Sir Thomas More's *Utopia* emerge as the unity of Western christendom gave way to modern nationalism? Did it not take a Civil War to create the colossal figure of Lincoln who, speaking in the midst of the whirlwind, could look ahead to a fulfillment of an American democratic destiny? Yet, though this book will deal with crisis, because this is a part of the very fulfillment of human potentialities, its emphasis is not upon crisis itself but upon the *potentialities which, in and through the crises of today and tomorrow, may find new fulfillment.*

• *The Nature of Today's Crisis*

The bombs that fell on Hiroshima and Nagasaki were toys compared with those now ready to be dropped at a moment's notice on the great cities of the world. In addition to the use of satellites and guided missiles, underground airstrips and submarines will soon provide launching points from which devastation can be spread, against which no adequate defense can be contrived. The circumstances which might lead the responsible decision-makers of the Soviet Union or the United States to launch an attack can scarcely be known to the outsider. In particular, the consequence of diplomatic or military defeat in any of several parts of the world might lead one or the other chief of state (or their lieutenants) to decide that retaliation is necessary and that risks must be taken. Where the duel will start is unknowable. So appalling are the prospects in terms of human destruction, suffering, chaos, destitution, and degradation that we automatically turn away and hope somehow to keep a certain number of months or years ahead of our rival, as he hopes to keep ahead of us, each grimly aware of risks too awful to be uttered.

It is true that as we pen these lines there are, here and there, some furtive signs of hope in terms of agreement upon the reduction or elimination of certain types of nuclear fuel testing, and for every such sign of hope we may be deeply grateful. We cannot, however, with any reasonable safety pretend that an agreement on high strategy for peace will put an end to a very long period of precarious and desperate uncertainty. It is as necessary for the momentum of the revolutionary Soviet world to keep moving as it is for the United States and the nations of the West to defend themselves. It is equally clear that an aggressive momentum is far easier to maintain than a posture of continuous, essentially static defense; equally plain that a large number of the neutrals of the world, whose power in Asia and Africa grows

daily, are more impressed by movement than by defense, more
ready to accept a counsel of risk-taking than of acquiescence in
the essentially defensive pose recommended to them by the big
brother of the West. It is more and more apparent that, over the
ease and casualness of Western civilization as a whole, a growing
shadow is thrown by the wings of a moving eagle whose magnificent vitality and power speaks both through peoples' movements
on the one hand and through the terror of concentration camps
and secret police on the other. Inspiring and terrifying, exalting
and shocking as the various aspects of the peoples' movements of
China and Russia are to the men of the West, they have, from
another framework, a vitality with which we of the Western tradition must be capable of coping or we are undone. We cannot
answer with postures of defense or promises of massive retaliation
alone.

Yet, does it not look indeed as if we were hopelessly trapped
between two equally awful alternatives? On the one hand is the
gigantic struggle between two powers so tremendous that either
one can lay waste and scorch beyond recognition the very body
of the other. The second alternative would be a form of capitulation, however gracious or ungracious, by which we would gradually yield the world to the authoritarian system of a small oligarchy equipped with all the attendant machinery of the secret
police, the concentration camp, the regulation of the press, the
indoctrination of the minds of children in terms of a highly dogmatic and authoritarian creed. Aside from the easy escape through
wishful thinking, is there in point of fact any possibility other
than these? If this much is faced in its full realism, and the
premises maintained that giants must either live as giants or die
as giants, there appears to be no escape for any of us but to hide
in the hills in the hope that radioactive fallout will somehow not
drift into our caves.

But before we look to see whether there are other realistic
possibilities regarding the crisis, it might be well to see whether
the *whole* of the crisis has actually been faced.

Today's crisis is not only the crisis of the cold war. We can
hardly maintain that with the cessation of the cold war all would
be well with humanity. Lurking immediately around the corner
where stands the threat of World War III stand other critical

issues which we in this century and the next must be ready to face. It is a period of seething new nationalism over half the earth's surface; almost universal problems of poverty and dis-ease; the inevitable new awareness of the have-nots that their lives are barren, as they cast a hungry look at those whose lives are lived in gentler circumstances. We face the struggle for power between economic and ethnic groups within and among nations, and with this a rapid realignment of forces; great instability in each momentary power aggregation; and through it all the con-tinuous search for ways in which the mass, though always rela-tively slow and handicapped, can in some sense regulate or con-trol the elite leadership which would so like to claim power over human destiny. All of these problems have their solemn messages and they must be heard for decades, yes if not for centuries. In-stead of saying that if once we can be sure of avoiding World War III all will be easy, we must face the fact that the survival of the Western democratic and technological society that we know is fraught with a million uncertainties in the decades ahead.

Despite all this, we have a kind of strength to which we have given little heed: the fact that human nature is changing at an extraordinary pace; that a new kind of humanity is coming into existence, rooted in current historical trends, especially trends arising from science and the urge toward discovery. Discovery of our own identity, belief in ourselves and in the use of the in-tellectual weapons of a democratic society—a science-minded and technology-minded society—can strengthen those moral, intellec-tual, and social devices without which, in such a world as this, there is no strength at all. The moral of a study of the unequal battle now being waged in the cold war and of our loss of many advantages which we could claim over the Soviet Union a few years ago lies not alone in the creation of powerful weapons. In-sofar as we understand what is happening to us, we can under-stand the strength that comes from that peculiar amalgam of science and democracy that is ours—and can be the property of all humanity.

This is equivalent to asking whether the basic human nature which carries the life blood of the giants can itself begin to change? Is there a possibility that rapid changes in our deeper probings into the structure of our nature as human beings may make possible not only some amelioration in the world crisis but a series of steps important in the handling of future crises? Is there a possibility that a closer look at human nature, its roots, its ways of development, its forms of control, and the directions in which it is now moving may enable thoughtful members of our species to conceive of outgrowing the present crisis, breaking out of the present strait jacket, and defining a mode of human living in which such struggles as the cold war will become anachronistic, stupid, self-defeating, and profitless? Such questions are questions relating to the origin of humankind, the nature of its first culture, the development of its many civilizations, the process by which human attitudes, values, standards, and norms get consolidated and rigid stereotypes of nationalistic, legalistic, and moralistic codes become entrenched. Hand in hand with these go questions regarding the devices by which something fresh, creative, hungry for discovery in human nature may break through the crystallized norms and codes, including the codes of culture and nationhood, to discover, especially through the ways of science and the intellectual children of science, a new kind of human living.

It is a chance to take. Perhaps the effort will be fruitless. In this era, however, with the threat so desperate and the ways of escape so hard to discern among the shadows, an effort at this more fundamental search for human nature and its ways of outgrowing its present tragedy must be made. This book is an effort to describe the sources available within human nature for the outgrowing of human nature, the constitution of new varieties of human thought, value, and aspiration.

• *The Choice among Futures*

This approach does not mean, however, that this book is crisis-oriented, or that it is concerned primarily with spelling out the exact nature of the kinds of crises and the possible modes of their resolution. On the contrary, though at the beginning and at one point or another in the course of the book—especially in Chapter 12—the reader will return to the crises as part of the background of the present task, his *primary* and central obligation is of a different order. It is to use the information about man which has become available in the period of science in which we live: information from the physical sciences, from the biological sciences, from history and the social sciences, and from psychology which indicates what sort of thing man is, what directions *current* biological and social evolution may give to his life in the years ahead, and the areas of freedom in which he may actually discern possibilities and intelligently select among them.

This task, though carried out in a sobering awareness of the hazards we face, may well give us courage and strength to view the possibilities that human nature will constantly take new forms. We have, indeed, new tools for gathering knowledge about men, ancient tools made new by much refinement and modern tools from chemistry and electronics. These last decades have, moreover, seen great strides in our understanding of the basic physical underpinning of life; the nature of the evolutionary process; the form of growth from fertilized ovum to adult; the nature of the organization of the living system, whether it be amoeba or man.

Amazing new light on human nature comes, for example, from the world revealed by the electron microscope. Within the threadlike chromosomes one can study the arrangement of the genes. Through the methods of the biochemist, we can study the profound effects upon the new life of nutrition and disease during the pregnancy period and the dependence of growth and stature upon nutrition, sunlight, and the environment. Through the methods of physiology and psychology we can understand the effect upon intelligence of early stimulation or deprivation of stimulation. We are beginning to understand the delicate interdependence of hereditary and environmental factors in sensitizing the individual to major mental disease; the role of parental standards and community supports in the development of intellectual skills, especially curiosity, fortitude, the drive to get the answers to life problems; the extraordinary range of cultural diversity and of individual diversity within each cultural group.

The rich data obtained from all over the globe in recent years on the structure of human culture indicate the dependence of adult character structure upon patterns of child rearing. We have become alerted to the modifiability of attitude and feeling through the interaction of a variety of biological and social agencies, including drugs, hypnosis, mass suggestion; withholding of information; the early molding of tastes and wants through "imprinting" or "channeling" (p. 60); the early sensitization of the mind to sources of conflict, planting the seeds for future unconscious struggle against oneself.

Psychoanalysis has gone on to probe into many corners of man's deeply unconscious nature and has laid bare the orderly meanings behind many a bizarre contradiction. Experimental psychology has defined more exactly the ways in which man sees, hears, learns, remembers, thinks. and imagines. Unrecognized new fields, such as parapsychology, point to unrealized potentials whose meaning is all too dim.

New perspectives on the past have come from the intimate fusion of the physical and the social sciences, as in the discovery of radioactive carbon, which can now date within a few years many remnants and relics of a life long forgotten and can confirm and support and give richer meaning to documentary materials throughout all the age of recorded history. Lynn White has shown how the combination of historical, archeological, and psychoanalytic concepts may, as it were, stretch out some potentate or chamberlain upon the analytic couch, giving sudden meaning where before all was chaos. Anatomy, physiology, genetics, pathology provide a living unity to the erstwhile confused evolutionary picture of man's development against the background of his animal ancestry. Psychology, sociology, anthropology, economics, linguistics throw light deep into the shadows of the supposed irrationalities of his collective behavior. Ours is an era of such enormous gains in these sciences that we may be justified in asking what glimpses and guesses can be drawn from it all regarding some of the directions in which man may move.

● *The New Ignorance of Man*

What a thing is man! After the Copernican revolution, it looked as if man had been belittled, reduced to a traveling position on a planet far from the center of things, and the astronomy of the last four centuries has made his earthly habitation more and more trivial in terms of the vastness of the known cosmos. Then the evolutionary theory of the nineteenth century showed man's derivation from humbler forms of life, his basic dependence upon techniques for adaptation to his environment in a manner not essentially different from that of other living things, and served to cast further doubt on any special position of importance which he might claim in this universe. Man became a part—a very humble part—of the cosmos and nothing more. Many people feel that this is the final or ultimate picture of man, offering full enlightenment and clear understanding of man's relation both to his cosmos and to his ancestors; and that enlightened common sense, systematically ordered in the ways of science, can do away with enigmas, mystery, mysticism, and obscurantism generally.

This confidence that man has at last discovered all the answers about himself is reminiscent of Gibbon's *Decline and Fall of the Roman Empire,* which assured us that man had at last fought his way out of superstition and confusion and had achieved a rational perspective on himself in the world, so that no longer need there be any basic revolutions or changes in human society. And Gibbon wrote just before the French and American revolutions! The dogmatic rationalism first uttered by Thomas Huxley, later to be echoed by Bertrand Russell, announced that for an enlightened, modern person ethics is clearly a local artifact of special conditions of society, and that man can count on no cosmic support whatever for any ethical goals with which he wishes to concern himself. These confident expressions are all interesting, if quaint, responses to the empirical and practical difficulty of determining where we are, where we are going, and what we are.

We have not outgrown this nineteenth-century nonchalance, this feeling that at last we have all the answers. After World War I the brilliant and inspiring James Harvey Robinson used H. G. Wells's monumental *Outline of History* as a textbook to give his graduate students a perspective of what could really be said at last about man. Robinson's view, vigorously and incisively presented, was that "the seven seals of the book" are now all removed; we at last understand the physical universe, its evolution and development, the proliferation of forms of life, the adaptation to the environment, the origins of humankind as a species, the gross forms of adaptation to various environments, and the accumulation of different types of human cultures; we understand the factors that led to the rise of philosophy, science, and the rationalist way of solving problems; and we see at last why the less rational methods have now begun to yield to the methods of science and order.

Our own dogmatisms after World War II are perhaps a little different. Possibly, however, with logical positivism, operationism, and a hardbitten insistence that we can know reality in just one particular way—namely, the way offered by today's science—we have found a new device for doing away with the haunting difficulties, the fuzzy edges which distort our vision of man.

Finding difficulties in understanding what is *inside* of man, we look *outside* of man, finding the same kind of receding vistas and expanding horizons in the realities upon which his life depends. The telescope and the spectroscope expand the cosmos; but cosmic rays carry us from the processes in the remotest star and beyond the galaxies to our own internal structure, for cosmic rays apparently mold the genes upon which heredity—and evolution—depend. We have not, however, found any easy way of telling what this means for human destiny. In the same way, we find it harder and harder to discover in what respects our own solar system can be regarded as really unique, or the properties of evolution so distinctive as to make it seem likely that man is different from everything else that the universe has ever produced.

We do not know, actually, as man reaches out to the cosmos, what there is in the cosmos that is like him or that can respond to him. In terms of living systems, energies, immaterial influences, or what you will, we are in no position to say that the little capsule inside of which our life goes on is all that there is to be said about human nature, and we do not know the resonance, the contacts, the supports that this kind of life may find, whether in spatial systems or in energy systems far beyond those that we can now scan. If the rest of the twentieth century is like that which is already past, the cutting edge of discovery will doubtless add to the difficulties rather than remove them.

Nothing could be more pathetic, glib, and futile than to say of any specific human act, "That's just human nature." The person might in any case do the opposite, and we might with equal glibness say, "That's just human nature." We do not know what human nature is. We have a limited glimpse only of certain historical and social expressions of it, and a few techniques for learning more about it. An attitude becoming a thoughtful, scientifically oriented student of human nature is one of gratitude for the richness of its apparent potentialities, the richness of his contacts with his cosmos, and the hope that more and more may be discovered that is capable of fulfilling and enriching that existence of which we today know so little.

We are, moreover, in the habit of thinking of scientific specialists as achieving more knowledge in order to ward off disease, produce more food, and help man to be more completely man, *as he is*. It has, however, been dawning upon us that science is doing much more than keeping man as he is. Man and woman today are much taller than man and woman a generation ago—and much healthier. They live longer; they avoid many of the scourges of a few decades ago. Not all the changes are necessarily "for the good." We are in no position to make final value judgments as to what is for the ultimate good or for the ultimate bad, but we are certainly in a position to say that man's newly acquired skills are changing not only the environment in which he must live but the very structure of his being. He not only finds out more about how he is made but, intentionally or unintentionally, is changing himself in the process, changing himself by what he discovers and by the fact that he sees with new eyes some hidden germs of humanness; and more and more such germs are about to be revealed in the decades just ahead. Potentialities are not just incompletenesses but radically new kinds of human nature, some of which we glimpse, some of which we will glimpse only tomorrow.

These potentialities which we have never yet seen bear the relation of acorn to oak tree, of caterpillar to butterfly, or of ovum to adult. We see them at various levels in their development by studying oak trees, butterflies, or human beings. We learn to detect earlier and earlier the signs of a possible form of growth. We begin to guess what the future may bring. In every study of life, however, we find that not only the germ but its environment must be understood.

In a book such as this one we shall have to consider the environmental conditions under which various kinds of human potentialities can flower; we must consider the social evolution that will bring into being different kinds of fulfillments of the germs of today. In so doing we shall keep in mind the principle, ever brought home to us more clearly by biologists, that no germ has an absolutely predestined future, its future depending upon the conditions of growth and realization, and that no conditions of growth and realization produce the same consequences with different germs. We shall have to consider, then, the kinds of potentialities about which we can make reasonable assessments, the kinds of futures to which they may be subjected, the kinds of outcomes which may ultimately be realized. We confront an infinite number of such realizations of potentialities, an infinite number of *kinds of human nature* that may ultimately supervene.

We are, of course, unready. But we are always unready for new vistas, whether good or bad. We are likewise unready for the possible solutions that wait around the corner. As David Riesman has put it, "One must go on imagining new goals, new aspirations, even if at any given time one cannot imagine their implementation." [1] As we shall try to show at some length, the timid process of extrapolation can often succeed well within a *small* space on the globe in a *short* span of time, but extrapolation is usually the wrong method for basic changes. What is needed is the shaking off of what Riesman calls the *"linear"* way of thinking—taking one gentle step at a time—and a readiness for boldness or even extravagance—a capacity for informed and serious guessing as to potentialities utterly different from those that a given epoch can directly suggest. We can often be wrong. In all such efforts, to be wrong fifty times is far more forgiveable than to be timid once.

So the one great reality that must never be forgotten is that there is always more. There is the rim of the sea beyond which one pushes, and there is land beyond. When the surface of the globe has been discovered, when we begin to look up into the stratosphere; when the known sidereal universe is scanned, there is the question of other universes; when the electron microscopes are invented, there remains the question of finer structure. Alexander wept because he had conquered all the world and there were no more worlds to conquer.

In every age men have conquered all there is as they chose to

[1] *Individualism Reconsidered,* Free Press, 1954, p. 303.

see it. Human nature remains largely undiscovered; or, rather, it will always turn into something that is new and strange from the vantage point of any given era. If we ask, then, whether it makes any great difference whether we look at the expansion of the mind in the old terms or in the new, the answer is that it makes a tremendous difference. On the one hand, the world outside, as it is discovered, changes human nature; on the other, sources from within human nature are themselves subject to endless discovery. The great problem is always the discovery of new dimensions, and the most universal of keys yet discovered for the unlocking of these mysteries is the study of the blind assumptions which make their existence remain unguessed.

Chapter **2:**

Three Kinds of Human Nature

Despite the amazing new knowledge of man and the accelerating pace of our techniques for bringing light into dark corners, the shadows continuously lengthen; the unknowns loom infinitely larger than the knowns. Confronting the range and intricacy of all that is known and especially all that is unknown about man, we may wish to attack our problem everywhere at once, and in a sense we have to do so. Cosmic structure throws light on nuclear structure. The living cell throws light both upon the organism of which it is a part and upon the molecules and atoms which compose it. Humanness gives meaning to the simpler forms of animality, and the evolutionary principle finds, in our emerging new ways of thinking and feeling, reflections of much that was foreordained from the time of the primal ooze.

• *The First Human Nature*

The life of today has developed through the processes of evolution, through processes which produced a *"first human nature"* —that human nature produced by the gradual development of a raw distinctive humanness differing from the nature of all other creatures and possessing sharper wits, greater capacity to learn and, above all, keener exploratory functions, the capacity to discover and use new relationships. It is from this raw—or "original"—human nature, that the more complex cultural processes have developed, the human nature that we see today. Endless variations in living forms have led to the formation of species and of well-defined relations between species and their environments, including the other species upon which they prey or with which they must come to terms in one way or another. The evolutionary process implies enormous individual variability, notably in the case of highly evolved species such as man—and, in a sense, individuality is one of the great achievements of the long evolutionary process.

At the same time, basic physical and chemical realities underlie all life, and in particular underlie the functioning of organ systems, the operation of the nervous system, and necessarily the functions of the brain—and the process of learning, the process of thinking, even the process of perceiving what is about us, reflect our own "biological individuality." There are, then, two broad principles defining the first human nature, one of which has to do with the *general* biochemical and nervous organization of human beings as such, their ways of knowing, of feeling, and acting, whereas the other relates to processes that guarantee some *individuality* from person to person, so that heterogeneity—a world of surprises rather than a world of uniformity—must eventuate.

• *The Mold of Culture*

The first human nature is essentially the product of the evolutionary process, and of the particular stocks from which man is descended; the emotional and impulsive equipment of man is essentially produced by his place in the evolutionary scheme. One of the fundamental features, however, of such a broad picture of man is the conception of sensitivity, modifiability, capacity to learn, adapt, adjust, remake the world in the image of his needs. It will therefore be not a fixed biological human nature that is involved but a human nature precariously balanced, always ready to be thrown into a new equilibrium. The first human nature will be not a frozen but a constantly changing model upon which ever-changing forces work. Thus there is a cultural molding of this biological framework—and there are further biological considerations in the question of how the biological stuff itself is changing today as a result of the cultural conditions that influence new health techniques, new types of family living, new types of blending of human stocks.

The emergence of culture means the establishment of a "second human nature"—that is, of devices acquired by individuals in the course of their lifetimes which can be transmitted, essentially intact, to progeny; devices by which ways of living not given by the hereditary equipment may become standardized and may be transmitted as a basic mold of life for countless generations following those who invented or first developed the techniques (Chapters 4-6). The world of language, of physical invention, of logical and mathematical reasoning, of religion and ethics, are, for example, worlds of cultural derivation, relatively standardized and relatively well transmitted over many generations, just as they may be transmitted, through migration, over large portions of the surface of the earth. The standardization of human nature that results within various areas in particular periods may easily deceive all but the most sophisticated student of history and of anthropology. What seems to be "just natural" or "in the blood" of a particular people, such as the warlikeness or the eye for beauty, may be dissipated like water into the desert sand when the conditions which support such modes of life are withdrawn.

There are, of course, many conditions under which cultural continuity and discontinuity may appear. The conception being examined here, however, is that of a human nature instilled, fomented, and impressed—almost, one might say, branded—into the soul of the people so that it seems like the first human nature, but may, as cultural conditions change, betray its true character as a part of a different cycle of humanness, a humanness depending partly upon the cultural stream rather than simply upon the stream of heredity. This *"second human nature"*—preceded by the biological human nature but evolving under the impact of culture into various kinds of human nature—involves the development of new ways of feeling, or "acquired tastes," shared by men with their fellows and transmitted blockwise to the world of the young, who grow up knowing only the culture thus transmitted to them.

But closer inspection of this pattern reveals that a certain rigidity, a certain arbitrary, "self-evident" quality results from this transmission. No longer is there wild, loose, rough, primitive, or flexible human nature ready to be molded in any direction. Rather, there is human nature molded, channeled, "cabin'd, cribbed, confined," made ready to move in one course rather than another, capable of enormous momentum if the direction be maintained but capable only to a slight degree of being deflected by mass effort, as in the time of great invention or revolution, into courses somewhat different. This is the fact of the great inertia, the great rigidity, the great refractoriness of culture to change.

• *Breaking through the Mold*

Despite all this, there is a still small voice, a tiny, dissident voice, which may at times erode and even ultimately destroy vast rigid blocks of cultural tradition. There are deep forces within us that strive fundamentally for gratification of the need to *understand;* forces resistant to standardization and the molding process; forces that nervously and restlessly cut through the chrysalis of culture. It is just as human to fight against cultural standardization as it is to submit to it; and, under conditions of modern living, the creative forces of curiosity and of artistic and scientific reorganization of the materials and ways of life may overpower many of the massive conservative forces of culture. This creative thrust of understanding is a *third human nature.*

The third human nature that we see coming into existence came to light in the urge toward *discovery*—the spirit of intellectual adventure as known to ancient Greece. It was given a renewal of life in the Renaissance and became the cornerstone of that science which in the sixteenth century began to bowl all civilization along in its own direction. Partly as pure science dealing with the physical universe, partly as a way of thinking that applied to living matter and in time even to the nature of man, the spirit of discovery has, through medicine and engineering, done much more than change the face of the earth. It has changed the face of man. It has changed the meaning of all that we see, has given new promise of understanding and application to every fresh fragment of information. It is the meaning of this thirst for understanding, this ordered demand for a conceptual grip on the universe and its meaning for us, that constitutes what we call the process of "breaking through the mold."

Nothing less than a thrust of such massive force as this could have broken through the mighty armor of the older Western traditions. The equally mighty and rigid armor of South and East Asia is today crumbling under the impact of the same battering ram, and men are becoming different almost over night. Science does much more than break down the encrusted walls of earlier formulated knowledge; it creates a new attitude toward the illimitable spaces in which the understanding may begin to move.

In this endeavor to show that culture can be overthrown, today's thinkers are certainly very small Davids contending with very large Goliaths, and it must be remembered that only rarely does a David ever actually bring down his Goliath. The forces in man fighting against tradition may or may not be stronger than those which define the continuation of culture. But the attempt to analyze the forces at work must be made. Nothing ever really becomes *finally* crystallized, and in the spiral of growth there is always more than the predictable spiral—always a countermovement against that which would involve standardization. There is lawfulness in this process, and it is the process of orderly selection from among lawful potentialities that completes the conception of man's discovery of his own potentialities.

This urge toward discovery, this living curiosity, beginning with a sort of "freeing of intelligence" from cultural clamps and moving forward in a positive way activated by thirst for contact with the world and for understanding and making sense of it, will begin to develop a society in which the will to understand is the dominant new component. Both science and the philosophy and ethics of a mass democratic movement provide reasons for believing that the whole thesis of a hopelessly uncontrollable culture can be annihilated, and that the conception of building a society largely motivated by the will to understand—including the understanding both of its place in the cosmos and of its own inner nature—may be fulfilled.

• *Self-directed Change*

Once we are convinced that the choice of a creative and self-directing society can be genuine, we shall have to face the most obvious of the immediate problems: Will this point of view be effective in relation to the immediate threats that face us in this half-century? Escape from these threats seems possible only through some unification of mankind within an industrial system based on curiosity and the application of the products of curiosity in the form of science and invention, while maintaining the spirit of freedom to ask questions through every range of philosophical, religious, moral, and personal inquiry.

As the struggle goes on between science as a gratification to man's quest for understanding, and science as a source of man's capacity for destruction, it seems clear that the vistas of understanding toward which we have made our way can be fulfilled only by recognition of "one world"; if humanity is to achieve a slow liberation and rebirth of the sort described, it will have to do it as one humanity rather than as two or three humanities contending for world supremacy. The problems are not altogether hopeless, since industrialized men will be largely the same men wherever they appear, and since forces have been set free in the modern world that will give science, humanitarianism, and even political democracy increasing sustenance. From this point of view, the crisis of which we are a part need not be the frustration of the vision that has been developed but can indeed be a catalyst to expedite the transition into the fulfillment, by a single humanity, of the three human natures already sketched out.

But assuming that humanity can, in such a perspective, complete the "long haul" through this age of crisis, how can a society fulfilling the third human nature give fulfillment also to the first and the second? Does not the first human nature in fact disappear as culture takes over the molding of man? And does not the process of inventiveness, by its intrinsic character, nullify the culturally stylized and ingrained characteristics? Probably not. Cultural change will act to accelerate *biological* change. And the problem of greatest challenge to human inventiveness emerges

when we recognize the interaction among the three human natures. Culture is being splintered by curiosity and creativeness;
yet culture is nevertheless being enriched. The central problem
is the fulfillment of the three human natures in their interrelations; the fulfillment, within the individual personality, of the
raw stuff of his being, the acquired cravings that he experiences
as a civilized human being, and the deep protest against both as
he seeks new meanings that transcend these first definitions.

• *Man-World Relations*

These problems can be solved not by providing for a three-cornered battle within the living tissues of a single individual but
only by searching out some concepts which may help to define
the relations of man to his cosmos. Kurt Lewin and other creative
thinkers in the land of "field theory" have undertaken to show
that the "life space" of man is a function neither of man's inner
existence nor of his environment nor of some bland formula regarding the interaction of the two but of *new creations of possible systems of relationship* between man and environment.

New interactions of the three kinds of human nature will come
into existence insofar as we are free to imagine and ready to take
the risks involved, seeing what may happen when utterly new
humanness and utterly new environmental possibilities exist,
each giving rise to new features in the other. New humanness
will give rise to new kinds of environment; new kinds of environment will give rise to new humanness in a mounting cycle
of elaboration and fulfillment. The heart of the book is this conception; but as is true of hearts in general, it will take much
preparation to find a way into it.

What is attempted here is not the statement of a wholly new
discovery. Rather, it is a speculative response to the congruent
force of many suggestions from modern science—physical, biological and social—showing the broad outlines of the conception
of three human natures; and indicating the urgency of fulfilling
the integration which they demand. The biological nature of
man, the cultural nature of man, and the protest against both all
have a place in this integration; and the immediate threats and
crises—social, cultural, political, economic, and military—which

face mankind are less desperate than this crisis—the need for the fulfillment of our humanness. This fact will be far easier to recognize if we keep our gaze focused upon long-range themes and issues which go to the very heart of the question.

The essence of this way of thinking is that the human nature of the future cannot possibly be predicted by a sheer extension of the trends of the present—a sheer continuation of the line of ascent, however steep we make it. The method of extrapolation by which we undertake to say that we shall have more and more of whatever has already manifested itself comes to grief as we view the dramatic transformations, the "emergents," the new creations that result from fresh interactions among components which never existed before. From this viewpoint the human nature of the future will be a product of both biological and cultural conditions different from those known today. A cycle of interactions between a changing culture and a changing biological potential will, as Julian Huxley has suggested, give us a spiral of transformations which in no sense grow directly from the patent trends of today. The fulfillment of the three human natures will involve not simply the separate fulfillment of biological potentials and of cultural potentials; it will involve new levels of human experience based on interactions among ingredients not yet in existence. *New components* and *new interactions* will produce a kind of human nature and human experience which will be as far from the present as our own is from that of our earliest Old Stone Age ancestors.

This "visionary" way of thinking is the only way of thinking that is left to us, in view of our insistence on outgrowing both our biological and our cultural heritage and getting ourselves involved in the kinds of curiosity and social reconstruction which it entails. God said of Adam and Eve that since they had acquired knowledge they were "like us"; they could never be childlike, ignorant, innocent again. Man, having discovered curiosity and, like Pandora, let it loose in the world, has no escape but to direct his own evolution in terms of it.

Here the classical ethical question arises whether we have a right to plan for our descendants; whether, since we qualify neither as philosophers nor as kings from a Platonist point of view, we have a right to make decisions. But life consists of progressively expanding decisions, and the failure to decide is itself a decision; the blind decisions arising from inertia are in all probability likely to cripple the freedom of our contemporaries, of our children, and of our remote descendants. The extrication of ourselves from the predicaments of today's thought is essential if we are to maintain any kind of peace and fulfillment in the development of the scientific and technological resources of today.

An autocratic élite simply cannot long survive, and decisions based upon thought and discussion among all who are interested in thinking and discussion—which is at least a large part of the democratic process—is the only control device within a scientific-technological society that has any serious chance of working. For freedom is largely a function of the availability of relevant information in the decision-making process, and reflection on our part will increase rather than decrease the freedom of those who in later years will have to make the decisions for which we are as yet unready.

The reader is asked to consider the possibility that man is (in a deeper sense than is usually reckoned) *a part of the sweep of the cosmos* and that his fulfillment is in a sense his realization of certain deeper contacts with cosmic structure than he ordinarily allows himself. Man is not an isolated portion, a little enclave pocketed off from the vast, cold, impersonal trends with which science is ordinarily conceived to deal. In a certain sense the substance of his life is a mirror of realities regarding the basic ground plan by which cosmic structure is defined. I suggest, tentatively and cautiously, that man's fulfillment need not depend upon cosmic forces that are utterly beyond his comprehension or, on the other hand, upon denial of his earthy participation in the stuff of which the world is made. Rather, his fulfillment depends on the fact that quite literally there are often no sharp boundaries between what he is and what the universe is.

Does this point have implications for the relations of men to one another? The logic already followed denies to the individual man any clear portion of reality which belongs exclusively to him as contrasted to his neighbor. The "life space" of Kurt Lewin appears to permit a man no sharp definition of what is narrowly his own. It is then the spiral of interactions between men and men, the spiral of reciprocities between mankind and the universe, rather than the existing state of human nature, which must be used in an effort at prediction. Human potentialities will be realized not only by drawing from its depths what is not evident but by the continuous creation of realities which are not a part of its present nature at all but will become a part of that redefined human nature which new interactions with the environment will bring into being.

So it is not so much a question of our changing *within* the world as of our changing *with* the world through an evolving pattern of fresh reciprocities. There is really no stable boundary between man and his cosmic environment; we are in the process of discovering new modes of interaction with our environment and therefore becoming *one with* our environment by virtue of this very process of self-discovery. The problem of whether we have cosmic support in our efforts to find our own direction and give it something nearer to the heart's desire will have to be faced in terms of what we can guess about the implications of science. Just as John Donne grasped the reality that "no man is an island," that each man is joined by a suboceanic continent to the solid reality of life of all other men, so this volume tries to demonstrate that the concepts developed here imply inevitably a richer fulfillment in the lives of our individual descendants— spaced as they are in generations the character of whose life we cannot even dimly comprehend—and argues also that it is only by the fulfillment of their life together, their reciprocity as members of a future community, that their fulfillment as living individuals can be realized. The man-world and man-man relationships, far from being foreordained by present trends external to man, can in some measure be so glimpsed that among them we may choose.

Where, then, does this thesis stand in relation to the spate of contemporary literature about human futures? Is it optimistic or pessimistic? Does it presuppose determinism or free choice? Does it assume the loneliness of man or divine support in his upward struggles? Does it assume that political and military problems must come first; that democracy and the moral stance of the West must be safeguarded before global human thinking can be successfully attempted? Does it believe that "as things have been, they remain," or that man may and does become something new?

To answer in a few words questions that the whole book must try to answer on a larger canvas, my belief is that mankind is still changing biologically ("evolution is still going on") and that his social-cultural evolution is proceeding at an extraordinary pace, destined for still more staggering acceleration in the decades just ahead. I believe that curiosity, the use of the mind, the craving to understand—always a major factor in human potentialities— has become the controlling difference between the men of the past and the men of the present era; that science is much more than technology, that it is rather a way of life extending its fingers into every cranny of modern existence; that technology in the broad sense, involving everything in our material existence from the corporate structure of business to the universality of vaccination and the improved agricultural yield, expresses the dominant idea of our era, the idea that man can and will *understand*. Part of this conception is that man can and will understand *himself* and his own society. A still more concrete exemplification of the idea is that all men in the science-dominated modern era can learn to understand one another, despite the colossal gulfs established by political, economic, and military cleavage; and that it is only through a common discovery of all men striving to understand that a "one world" fit to live in can be discovered.

This is, perhaps, "optimistic" rather than "pessimistic." It presupposes, however, that the thoughtfulness and the craving to understand more fully can and will go on accelerating. It is not fatalistic—in the sense that forces external to man are believed capable of blocking his way—nor, on the other hand, is it ready to assign man's salvation to the "arbitrary spontaneity" or individualistic free choice of persons acting outside of, or despite, the massive force of their own cultural outlook. On the contrary, it is the belief that in a society such as ours men can and will develop increasing understanding and will use this increasing understanding to increase their freedom, their capacity to make intelligent choices. This is the belief that prompts the writing of such a book.

Chapter 3:

Man as an Animal

To chart the *directions* in which human nature can change involves the question of how we have arrived where we are. What sort of thing is human nature? To what degree is it fixed, to what degree modifiable? What are its emotional roots, its intellectual capacities? What do the varying types of human culture mean as expressions of a latent or uniform human nature?

Many of the answers are suggested by the evolutionary view of life. About the origin of life we have little knowledge. It is clear, however, that the ability to maintain an internal organization against the tempest of outer reality was a first essential. After a long series of cumulative changes, an organization of particles arose which could maintain itself, grow, repair its own injured tissue, and reproduce its kind. There was at first no sharp separation between the portion of the individual that was destroyed in the vicissitudes of life and the part that contained the potentialities of transmitting the characteristics of the stock to new individuals. In all higher forms, however, the differentiation exists in terms of *body cells* and *germ cells*. The germ cells contain the tiny particles—the *genes*—that regulate the development of the new individual formed by the union of male and female elements.

Through the eons during which the aggregation of the appropriate matter and the struggle for existence has gone on, the genes have been formed and selected in such a way as to preserve life and to permit attunement to a specific environment. They fit the new individual not only for life in general but for a particular life; not only for environmental vicissitudes but for particular vicissitudes. If we ask, then, "For what particular kind of an environment were our animal ancestors equipped?" we can answer in terms of three specifications: First, to meet the physical requirements in terms of warmth, water, food, and safety from enemies; second, to respond appropriately to the other members of the group to which in early life they are exposed, developing the necessary types of interdependence which make adult group living possible; third, to develop specific selective response to members of the other sex group adequate to permit sexual, as well as social, function.

But every form of life has to compete with *other* forms of life. Charles Darwin, after showing how each individual owes its existence to its place in competition with other individuals, its capacity to survive in the "struggle for existence," went on to defend the interactions of *species,* acting as hosts and parasites, or as hunters and hunted, or as competitors for the same food supply. In the intricate interdependence of the living world, the process of adaptation means the extinction of those which are not in tune with the specific requirements of a particular way of life, while competing with, or adapting to, other species.

For a long time, for example, the basic attributes of mammals have been developed and selected by the struggle for adaptation in a niche offered by the geographical environment and the food supply. Then within the mammalian stock were developed and selected various groups—genera—of mammals, each filling a specific niche in the face of environmental possibilities.

• *Simian Traits*

One of the ways in which the mammalian stock could develop was to increase the size and complexity of its central nervous system, and thereby its learning ability and its intelligence. It was the lot of the primates, a relatively defenseless but agile and adaptable stock, to undergo this transformation in the direction of intelligence. Their emotional and impulsive life, colored by a high degree of curiosity and sociability, remained a part of the package; primate *temperament,* as well as primate *intelligence,* developed beyond all bounds previously seen on the face of the earth. There is a huge amount of "primate nature" within us. It was suited to the arboreal existence which characterized our progenitors for a very long period. In fact, the length of time since "we came down from the trees" is slight indeed. And the arboreal was merely a one-night stand compared to the evolutionary sequence as a whole.

The thought of animal-like men and manlike animals has charmed every generation of children and puzzled every generation of philosophers. A half-century ago there was a wave of fresh awareness of man's kinship with the world of birds and animals. From John Burroughs and Ernest Thompson Seton to Rudyard Kipling and Jack London, vigorous minds proclaimed, like Whitman, their kinship with the animals, and taught us to find what was like ourselves in each one of them and like them in each of us. Then all this became either "anthropomorphic" or "sentimental," or both. We waited until the thirties and forties to rediscover (and now with a fresh accent) the extraordinary humanness of beast and bird. The animal studies of Lorenz and Tinbergen are the apex of a pyramid of scientific lore and folklore in which we all avidly discover ourselves. The sense of community with animal kind appears to be with us again. In this new sense of a common heritage we discover at the same time how deep within us are the loves and fears, the raw keen sensitivities of ear and nose, the wild impulses to shout, scream, tear, and run, which we see among all lower mammals.

We have solemnly learned that monkeys are not apes, and apes are not men, because of this or that special evolutionary quirk which meant that something new had been added. When the psychiatrist E. J. Kempf, however, studied tyranny among monkeys, we found our own nature there in the midst of the picture, and when the psychologist C. R. Carpenter "trapped out" the little Hitler in a free-roving monkey colony on a Caribbean island, we noticed the transformation of the monkey world along lines not so utterly alien to our own political observations. Above all, we have learned in the last few decades, thanks especially to Robert M. Yerkes and his Florida colony, to ask clearly just what the great anthropoid apes can do and can become, at what points their "striving to be man," if it be such, comes to an end. Although their sensory and motor virtuosity are superb, the superiority of the apes to the monkeys is apparently due not primarily to the sensory and the motor skills but rather to the cognitive, the *comprehending* aspects—that is, the way in which things are sensed to give perceptual meaning, the way in which they are acted upon to give meaningful behavior-constellations.

When we muse on this *closeness* to our animal brethren, we often gain fresh perspectives from it. Indeed, one of the greatest achievements of our human fantasy, erring always in the grand style and committing untold extravagances, but bringing us back to ourselves with a renewed realization of potentials, is this perennial fantasy of animals thinking, talking, and acting like men, and of men thinking, acting, and talking like brutes. In Swift's Gulliver, for example, humanity appears in a lens, distorting sufficiently to bring out with staggering realism many of the attributes which we are too blind or defensive to observe, or glossing over other counterbalancing attributes, upon which we lean in comfort in the moments when the despicable features of human nature are thrust upon us. Swift traced human potentialities by showing what would happen if some of the traits of humanity were unrelieved by others and were sufficiently exaggerated to determine a primal law of human life.

Even more skillful, perhaps, is Clarence Day's portrait of mankind and of the relatives of mankind in *This Simian World*. Day asks us to remember that we are simians, that our basic temperamental and impulsive attributes are those that have been developed over eons in the primate stock. He points out that much that we have attributed to the sheer development of intelligence really has to do with our endless sociality—our need for one another —especially our need to waggle our tongues at one another. It is true that language could have developed through the utilization of other parts of the body than the vocal cords, and it is true that the use of symbols is a far richer thing than the making of sounds. Still, the basic need of the primates to share, to dominate, to be dominated, to attack, to defend, to make and receive signals, to live in a world of sociality, marks them off from many of the other more highly developed forms. And their sociability is not the brute cohesion of bovine or equine stocks.

It involves the need to nudge, to push, to make sounds at, to direct the attention toward and away from this or that. Such sociality is the nervous, preoccupied, interpersonal, diadic, group-dynamics-oriented, center of simian character. There is pathos in Köhler's accounts of the agonized sympathy of the group toward the sick chimpanzee, and of their joining their comrades in protest when the experimenter disciplined one of them. Much of the basic simian character is apparent in the Central African dance in which the chimpanzees whirl about a central hollow tree, thwacking it like a drum as they dance in procession.

Human beings, in this sense, may be viewed at the same time as intellectually by far the most highly developed on the face of the earth but also as the most complete elaboration of a fundamental and primitive simian quality. It is not the same thing to be an intellectually developed simian as to be an intellectually developed cat or horse. In fact, Day goes on to point out the different attributes which the great felines would have cultivated had their fundamental temperament been graced by the over-arching cerebral hemispheres—had the evolutionary process turned these particular beasts into the symbol-manipulating, and therefore the dominant, group of the world. It is not simian quality alone, of course, but simian quality in relation to long selective processes at a biological level and long symbol-manipulating processes at a cultural level, and many interactions between the two, which have given us modern humanity; it would be absurd to argue that the simian qualities are alone incarnated in modern life. It is the simian qualities in relation to a particular development of the central nervous system and all that that means. Nevertheless, it remains a biological cue of very profound and almost universally neglected importance.

One of the most profound of modern expressions about the relation between sheer intellectual development and the basic temperament which goes with the stock is contained in the extraordinary fantasy of Olaf Stapledon about the dog Sirius.[1] Sirius is a brainchild of a Cambridge genius, whose biological inventions made possible the breeding of extraordinarily intelligent dogs. The resulting superdog, the Alsatian Sirius, has a human

---

[1] W. O. Stapledon, *To the End of Time,* Funk and Wagnalls, 1953.

intelligence in a dog's body. The pathos of being fully immersed in human society, fully loving and being loved by human individuals and still "just a dog," is carried to superb heights of grandeur and pathos.

The essential germ of this story, its basic meaning, lies in the highlighted difference between sheer accumulation of intelligence and the accumulation of intelligence within a simian and, more specifically, a human framework. Any attempt to forecast human potentialities must consider not only the satirist Swift and the fantastic dreamer Stapledon; it must reckon with the fact that a strange blending of the temperamental attributes of the evolutionary stock with the potential for intellectual, esthetic, and creative achievement must be earnestly studied in any attempt to look into man's future.

This question of our core biological nature is one of the greatest challenges which can ever be directed to the conception of a future for humanity which is basically different from all the pasts which it has experienced. If there is a fundamental mammalian stock with its inbred characteristic traits, and if, somewhat specialized and superposed upon this, there are *primate* attributes, and if, within the last few moments of the evolutionary process, there is an opportunity for some subtler *human* attributes to be developed which are essentially a gloss upon the margin of the huge manuscript of time, we must accept the basic humanness of all the human acts through history: the nobility and depravity, the gentleness and the sadism, the generosity and the meanness.

• *The Emergence of Humanness*

From this point on the path there are two possible directions of thought about human nature. On the one hand, it may be held that this pattern of simian emotions and impulses, ways of perceiving and understanding, needs only to be enriched by the growth of man and the consequent increase in the aspect of ability to learn, to understand, to imagine, even to think in terms of symbols. Individual variations in response to like challenges, stimulated or held back by this or that social factor, may be held to mark out the general domain of human nature from which nothing much can be subtracted and to which nothing very much can be added.

Though speaking in terms of the cultural richness of man's future, those espousing such a view assume that somehow the built-in genetic attributes anchored throughout all of history upon this primate stock can yield no essentially *new* responses; the most that can be done to change human nature is to enrich and develop certain aspects of this human nature, and to mute or weaken some of the others. Many psychologists believe, for example, that there is a raw or "original" human nature which consists of *"primary drives"*—hunger, thirst, sex, the cravings for oxygen, warmth, rest, etc.—and primary aversions—fear, rage, disgust, avoidance of pain, etc. They believe that mankind shares these primary drives with their mammalian brethren—in particular, their simian brethren—and that human nature transcends these drives only by virtue of learning more, being more intelligent. They are certainly partly right.

But this conception does not necessarily exhaust the picture of "original human nature." For there is much to suggest a very different conception of the range of human sensitivities, which we can examine in broad outline here and return to from time to time as new problems require it. The process of evolution has done more than provide specific organs to meet specific needs: respiratory apparatus for breathing, teeth for biting and chewing, and the neural mechanism for such specific drives and aversions as hunger, sex, rage, and fear. Nature has done more than develop much more *general* adaptive and integrative mechanisms, permitting a huge amount of learning in the lifetime of the individual, the modification of response through experience and even the capacity for dealing with the *imagined* environment. Such capacities imply new *motives*. The *capacity* to deal with a complex world of here and there, and with past, present, and future, the *capacity* to deal with abstractions which give general laws cutting across the maze of particulars has entailed *the urge to do all of this*. The impulse to perceive, to understand, to imagine is just as much part of human nature as are the specific adjustment processes which we describe in terms of visceral drives.

Some have maintained that all of these devices for learning and

thinking are simply passive *means* to bring to us the major satisfactions which our vital requirements define. Let us see. Infants, having got over the shock and stress of the birth experience
and beginning to be awake more and more of each twenty-four
hours, begin to take active note of the world, begin to do more
and more looking, listening, touching. The eyes explore, and
active smiling and other facial expressions indicate the degree
to which the environment is in itself important, quite aside from
its leading toward a goal; in fact, the goal may become unimportant in the child whose curiosity outweighs his hunger. Even
in the monkey, this exploratory or curiosity drive may far outweigh the importance of his food cravings. He will work for
hours to solve a problem even when there is no food or other external reward; indeed, he will work just as hard at the problem
when he has eaten *before* starting the problem, or when there is
food at his side to be enjoyed when he chooses.

The human young are even more curious. When children in
the third year of life are studied with such "sensory toys" as
velvet, sandpaper, cold cream, many of them show a huge amount
of interest in the tactual, olfactory, and muscular sensitivity. They
will immerse themselves in the world; they soak themselves in its
rich qualities. Its endless problems and challenges are intrinsically appealing. Now and then it hurts them, and they learn how
to avoid the recurrence of such hurts; but in general it is a rich
and commanding world which they must understand and with
which they must come to terms. Often the child has to be dragged
from his sensory and motor satisfactions to swallow the food
which adults think necessary to meet his "primary needs," or
dragged to bed against the competition of excitations which
stimulate his sense organs and later his imagination. Human
nature, as directly observed, is no matter of the viscera alone.
It is a matter of exploring the possibility of the surfaces, lines,
colors, and tones—and, later on, the symphonies, mountains,
and stars.

Where do all these rich interests come from? Often one needs
only to expose the child to these gratifications to see him immerse himself in them. It is true that he "learns" such interests
in the same sense that he "learns" his interest in milk bottles,
tomato juice, ice cream, or comics. There are crude and primi-

tive wants which undergo specific channeling under particular environmental conditions. There is, however, no group of human beings which has not cultivated devices for enriching contact with the sensory world, and none which has not philosophized and attempted to derive satisfactions from understanding and manipulating, as well as touching, smelling, tasting, and exploring the world.

The word ordinarily used to describe this class of satisfactions in the world around us is *esthetic*. It might be better simply to use the word *sensory*, as indicating primitive processes long before they undergo that elaboration to which the fine arts give their attention. The esthetic is simply a late and derived form of a very much deeper and more general human preoccupation with the sensory attributes of the environment. Along with this goes satisfaction, manipulation, and recombination of the sensory attributes: the use of brush, hammer, bellows, the world of craftmanship. But craftmanship in all its forms produces much more than sensory recombinations; it provides the satisfactions of activity, the satisfaction of using the muscles; also the achievement of a goal; ultimately, a sense of ego-fulfillment (cf. p. 74).

To these more complex motives we shall turn later on. Here we are concerned mainly to indicate that the *potentials for becoming a human being,* as compared with a less complex kind of animal, *lie largely in this enrichment and elaboration of the sensory and motor ranges of experience* and the life of symbolism which depends upon this. The sheer fact that we have a nervous system, the sheer fact that we can learn, means that we can prolong and complicate sensory and motor satisfactions, can make them richer, can give them more connections, can avoid boredom, can recombine them, can feed upon them, can become immersed in them and make them a part of ourselves. In all these respects, we are most completely human. Moreover, to suggest that the carpenter uses his saw or his plane only to earn a living is to show very limited acquaintance with carpenters, just as to say that the congressman strives for re-election only for the sake of his salary shows a very limited concern with the psychology of congressmen. My primary thesis is that there is satisfaction in using what we have—in using the equipment that makes us human—and that this entails not only the sensory and motor equipment but that central nervous system upon which the learning and thinking processes depend.

But there is a further point. *The very processes of learning and thinking may in themselves become satisfying.* There may be a movement from the initial satisfaction in color to the delight in manipulating the colors to produce a picture. In time there is a still further elaboration by which one becomes interested in the fact that different kinds of pictures require different kinds of media, that different kinds of people paint different kinds of pictures—permitting different kinds of satisfaction in the process of selection and abstraction which makes possible the sensory and motor gratifications described. This means a "higher pitch," becoming interested in all those activities which are one step removed from the immediate environment as such. The same delight in watching the mind work also applies, of course, when the tableau of present excitation is withdrawn. We close our eyes and till the fields of memory, drawing back and holding close the special impacts which meant something yesterday or years ago.

We seem, then, to have come to a very paradoxical conclusion. The first line of evidence had suggested to us that man has not had time in the evolutionary process to develop any new needs beyond those of his mammalian ancestry. He was inevitably pre-occupied with a few primary visceral drives, the satisfactions of which constituted the goals of living and the frustration of which constituted the basis of psychic pain. We seemed to find, in our preoccupation with the viscera, no essential respect in which man differs from pre-man, except in the complication of the devices by which the visceral goals may be reached. Yet, in fact, more attention to the nature of these devices, more attention to the meaning of the development of the central nervous system, has shown us how the very fact of possessing a complex nervous system has resulted both in the enrichment of sensory and motor satisfactions and in the development of a type of satisfactions which are less directly dependent upon sense organs and muscles. We have, then, a tremendous range of human motives which are organized around the central nervous system and its processes.

It follows that the future of humanity, so far as we can see it, must do more than continue to provide a deep and healthy concern for the visceral requirements; the hardly explored realm of sensory and motor gratifications also has an enormously rich potential before it, even if the biological structure of man changes but little in the next few millenia. It is highly probable that sensory gratifications, including those through the arts, and motor gratifications, including those through competitive and cooperative effort, discoveries, sports, and progressive refinement of motor skills related to vocations and avocations, will all grow progressively more and more complex and make up a larger and larger part of life.

There is much in this way of thinking that runs closely parallel to the conception that the erotic energies are channeled into higher activities very different from their lower, primitive expression. This conception of the delight obtained from the senses is not, however, dependent upon any theory of the erotic. The primitive delights which even kittens or puppies take in the sensory objects about them can become richer as more is perceived, as differentiation goes on; and in the case of human beings it is not long before habits of close attention, habits of differentiation, the use of names, the use of terms of endearment serve in various ways to enrich the sensory delights which were present even in the first weeks of life. It is a good, sweet, rich world, this world of color, tone, touch, smell, this world of movement, this world of discovery and challenge.

There is, however, *still* more here. There is the satisfaction that comes from progressive differentiation, closer looking and listening, the fresh combinations to be made. There is a sort of rolling the thing about in the mouth, snuffing it up into the nostrils, a sort of deliberate intensification of it. There is the added delight that comes from getting ready for it. Distance lends enchantment to the view, and we look forward to fresh delights, enriching them in the imagined and anticipated consummations. There is, moreover, a process of self-love similar to Freud's narcissism in which, like Little Jack Horner, we delight in that which we sense and in that which we do. It is good in itself, but it is all the better because it is our own. This book will have a great deal to say about the origins of these satisfactions, these potentialities, which do not appear to be direct derivatives of the life of instinct—as contrasted with sensing, perceiving, thinking

—at all. What we are calling the "first human nature" is the integration, as man came into existence, of the mammalian, specifically the simian, system of interests and motives into the elaborate sensory and cognitive preoccupations which are found everywhere where there are men.

The core qualities of humanness, as thus conceived, including both the *raw materials* of impulse and the *ways of learning*, include the following: First, intense, though often diffuse, vital needs which have a biological aim and mode of resolution but are considerably modified in their intrinsic form and very greatly modified in the objects which will satisfy them.

Second, even more diffuse, but frequently imperious, demands for certain types of activity, especially those involving curiosity, rhythm, manipulation, exercise of the muscular and other systems. The more complex and prolonged the realm of experience during man's long period of immaturity, the richer the potential outcomes.

Third, a need to learn and a capacity to learn, appearing specifically in the capacity to form associations, the capacity to channel the drives in specific directions, and the capacity for organization, as we shall see in detail in Chapters 5-9.

This view of human nature is so simplified as to be an abstraction, but it seems useful as a springboard. I believe that it is legitimate to find a place, as I have attempted elsewhere (p. 306), for all the very complex motivations. They are seen to be just as *human* as the single ones if the cognitive needs and the need to learn are given their due place. The relative nonreversibility of many types of learning, especially canalization and structuring, call for emphasis, too.

From such a point of view, part of the essential nature of humanness lies in the specific evolutionary trends that underlie the many demands of mankind upon life, but much likewise develops from the elaboration of the cognitive life and the rich blend of cognitive and affective tendencies in social, esthetic, religious, political, philosophical, and scientific life. Human nature would therefore seem to be dependent both upon a raw matrix of general mammalian predisposition upon which is superposed a system of attributes formed through the simian line and upon the enormously rich gifts of sheer cognitive intensity and plasticity from which inevitably follows a high degree of unfulfilledness with respect to any specific potentialities. *There always has to be more.* There always has to be a movement toward satisfaction of unresolved balances and the creation of new instabilities pressing toward their own solution in turn.

• *Individuality*

But the sheer presence of dramatic individual differences in learning ability and in temperament give human nature another dimension implying division of labor, differentiation of role, polarity of leader and led, and the subtleties in the orchestration of diversities upon which a complex society depends.

The evidence from evolutionary biology indicates that the human race arose once, not several times; that all living human beings are the descendants of one central human stock which developed a million or so years ago in a specialization of life upon the earth and in contrast to the life in the trees that their own ancestors had maintained. This one stock was itself highly complex, with an enormously complicated mechanism built within it for the reproduction of a wide diversity of traits. So it was possible, when various subsections of this great family moved into various areas, for some of the latent hereditary traits to develop and become fixated as appropriate adaptations in each environment while other groups, essentially the same but having the same enormous variability, gave rise to different types of adaptations. Some of the hereditary potentialities which were favorable in one environment were not favorable in another.

There was, therefore, an elimination among the Northern stocks of many of the attributes (heavy pigmentation, etc.) which developed in the tropics and vice versa. The actual survival value of many of the genes was probably not put to a test at all; that is, undoubtedly much of the development of the separate races was due to "accidents" of various sorts, not involving specific responses to the severe demands of the environment. In general, the diversification went far enough to give recognizable biological types but not far enough to prevent the possibilities of fertile matings between the members of the various groups. The human stock, in other words, never developed into more than one species.

With regard to most human attributes, the enormous *individual variability* already described maintained itself within each of the derivative races, so that today, in most of the attributes which can be scientifically measured, the difference between the average white man, the average Chinese, the average Negro, is very small compared with large *individual* differences within each. In other words, there is the necessary raw material in the Chinese stock to develop the civilization of ancient Peru or the civilization of contemporary Boston; and there is in West European stocks the range, variability, and plasticity necessary to give us men like those who painted the Sung dynasty paintings of China or produced the philosophy of the Upanishads and the Indian epics.

Such ideas would be debated violently by the proponents of some of the currently popular "racial" theories, but they are unarguable if the nature of human variability and the nature of human plasticity are fully grasped. We shall not maintain (as some have done) that there are *no* distinctive racial characteristics or that there are *no* gross differences in averages among the various subsections of the human family. We simply do not know. Of this, however, we can apparently be fairly certain: there is enough variability anywhere in the human family to support any of the major cultural trends which any portion of the human family exemplifies at any given time.

All of mankind learned to use tools, fire, and domesticated animals before there was written language. In the process of "holding back the jungle" and in the process of meeting environmental challenge, the men of several great river valleys discovered ways of getting enough food, shelter, *and leisure* to develop a taste for the amenities—in other words, an opportunity to satisfy their eyes through lovely things to wear, their ears through making musical instruments—comforts and gratifications of a sort that were good in their own right. These were rapidly built into aspects of the prestige system of chieftains, kings, and whoever was dominant at any time and place; depending upon different environments and resources, different kinds of products expressed the different civilizations. Often it is hard to tell which is "higher," just as it is hard to tell in the rich poetry of the Dakota Indian what is higher, what is lower, let us say, than in the poetry of John Donne or E. E. Cummings.

Different civilizations achieve different emphases. Some of these emphases were easily copied and shared by civilizations in communication with them. In general, the practical arts were easier to lend and exchange across cultural lines than were the esthetic arts, though no absolute rule can be set down. There was an elementary priority of the "economic," in the sense that physical objects could be exchanged for one another, whereas ideas and attitudes, though they could flow, could in no easy sense be "exchanged." They could hardly be taken on a long journey for export purposes, with the hope of returning with something which would surely be valued as much by the originators of the ideas. Economic cravings made men explore—made men make contacts—and led, both in their own right and in the associated ideas and in the contacts that went with it, to the amalgamation of ways of thinking and feeling. Starting on a very small scale, on a house-to-house, village-to-village basis, the increasing coherence and like-mindedness of people who could carry out the exchange of things and ideas began to spread, until it became literally an imperial system. It contained within itself no absolute necessity for coercion; and in general over the face of the earth international trade has been regarded as a peaceful force.

From all of this it follows that there has been differentiation of human cultures and that there has been exchange of ideas as fast or almost as fast as there has been differentiation. The process of pulling apart and drawing back together has been found throughout history; and the accretion of many physical objects, many productive arts, many ideas, has characterized the building of great states and empires.

Ruth Benedict has placed us forever in her debt by lucidly suggesting the way in which the variability in raw human nature may play into the various requirements of different societies. If we assume a wide variety of latent human personalities contained within the germ of our being, different kinds of latent or ready predispositions may be drawn forth and finally stamped in by a culture that favors them, whereas those attributes further from the requirements of the culture may lie dormant or may, if colliding with culture, lead to stress. It is indeed possible that there may be such a thing as sheer stress in trying to cope with the pressure of cultural demands—"culture shock" —not only through the failure to meet specific requirements but, in a broader sense, through the failure to meet cultural requirements at large. There may be both a certain kind of resonant flexibility which makes children ready for the cultural assimilation process and a certain kind of basic reluctance, as it were, to undergo the impress of cultural norms. The little tyke expected to wear gun and holster today may be vaguely pleased, but inwardly insecure. However this may be, any conception of the fulfillment of latent man by a given culture must recognize the stresses involved in different cultures in relation to different latent potentialities—and, in particular, the virtual universality of a stress process, both of the specific types suggested by Freud and of those general types which modern personality and culture theory suggest in terms of the very long time that full assimilation to cultural norms requires.

Ruth Benedict's ideas could, indeed, be developed in a useful direction by applying our knowledge of genetics more specifically. We have now about as good evidence for constitutional temperamental variability in mankind as we have in the many other species which have been studied. Such studies indicate that in the complexity which makes up mammalian temperament, as such, wide individual variability is to be expected, unless strains are inbred for a very long period specifically to reduce such variability.

Finding it necessarily very difficult to be objective regarding human temperament, we are prone to forget that different temperaments move more easily or less easily in response to the kinds of requirements standardized in different groups—more ready or less ready for any specific cultural adaptation, any specific social task. We should prefer not to speculate much about the matter of body types, but to remain on the safer ground of *wide human temperamental variability* and the fact that any society whatever which the future may bring is sure to lead to the release of different kinds of potentialities with varying degrees of satisfaction or stress among individuals with various genetic dispositions.

There is, however, some danger of freezing the present viewpoint into a rather static conception—namely, that there is a kind of person suited to each kind of culture. One of the fundamental attributes of the higher forms of life is variability from situation to situation and from day to day in terms of the great complexity both of the inner adjustive mechanisms and of the environmental demands. It follows, therefore, that sheer *variability around one's own norm* is itself a basic biological attribute which varies greatly from person to person. Some people can be "depended upon" in the same situation; some can be "depended upon" even in very different situations; some are notoriously undependable or, if you like, flexible or, if you like, volatile, because of their own variability around their own norm. It is entirely probable, as we shall try to show (p. 113), that there are already factors at work in human life which are tending to intensify our protest against cultural rigidity; one of the difficulties with an "ideal society" is that it must fail to take into account the fact that one of the most "ideal" attributes of human beings —namely, the capacity to vary in accordance with outer and inner demands—implies that a rich, flexible, and ultimately open and unresolved society may be a better one for such persons than one which can be fully specified with respect to its norms and demands. The Utopia will be a better one if there are many unfinished regions in the canvas; indeed, if much of it is unfinished.

The first human nature, in summary, is a system of biologically given dispositions varying in their rigidity or flexibility and including many which are so flexible, so sensitive to changing requirements, that the "human nature" which they represent easily moves into a wide spectrum of different realizations. Despite common features, cultures move apart from one another not only in specific techniques of weaving or speaking or making war but also in fundamental feeling tone, ways of facing or dreading or trying to control the universe. Each of these diverse cultures, however, develops its own gradually hardening mold, so that the soft little bits of living stuff born into it become, be-

fore long, case-hardened—become representatives not of humanity as such but of a formalized or standardized kind of humanity
that sees, feels, and thinks as the mold determines. To this
"mold of culture" we turn in Part II.

PART II

The Second Human Nature:
The Mold of Culture

Chapter 4:

The Invention of Culture

The first human nature, then, was a rich amalgam of instinctual drive, delight in the environment, effort to understand, and general learning ability. From this—as evolutionary processes steadily enriched the size and complexity of the brain without very greatly modifying the other basic attributes—came very rapidly the further enrichment of the ability to learn. The second human nature began to emerge. As men learned a little, they shared it with their children; and as the children grew up and learned a little more, they, in turn, shared it.

Students of society like to argue whether the culture that man thus built was akin to man or alien to man; whether man built himself a home or a prison. Indeed, since the time of Thomas Hobbes and John Locke three hundred years ago, the issue has been sharply drawn in the controversies of the social theorists as to whether man has to be "socialized" or is *by nature* social; whether the natural state of man is a "war of all against all" or a seeking of contact and of reciprocity.

The study of the instinctual life has given strong support to the conception that there is much in man that is primitively self-centered, nonsocial, or antisocial, but it has also shown clearly that the craving for the social is real and vital within the structure of human nature. The social sciences have yielded much rich material on the primitive social cravings of human beings over the face of the earth, and pathology has more and more clearly shown that the failure of such contact and communication is a major failure in the achievement of human nature itself.

Man needs to be social partly because he needs *other men;* partly because he needs *order.* With great delight the six-year-old announces: "We have *rules* at our school." For many a child there is enormous satisfaction in establishing order. This is partly a matter of response to adult requirements, but it also expresses in-group satisfactions—not only satisfactions of mastery but also satisfactions in learning to grasp and conceptualize relations among persons. The rules may, indeed, change the activity, by offering greater intellectual satisfactions as well as complicating and enriching the social relationships. Children spend an enormous amount of time in getting the rules straight and in arguing about every possible digression and exception. Sometimes, of course, the purpose is to establish a point and to assert one's competitive superiority over those who cut the corners and break the rules. Yet there is sheer delight in the rules as such, sheer "virtuosity" in mastering and using this, like other forms of the social network which holds us together. A major aspect of the "latency" period as conceived by psychoanalysis is the outgrowing of the primitive urgency of unsocialized needs in favor of the processes of identification with parents and peers which both maintain order and increase the area of social satisfactions. In many a child the social and the cognitive gratifications vie with one another for supremacy at a given moment. Children, as well as adults, seem to crave order—indeed, an order from which they cannot escape.

There is, however, a double paradox here. The intensity of the visceral needs (of both children and adults) is so great that it is hard indeed to see how they can be put aside in favor of sheer order or external control; and if on top of this there is residual guilt regarding visceral cravings, there is much unfinished business with which to struggle in the growing-up years. Why don't children have far more trouble than they do? They must want *people* and *order* more than anything.

There would seem, then, to be strong reasons for human beings to cling together, even beyond the period of dependency of the young. Often, of course, economic considerations in the broad sense are paramount: the group must be big enough for defense against animals and enemies, and to allow some division of labor. Man gains in so many ways from his association with his fellows that "hermits" are rare, holy, queer, or pitiful. Man wants safety, order, protection against the unknown, and, on the positive side, companionship, love, and dependable cooperation.

Man, developing his "second human nature" and acquiring the rudiments of culture, began to share skills, ideas, feelings with his children in such a way that they in turn transmitted such skills, ideas, feelings to their children.

• *The Ability to Learn*

This ability to learn entails at least five processes:

First, the ability to form simple associations—*e.g.*, to withdraw from danger signs, and pursue signs that may mean success.

Second, the development of gesture and vocal sound to stand for present or distant or future objects, communicating with oneself and with others, standardizing a language of symbol.

Third, the utilization of such symbols to develop the higher capacity to think abstractly, to grasp that what is true of four apples and three apples is also true of four pears and three pears.

Fourth, the capacity to invest feeling in specific objects (a process to which we shall give much attention below), the capacity to form stable objects of deep personal significance.

Fifth, the capacity to systematize both these investments and these forms of symbols so that they become socially shared, and indeed are shared with the young, establishing a continuity of group attachment and ultimately a culture.

This is not the place to elaborate upon the processes by which culture was invented. Certainly it is true that mammals and birds, too, have at times invented ways of building dams or nests; to some degree we can watch them "explaining" or "showing" to their little ones the processes, however rudimentary. But building a culture takes more brain and far more symbol and far more capacity for abstraction and standardization through abstraction than any simian prior to man was able to muster. We may, for this reason, say that the first human nature, which consisted essentially of the enlarged simian nature, underwent a very profound metamorphosis in the elaboration of the five attributes described above—a metamorphosis so profound that we may speak of the genesis of a second human nature. This is a human nature organized around symbols and values and capable of sharing them over regions of space and—far more important —over regions of time, in the sense that the progeny carry forward to their own progeny the slow accretion of standardized thoughts and values. This beginning of culture makes man a different kind of creature and human nature a different kind of nature.

The steps through which culture was discovered and first disseminated are held by archaeologists and anthropologists to have been rather similar in different parts of the earth. We shall not recount the familiar story of the domestication of animals, the taming of fire, the chipping and polishing of stone implements. Our purpose here is merely to note that it was the human family as a whole that had the requisite attributes of sense and brain to make such discoveries. It was not one subdivision of the differentiating human family that mastered these problems; it was man as a species.

The diversification of human stocks did, indeed, occur, and with this went on, in different parts of the world, different kinds of cultural inventions. The inventions, according to the present thesis, however, are in the first instance common to all humanity. The discovery of language, for example, was vastly more important than the discovery of glottal stops or modes of inflections or devices for indicating the subtleties of duration and recurrent action. In the same manner, the discovery of the family, if we may use the phrase, the discovery of stable groupings of persons around the procreative and child-rearing functions, the discovery of modes of adjustment between mates and between parents and progeny within the larger group, although showing very large variation, entails everywhere what may be called basically one central human preoccupation passing from the impulsive and temporally isolated reproductive act to the enduring ties of personal meanings, social responsibilities, and above all cultural coherence through parent-child interaction and transmission of ideas and values. The invention of language, the invention of the family, and some other inventions related to the crafts for dominating the physical world and maintaining life against enemies and against starvation and disease are common and universally shared human preoccupations. Individual differences in success in their solution are far less important than the common humanness of the adventure.

● *Cultures Do Not Bring out All that Is Human*

We might be tempted, therefore, to conclude that all human culture is essentially the expression of one central fact about human nature and that the things that are shared by *all* cultures represent that which is potential in all human nature. If so, it would be the unity of human nature that would show itself in the unity of culture. This seems at first to be obvious and self-evident. But there is a serious flaw in the logic by which these statements are derived. The fact is that only a small part of the first human nature is actually incorporated in *any* culture today. Culture is the elaborate development of certain very special aspects of human nature, leaving a large part of this human nature uncultivated and undeveloped. It is the human potentialities as a whole, springing not only from the currently culturized but also from the vast reaches of *unculturized* aspects of human nature, with which a book such as this must necessarily concern itself.

We can put it in another way. Since all human beings over the face of the earth known to us through the methods of history and archaeology have a great deal in common with regard to their wants and their ways of learning and thinking, it might be assumed that the known cultural arrangements sample fairly well the various kinds of cultures which might exist. One might go on from this point to assume that we really know a good deal about human nature, since, within the widely varying known cultures, it varies only in certain respects and reveals striking uniformities.

This is, however, misleading. All the past and existing societies have arisen within a rather narrow range of possibilities in comparison with what can easily be imagined. It is true that all known human cultures make use of fire and of domesticated animals; all respond to an unseen environment in a pattern that we call religion; all are organized around a family system with a sex differentiation much sharper than modern biology and psychology would seem to require; all involve economic surpluses which lead into activities far more complex and luxurious than would be found at the level of sheer fulfillment of elementary life needs. But at higher technological and artistic levels, the similarities are often dwarfed by the diversities. Many different kinds of latent potentialities emerge. *And in any culture these are only a few of the potentialities that lie latent.*

The learning process is sometimes "reversible": one may unlearn and start over. Often, however, it is relatively irreversible. As one makes one's bed, one lies in it. Indeed, the bed becomes a plaster cast of one's body. It is this process of progression toward rigidity, this process of crystallization of human learning and therefore of human culture, that we must examine if we are to understand the second human nature—the acquired human nature that becomes fixed and standardized.

In particular we must consider one aspect of human nature which results from the five attributes we have just discussed: the consolidation of *ways of perceiving and thinking under the pressure of wants;* the tendency to perceive, to think, and to standardize culturally the ways in which members of the group must perceive and think. We shall see that man, in becoming a culture-making animal, has often sacrificed one of his potentialities—the capacity for exploratory perceiving and thinking—to the exigencies of cultural requirements at a given time; and that the resulting ossification of creative thought is a basic obstacle in facing the task—the emancipation of new human natures—to which this book is devoted.

• Perception and the Sifting of Reality

We may well look first of all to the senses and the process of perceiving—our main tools in maintaining contacts with our environments.

Mankind generally assumes that it is in good contact with the world. The stuff of which we are made reveals how intimately we reflect the stuff of the world. Since living things arose in the sea, their existence depended upon continuous commerce with these environments; and the salt of the body fluids reminds us that the sea is within as well as around us. Life is of the substance of the sea. Later, reflecting evolution, living stuff reflected the substance of the soil and of the free air that moves about the soil. The inner world is never absolutely sundered from the outer, and the fulfillment of an interior self is never possible except through the delicate utilization of the bonds between the inner and the outer.

The more delicate processes that we define by the term *perception* are derived from these same processes of commerce between inner and outer. In the evolutionary process a sensitive spot on the surface becomes more and more sensitive to the particular types of external energies that it is specialized to receive. Sense organs, such as the eye, develop through a long series of complications from these original sensitive spots. At the same time, the sense organs become linked with muscle groups that bring about, in the responding individual, appropriate behavior in the situation that the sense organs report.

A sense organ must be truth-yielding, contact-making, "veridical." Moreover, the various aspects of the environment must be simultaneously reported; sight and hearing, for example, must give one another corroboration and mutual correction. We respond not to one object and then to another but to the joint or organized impact of the two. A world of many impressions is integrated into a totality. As Gibson[1] puts it, "the visual world" differs from the "visual field" in two basic properties: First, it is a synthesis of the many different visual fields that one might achieve by casting the eye about in various directions; and secondly, it is a summation in time of all one's experiences with many visual fields of the past. The visual world remains essentially the same as we walk along the road, turn from left to right, look up and down; the visual field at any given moment is a snapshot, a slice. By means of the visual field alone, we could not maintain orientation to the road or the world to which it leads. We construct in each modality (sight, hearing, etc.) a world appropriate to it and, by linking the various modalities, develop in time a world in which to live. The time sequence is

[1] J. J. Gibson, *The Perception of the Visual World*, Houghton Mifflin, 1950.

important both in the linking process and in the primal assumption developed by each of us that the world will still be there when we come back to it from around the corner and will still be there tomorrow when we awaken from sleep.

This modern picture is essentially in harmony with the conceptions developed by Herbart a century and a-half ago with reference to the process of "apperception." Each given sensory impression, said Herbart, is linked with other sensory impressions simultaneous with it, preceding it, or following it; and in time, clusters of associated sense impressions are formed. These act as sense masses to which new elements adhere, from moment to moment, like a sticky cluster to which new elements may always be added. In the process of learning, one always approaches each new problem in terms of the existing "apperception mass." A creaking sound, a dark cloud, a pungent odor in a given context gives rise to associations, memories, expectations which are parts of the apperception mass in which it is apperceived. Each new experience is in part determined by that which is already there.

This is the primary basis for the universal phenomenon of judging in terms of what we already know—the process to which political scientists and psychologists apply the term *stereotyping*. One interprets in the light of past experience; one expects a saw or a canary to behave as other saws and canaries have been found to behave. This is an expectation and anticipation that gives meaning and, unless frustrated through the failure of the object to conform, confirms the experience and strengthens the stereotype for further use. This is the same process by which, through fortunate or unfortunate connotations, processes of expectations of human beings are formed. When one individual is judged in the light of experience that does not truly define his character, the result may be a misjudgment. But the anticipation, expectation, classing, and conceptualizing of individuals on the basis of common features and experiences with them is simply the general psychological process by which, with many successes and many errors, the world of classes and concepts, the stable world for which there are names and to which there are attuned habits of response, is formed.

This means that not only recall and thought but the very

process of perception is itself warped from the beginning by prior experience. One sees and hears in terms of one's expectations—expectations that are almost never free of affective coloring. One expects a thing to do one good or ill—to help or hinder one's progress towards a goal. How far we have gone beyond dinner time is a factor relevant to the likelihood of our noticing things connected with food or even of our distorting the evidence so that we "hear" a call to dinner when it has not been given.

There are, then, two principles in the organization of perception: (1) the sheer *regularity* of our experience, by which one experience arouses expectation of another; (2) the relevance of the object to our desires (and fears). Expectancy is not the same as desire, but both are activators of perceptual responses. Desire (and fear, cf. p. 56) may make more vivid the associations between the given object and that apperception mass which belongs to the consummations of our needs. That which within us is waiting to move—the desire waiting to be fulfilled—sensitizes the act of perception to apprehend that which is already waiting to be apprehended. An indistinct, incompletely structured feature of the environment can always be thrown more readily into a structured form fulfilling the inherent trends of the apperception mass.

From these considerations follows the widespread tendency of human minds, like animal minds, to become crystallized in terms of outlook, mental habit, form of interpretation, the conception of what is to be expected; and from this follows the order, reasonableness, and good sense of a stable society. The very things that might be added through new contact with the environment and that might therefore jostle and disturb the existing apperception mass are repudiated as absurd. All this will occur even if there is no special vested interest, no special subject of preference for one experience rather than another. In his admirable study of the steps involved in recasting the structure of science, J. B. Conant has shown that new facts are accumulated by the dozens around the solid core of an established scientific outlook, but facts not easily squared with it do not change the outlook until, in time, they become numerous enough, interdependent enough, solid enough to suggest a new *theoretical structure,* which can then contest and ultimately overthrow the outlook that had been standardized. New facts, no matter how thoroughly established, do not gain general acceptance until there is a theoretical structure to accommodate them. *The second human nature is the stylized, habit-bound, culture-bound way of seeing which represents the (nearly) irreversible acquired pattern of a human nature which man has learned but cannot unlearn.*

The case becomes more dramatic, of course, when, in addition to sheer order, reason, common sense, and repeated experience as a basis for conservative viewpoint, there is a vigorous vested interest. Attacks upon techniques in the handicrafts, for example, will be relatively unimportant unless the handicraftsman is a person of prestige and power in the community. Attacks upon forms of government and forms of interpretation of the unseen world are more serious, for here neither the technique nor even the position of advantage of a single practitioner is involved but rather the power and status of a dominant group that can fight back. Thus when the Knights Templar achieved such great power during the Crusades as to constitute a threat to the dominant elements in church and state, it was only through torture and execution that their power could be broken.

In a society in which power is more widely scattered and no one vested interest secure enough upon its throne to command the rest, ways of thinking that defy the rules are countered with trepidation or a sneer rather than torture, imprisonment, and execution. Even here, however, when new forms of observation develop that appear to upset traditional viewpoints, as when the use of the microscope permits new aspects of life to be observed, the seats of power are in some degree shaken. The more unstructured or indistinct the data fed into the sense organs, the greater the role of our wishes and fears.[2] It follows necessarily that in the social sciences, where simple facts are difficult to come by and generalizations more difficult to document, the findings meet a massive resistance seldom encountered in the relatively simple structure offered by the physical sciences.

All the behavior that we have tried to recount, from the simplest act of perception to standardized limitations and preju-

[2] "Or in the night, imagining some fear,
How easy is a bush supposed a bear!"—*A Midsummer Night's Dream*

dices of a community, is utterly human and at root no more surprising than walking or sleeping. The castigation of one's fellows for their limited or warped outlook is comparable with the castigation of the heart for beating.

● Levels of Organization

Using a pyramid as an aid for the visualization, we may conceive of personality in terms of a series of *levels of organization*. Elementary biological phenomena extend over a very broad base, and at various levels above the base there are *derived* phenomena, expressions of functions dependent upon the basic ones, but reflecting learned—especially culturally learned—habits. This hierarchical organization would reveal at the top of the pyramid certain ego functions or integrative functions, organized around the individual's concept of himself.

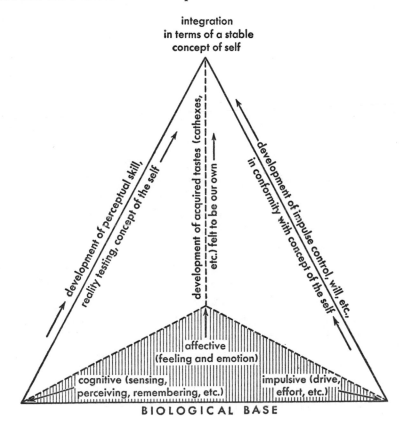

The present hypothesis is that throughout the whole human family the elementary biological phenomena shown at the base of the pyramid are essentially similar except for quantitative variations. Human beings have essentially the same drives, tastes, and interests, except insofar as these express individuality (cf. diagram) in dispositions toward distinctive growth and learning related to the development of (1) cognitive differences: ways of exploring the world, (2) affective differences: ways of feeling in response to it, and (3) impulse differences: ways of acting toward it, and the gradual achievement of integration of these under the aegis of a concept of oneself.

From this point of view, culture would not be conceived to modify the basic drive components—or even those complex structural relations of drives that we define as temperament—except through *connecting them with specific outer and inner stimuli and with one another*. Some forms of personality style, such as perseveration, or grace, or impulsiveness, or dissociative trends, may well likewise be basic in the sense of expressing a genetic structure. Moving up the pyramid, however, we should encounter responses that vary strikingly with the environment. The things that make people angry—and the things that they love—will differ.

Personality style within a culture area will represent some degree of standardization of such attitudes. Members of a cultural group will manifest sometimes narrow, sometimes wide, variations, including standardized responses to norms and codes. To the question: "Is human nature always the same?" we must reply: (1) that the basic attributes are roughly the same, though there are qualitative and quantitative variations; and (2) that the *derived* patterns, whether in the form of temperament or cathexis or culturally ingrained cognitive-affective-conative responses to situations, may appear on the surface to make human nature a chameleonlike adaptation to circumstances, but, when viewed developmentally, still carry us back to an essentially uniform initial human nature, reflecting profound individual differences in the strength of the various tendencies but not enough to require different maps for different people.

Phrases used to suggest that "you can't change human nature," usually reflect, through naive cynicism, a system of culturally ingrained patterns (conceit, energy, laziness, etc.) and have but little to do with the "basic" human nature considered here. But to assume the unlimited plasticity of human nature is equally far from our thesis. The degree and form of human plasticity is at the heart of the problem of personality and culture.

The thesis developed here is that as one goes up the pyramid (from biological potentialities to cultural and personal actualities), one forgets how to climb down. The second human nature is a rich but rather rigid system of patterns that we do not know how to outgrow.

Chapter 5:

How We Come To Want
What We Want

In the preceding chapter we saw mankind clinging to a cultural system that involves a rather considerable degree of blind and rigid investment in a way of looking at life. The task of the present chapter is to try to understand this immensely valuable, though blind and rigid, investment. For this chapter discusses "how we come to want the things we want"—how our inborn needs are channeled—or canalized—so that we want specific things, acquire specific tastes, build a world of *values* which expresses our own individuality and from which we seldom escape or wish to escape.

● *Human Needs*

We shall assume for convenience that it is possible to classify our inborn needs in four main categories:

1. Visceral needs—that is, needs directly related to the vital organs. These include, among others, needs for food, water, air, etc.; needs related to the reproductive system; needs related to protection of the body from extremes of cold and heat.

2. Activity needs. These include the need to explore and manipulate and the urge to "keep going" which differentiates a healthy child from a very tired or sick one, and a normal adult from an isolated psychotic adult.

3. Sensory needs. These include needs for color, tone, rhythm;

the need to orient ourselves to the environment; the need to escape confusion; the "urge to perceptual clarity."

4. The need to avoid or escape attack, injury, threat, shock, or unbearable disturbance, as exemplified by fear, disgust, rage, and many other "emergency responses."

But suppose we agree on the universality of human needs. Suppose we agree that all men grow hungry. This does not tell us what *particular* food a particular man will like—cheesecake, oysters, or spaghetti. Or suppose we know that they all love rhythm; this does not tell us whether a given man will crave Bach or Berlioz, Gershwin or Irving Berlin. Our present essay is a study of the *way in which the universal human needs become specific.*

• How Needs Become Specific

We immediately encounter two kinds of hints: (1) those provided by general social background, and (2) those provided by personal history. There are some things which all (or nearly all) members of certain social groups desire, such as long feathers strung around the head and down the back, as with Sioux Indian braves, or strings of letters after one's name, as with American academic personages. Other wants or needs are highly personalized. One may dream of going back to one's childhood home and finding the old man who could tell such wonderful stories about pirates. If it is true that life is made up of the pursuit of goals, it seems to follow that there are some goals that *all* members of a social group *share* and other goals that must be seen in terms of the *unique story of each individual.*

Let us turn first to goals which are shared by members of social groups. Even in such a simple matter as needing food to keep the body going, human groups differ enormously in the things they regard as food. Most of us would not consider the candles on the mantelpiece as food. With the Eskimo and his need for fats, it is easy to see how the children are early exposed to the eating of tallow and blubber and how the acceptance of these fats becomes deeply ingrained. There may be individual experiences, however, which are not so easily explained. The tiny brown stone with its little white spot which was to me the symbol that fairies had visited the creek was to my five-year-old imagination an object of enormous value. The "old oaken bucket," the "little red schoolhouse," the pressed flower from an album made up in childhood days—all these and countless other objects are precious to the person in whom they have fulfilled some specific need at some time in life. These needs range all the way from simple food needs, such as the "doughnuts that mother used to make," to very complex social needs, such as the need for a particular form of prestige—*e.g.*, the need to be pre-eminent in the Masonic order.

The basic psychology of all these processes is the same, whether they deal with simple physical needs or with more complex needs of the ego or of the member of a social group: in all these cases the *raw material of primitive human needs has been socially molded in a specific way.* A man is not just hungry; he is hungry for a T-bone steak. He is no longer just a lonely man; he is a man who wants the intellectual companionship of someone who can out-argue him in discussing Tolstoi. He is no longer just a man who enjoys color and tone; he is a man who wants Van Gogh paintings or the music of Brahms.

This process by which the diffuse needs of early childhood have been channeled into specific form is what we are calling channeling or canalization. This is the phenomenon of "acquired taste." It is a primitive form of the universal human process of developing "values"—developing an orientation that "this is good," "that is bad." The world is classified into that which *does* and that which *does not* satisfy our needs; and the process of channeling is a guide to the understanding of this process.

All human societies instill in their members the ways in which desires are to be satisfied. Thus, from a remarkable study of white children captured by American Indians, we learn that the great majority grew up as Indians and never wanted to go back. "Indian education, quite independent of the incidental color of their hair, eyes, and skin, had cast them into a certain form, had pressed upon them a certain cultural pattern; and one cannot throw away, like an old shoe, a firmly acquired cultural pattern at a moment arbitrarily chosen." [1]

[1] E. H. Ackerknecht, "White Indians," *Bulletin of the History of Medicine,* Vol. 15, 1944, pp. 15-36.

- *Canalization vs. Conditioning*

Canalization is clearly a form of *learning*. The reader of this book has undoubtedly already encountered a description of another type of learning called *conditioning*. Canalization can easily be differentiated from conditioning if attention is given to the nature of the satisfactions which play a part in the learning process. In the classical (Pavlovian) type of conditioning, there is a signal which is presented along with or just before a stimulus which evokes a response—for example, a buzzer to be sounded before or during the process of presentation of food to dogs. After a few trials, the buzzer initiates the flow of saliva as if the food were actually present. The buzzer does not, however, *become food;* the buzzer is not eaten and digested. The buzzer plays no direct part in the actual satisfaction of the drive; it is simply a signal that a satisfying object is to be *expected*. And no amount of simultaneous subjection of the individual to buzzer and food will make the buzzer into a drive-satisfying object. *But in every case of canalization, the stimulus is a satisfier from the beginning.*

In the course of experimental work on the acquisition of food responses in animals, P. T. Young has amassed much evidence that sheer repetition in eating certain classes of foods makes them more acceptable.[2] Other things being equal, it is the object that has been repeatedly used, that is standardized as food. This raises the question whether sheer *familiarity* is sufficient explanation of the phenomenon of channeling or canalization. Sheer familiarity as such, without repeated commerce with the object in such a way as to satisfy a drive, does *not* appear to lead to channeling. "Familiarity breeds contempt"; but familiarity may also at times breed indifference. By itself it cannot explain this universal phenomenon of "learning to like" that which has frequently been used as a satisfier—a progressive increase in the positive attitude toward objects because they have afforded the specific way in which our needs were met.

[2] P. T. Young, "Studies of Food Preference, Appetite and Dietary Habit. VI. Habit, Palatability and Diet as Factors Regulating the Selection of Food by the Set," *J. Comp. Psychol.*, Vol. 39, 1946, pp. 139-176.

• *Canalization as a Form of Learning*

Since canalization is only one kind of learning, let us take a broad view of the process of learning and see how canalization fits into it. We need some clarification of the ways in which responses are modified—the ways in which we "learn." Psychologists include under the term learning not only the memorizing of factual items such as the capitals of the states or the irregular French verbs but all interaction between the living individual and the environment which results in changed behavior patterns. The following are some of the commoner kinds of learning:

1. Simple Pavlovian conditioning, just described.

2. The *operant conditioning* described by Skinner[3]—the reinforcement or strengthening of a response by rewarding it, *e.g.,* giving food after a man or animal makes the "correct" response.

3. The simple *associative linkage* between experiences, as in connecting lightning with thunder (which throughout the history of psychology was always regarded as a prototype of learning until in recent years the emphasis turned from ideas to behavior).

4. The *reorganization of perception,* as in the sudden grasp of a situation, the "aha phenomenon," the sudden insight emphasized by students of creative thinking.

5. The more general *reorganization of the whole outlook,* involving not only perception but also memory, thought, imagination; not only purely cognitive responses having to do with fact but also feeling and emotional and impulsive factors which make the world seem different this morning from the way it seemed yesterday evening.

6. The *canalization process* now being described.

Perhaps all these forms of learning can be reduced to one general form; perhaps all learning is the *forming of connections*—connections between sensations, connections between acts, connections between ideas, connections between an idea and an act. From this point of view canalization is the *connection of a need with a specific way of satisfying that need.*

[3] B. F. Skinner, *The Behavior of Organisms,* Appleton-Century, 1938.

But this would not obliterate the practical distinction between channeling and the other types of learning. For example, the fact that a conditioned stimulus, such as a buzzer or bell, does not reduce the drive tension—*i.e.*, the fact that the organism does not ingest and digest the buzzer or bell—sharply distinguishes conditioning from channeling, for in channeling there is direct commerce with a satisfying object.

• *Are Canalized Responses Ever Lost?*

The practical distinction between canalization and conditioning becomes important when we ask what will happen if the drive is aroused but the gratification not given. In the case of Pavlovian conditioning, the substitute stimulus which elicits the response need only be presented a few times *without* the concomitant use of the food in order to lose its stimulus value. If the dog is not given food when the buzzer sounds, the response soon fails to appear. In the same way, in operant conditioning, if the drive-satisfying reward is not given after the appropriate behavior, the latter soon ceases. The process of "extinction" is the loss of connection between substitute stimulus and response.

Everyday habits based on conditioning, such as little courtesies and etiquette behavior, drop out if they bring no smiles or approving responses. There is nothing clearly corresponding to this in the case of canalized responses. The reader will remember many experiences from childhood in which strong attachments, enthusiasms, acquired tastes, were formed which have not died out. One encounters again, with joy, a face which one has not seen in many years. Dad gets down on his tummy on the living room floor to play with the electric train that he has just given Junior for Christmas. American Legionnaires behave like boys when they step out into the delights of a Fifth Avenue parade. On the surface, at least, canalized responses do not "extinguish."

Indeed, does the canalized response ever have a *chance* to extinguish? If in Pavlov's experiments the buzzer is repeatedly sounded in a nonfood situation (in which case it functions as an annoying or meaningless signal), the normal response to such an annoying (or meaningless) signal is to turn away in boredom or disgust. It is not the passage of time that caused the response to the buzzer to disappear, but the fact that the two responses—one, buzzer-food presentation, and two, buzzer-no-food presentation— have competed and the latter has become victorious. There was a genuine and dynamic reason why the response extinguished. When canalized responses do not extinguish, the reason may be the fact that they represent cases in which the situation has consistently brought direct commerce with something affording satisfaction and has never brought a contrary response.[4]

The problem is to identify what kinds of situations there are in which no opportunity is given for extinction. This calls for an inventory of such direct satisfiers in terms of (a) culturally-bound situations such as those described on page 61, and (b) individually unique situations. Drinking beer or soda-fountain beverages would be an illustration of the first; so also would be the types of music and dance which express distinctively the culturally molded esthetic demands of any given group. The specific personal gratifications that each of us enjoys—the pattern of hobbies, mannerisms, humor, pensiveness, and whimsey that characterizes each of us distinctively—such as a taste for Turkish coffee, or goat's milk, or Stravinsky, or Benchley—would represent the second.

In discussing with students the question of the nonextinction of canalization, I have always found special interest in the question of what happens to those childhood hobbies which are supposed to "drop out" as one grows older. I suggest that these canalizations are not entirely extinguished. They come back in dreams; they come back in moments of fantasy. We discover in the attic a toy that we played with as a child, and a glow of delight spreads over us. What has happened is not really the elimination of the response, but rather the reawakening of an old response that had been *overlaid* by other responses which are ordinarily more appropriate to the tasks of an adult. "When I was a

---

[4] Another way of saying this is in terms of the distinction between *"precurrent"* responses such as pricking up the ears and *"consummatory"* responses such as digesting food. The canalized stimulus is one which brings about a *consummatory* response every time it acts upon the individual. Such being the case, there is no opportunity for a consummatory response to fail to occur. Cf. C. S. Sherrington, *The Integrative Action of the Nervous System,* 2nd ed., Yale, 1947, pp. 329-333.

child," wrote St. Paul, "I spake as a child . . . but now that I am a man I put away childish things." It seems likely that we are so busy being our present adult selves that we cannot "live the past along with the present." If, however, the two responses do not conflict and there is a "pause in the day's occupation," the children's hour may certainly come back, inserted, wedged in between the hours that belong to adulthood.

But the process of forming new canalizations is never ended. The infant, the adolescent, the mature man and woman, and the aged are all seen avidly acquiring new tastes. The height of vigor in the prime of life may entail an enormous capacity for fresh discovery of things worth pouring oneself into, and an old age not too blighted with loss of vigor may still have its great delights in self-discovery. To be sure, the canalizations of any period are to some extent transferred or generalized from earlier periods; but if there is no genuine newness, there is no true transfer, but just a replication of the old. Indeed, newness is an essential feature in the craving for experience which we have already sketched in terms of sensory and activity drives. Canalization entails a world of discovery, not a gliding through endless well-worn grooves. The *making* of the grooves is the canalization process, and new grooves can always be made. But something is conserved from all canalizations, and this something always takes part in the freshly acquired canalizations of each new period.

- ● *Concepts Which Resemble the*
  Concept of Canalization

It may be worth while to glance at a few other concepts which seem to be related to the concept of canalization.

First, Freud's concept of cathexis, literally, "investment": Instinctual energy is invested in a particular object which gives satisfaction, such as the breast or the whole mother, or the system of symbols associated with her. The world is thus structured largely in terms of such investments, and only with difficulty can the structure undergo fundamental change.

The concept of cathexis appears to do much that is attempted above in the utilization of the concept of channeling. There is the idea of mobile energy which takes a specifically channeled form. On the other hand, Freud recognizes the possibility of withdrawing an investment from one region and assigning it to another. This is an idea quite different from that of the irreversible nature of canalization. Looking still more closely at the analogy, cathexis means basically the investment of energy in an object, rather than the satisfaction of a drive. And of course Freud's theory of *libido* is presupposed. On the whole, then, the analogy with cathexis should not be pushed very far.

Closely related to the concept of canalization is William McDougall's conception of the formation of *sentiments*.[5] Believing in fundamental propensities which can be directed upon many objects—many objects, for example, arouse wonder or feelings of self-assertion—the individual builds up a personal structure of sentiments involving a cluster of instincts organized around an object or person. One may, for example, feel love, wonder, self-abasement in relation to a father-figure, and the feeling connected with each of these instinctive tendencies may be fused with the others in one composite feeling. This is a sentiment. McDougall's idea is of great value, especially in connection with the way in which he described the derivation of feelings toward the self. One may love, hate, and fear oneself and respect, be amused at, be bewildered at oneself. All these responses make up the "self-regarding sentiment."

In protest against McDougall came attempts to find fundamentals of human motivation which were *not rooted in instincts at all*. One of these protests was R. S. Woodworth's *Dynamic Psychology*.[6] Woodworth developed the thought that a habit may, after much use, become an ingrained part of the person and may continue to function *without needing the support of the original instinct*. Thus, even when no longer governed by the original self-assertive instinct a man may play the "great game of politics" for a thousand different motives. After finding himself a small niche as a "power behind the throne," he may play politics as one plays solitaire, as an intriguing way to spend his time. Such habits, originally developed in the service of an instinct, become independent. Woodworth, therefore, offers the thesis that "a mechanism may become a drive." There is no practical limit to

[5] W. McDougall, *Introduction to Social Psychology*, 15th ed., Luce, 1923.
[6] Columbia University Press, 1918.

the number of drives which may in this way be derived from a few instincts.

Twenty years after Woodworth's thesis, a somewhat similar thesis was offered with great vigor and skill by Gordon W. Allport.[7] Allport emphasized the *integration* of personality rather than the separate instincts and the process of *understanding* which, at the cognitive level, corresponds to the integrated life of motivation. He applied the conception of *levels,* by which higher integrations must be considered in terms of laws of their own rather than be constantly reduced to simpler principles. From this vantage point, however an activity arises, it reaches a point where it is self-maintaining and may then be continued for its own sake independently of the original instinctive energies which started it. This is the doctrine of *functional autonomy.*

The canalization principle differs from those of Woodworth and Allport. The canalization hypothesis is based on the premise that the original drive, whether visceral, sensory, motor, or the emergency type (cf. page 60), is still the core of the activity. It is not transformed or hidden. Rather, it comes to be satisfied by a *particular object,* and this process goes on progressively, so that there is a more and more intimate relation between the drive and the particular object.

How, then, may we account for the wide range of activities, such as politics, religion, art, sports, wit, and folklore, that seem to go on autonomously? It is hard to name any specific drive or combination of drives which must necessarily underlie the delight which fifteenth-century painters experienced in learning to master the third dimension, ceasing to paint in the flat, and painting persons and scenes in full perspective. One might perhaps say that the young artists of the era delighted in outdoing their teachers and that an instinct of self-assertion was involved. But the argument is put the wrong way around. If there is a delight in skillful representation, skillful representation will become the sort of thing in which people compete. People do not, as a rule, compete in activities which have no intrinsic value— such as finding the largest number of different colors that can be used in painting a house. Even when small children compete as

[7] *Personality: A Psychological Interpretation,* Holt, 1937.

to who can say a doggerel rhyme most rapidly or who can spit the farthest, the activity is something that is fun to do anyhow, something that expresses the self and is thus worth making a competitive game out of.

Canalization exemplifies that vast world of delight in sensory gratification which is represented by the arts, literatures, and amenities of civilized life—the complex skilled activities of eye and hand, or of the whole body, as in theater and dance, craftsmanship, sports, and self-display. These activities are related to human wants which appear very early in life. Joy in color and tone is one of the most obvious of infantile delights, and joy in mastery of the body and in increasing skill in controlling the body and the environment is one of the most obvious early satisfiers. They belong to the activity drives and sensory drives discussed above. The trouble with the doctrine of instinct, as it got started in the early years of modern psychology, was that it was limited to *visceral* drives. It was modeled upon the food-getting, electric-shock-avoiding patterns of experimental animals, omitting the fact that in the higher animals there is an enormous amount of vigorous activity in the pursuit of goals which is not "instinctive" in the narrow sense of serving the visceral needs. In fact, it would be extraordinary if canalization did not occur in the case of response to color, tone, physical movement, skilled manipulation, which are among the most obvious examples of complex human activities which can be gratified in specific ways and which therefore tend to consolidate into recognizable forms, both personal and social.

If the sensory drives and activity drives may be canalized, and if such canalizations play an important part in the adult world of values, we may judge why the world of hobbies, enthusiasms, absorbing preoccupations, is so often more useful in predicting human activity than reference to the "basic drives." Men live not by bread alone—nor by the gamut of all the visceral drives alone. They fuse these visceral drives with other interests, as color, odor, and spatial arrangement in a Japanese flower arrangement are related to symbols meaningful for the whole person and the whole culture and as, in the Western world, love-music combines the erotic impulse with the vast subtleties and riches of tonal and rhythmic satisfactions. Often, as in the aggressive struggle to master a problem which will not let us go to sleep or in the attempt to complete an unfinished task, the aggressive effort may be fused with the intellectual pleasures of discovery.

This fusion of motives seems to be as typical of the small child as it is of the adult. How often the solemn adult finds it impossible to get small children interested in the "need for rest" when an exciting mystery or hilarious comedy is presented on TV or on films or in the comics! The aggression of slapstick, for example, may be combined with pleasures of recognizing familiar faces, and with a new and intriguing manifestation of the storyteller's art. I attended a Thanksgiving dinner not long ago in which the adults munched ahead manfully, while the small children, after one tiny dab of the turkey and stuffing, wanted only to get down and play with the toys and games on the floor. How often the aggrieved mother finds that food is not enough to keep the excited or restless child at peace! There are realities more interesting, more burning, more demanding in our world of fascinating values embodied in things that can be looked at, pulled apart, put together, combined, made to recreate a fresh world.

It would appear that the visceral drives, the sensory drives, and the activity drives can all be canalized, sometimes separately but usually in combination, and form the firm basis of personal values. The question arises whether our fourth category, the avoidance drives and emergency drives, such as fear, rage, disgust, shame, and the response of extreme pain (p. 61), can also serve to form canalizations. Common speech, which is so often a useful guide, speaks of "pet peeves," "favorite hates," or, as the French have it, *bêtes noirs* (black beasts). This may mean that certain objects are more firmly tied to the avoidance drives than are others. We might say that people come to dread a particular pain, such as the pain from the dentist's drill, and that this becomes more powerful than other pain-avoidance drives which were at first equally strong. Things which small children fear, like dark rooms or grimacing masks, may become gradually more unbearable. It would appear, at least, that these "canalizations of avoidance drives" might be analogous to canalizations of the visceral drives.

Let us resume our comparison of canalizations with other dynamic principles. There are still two more conceptions in modern psychology that are similar to canalization, and need to be considered. The French make use of the verbs *canaliser* and *drainer* to indicate a channeling process. In the work of Pierre Janet, the suggestion is made that the diffuse energies of a patient may pour into a channel which is already being used.

The most stimulating use of the term *canalization* in the psychology of the English-speaking world is that of E. B. Holt who, in a monumental volume, *Animal Drive and the Learning Process*,[8] undertook to describe the way in which bodily energies are channeled during the embryonic period into particular action patterns.

Oversimplifying his statement: when a drive is aroused, the details of the situation—for example, the odor, taste, and appearance of food—serve to draw the individual on to the consummation of the activity which satisfies the drive. The arousal of the drive will lead the individual deeper into the "trap." Thus, Pavlovian conditioning leads into canalization.

We can use Holt in another way. He suggests that, just as the organism is trapped into positive responses which relate to its satisfactions of its needs, so, in general, gross injury leads to disorganized response which, in the long run, will knock or kick the object away. I believe that those who have seen young infants or little animals in such stress situations as being bitten, drenched, or otherwise hurt or upset will agree with Holt that first response to injury or disturbance is often of this disorganized sort, rather than a specific avoidance reflex.

Nevertheless, there are also instances in which a *disturbing stimulus traps the organism*, just as a satisfying one can trap it, and, so to speak, holds it in its grip. A familiar example is the man who has hold of a high tension wire. The current causes a spasm of the forearm muscles, and as long as the current continues to flow no act of will can break up the response. The involuntary clutching is the very activity that causes the hand to hold on to the wire. There are many life situations in which we are, in a similar way, "trapped" by disturbing or damaging stimuli from which there is no escape—no escape except by the impact of some

[8] Holt, 1931.

other vigorous stimulus which would forcibly pull the trouble-making stimulus away from us.

In psychoanalytic doctrine, Freud has described many cases of continuous or repetitive reliving of painful stimulation, using the term "repetition compulsion" to describe the phenomenon of going back, back, back over the most painful memories. From the present viewpoint, when once the brain has received the impact of this disturbing stimulus, we are likely to be trapped in the same fashion and to find no escape unless a vigorous counter stimulus pulls us away or pulls the situation away from us. This concept of being trapped by a situation, whether in Holt's or in Freud's formulation, is basically appropriate to what is here called canalization.

But, of all the concepts of modern biology and psychology most closely comparable to canalization, the one to be most emphasized is the concept of *imprinting* as developed by the naturalist experimenters Lorenz and Tinbergen. It is clear from their work that there is a specific capacity in the newborn of many species, bird and mammalian, to respond specifically to some visual or other cue. For example, the beak or the outspread wings or the cluck of the mother bird may have a highly specific releasing effect on the young animal's readiness to respond. It may "trigger off" an appropriate response in the young. We might, at first glance, get the impression that throughout the whole span of its existence on the earth this particular species is selectively attuned to a few specific stimuli of this type and that heredity therefore limits its repertory of behavior. Experiment shows, however, that what is *first* brought to bear upon the little animal or bird at the appropriate period in its development has a profound and lasting effect. The graylag gosling, for example, normally sees the mother's form *and follows her*. But suppose that, instead of the mother, there is at the appropriate time the figure of the *human investigator*. He moves and the young follow *him*. Indeed, thereafter they will follow him rather than the mother. It is what acts *first* that fixates the response. It is almost as if energies were invested which could never later be withdrawn. This is close to the conception of irreversible, inextinguishable canalizations. It is certainly not identical with it. For one thing, the imprinting process in the animals and birds studied must occur at a specific phase of development, and before or after this phase it cannot be established. My interest here is in a broad similarity, not in identity.

The reference to these other ways in which new tastes are formed is not meant to suggest that any of them is an exact equivalent of the canalization process. Nor is it meant that one must choose between one or another of the formulations here. Perhaps several of them, perhaps all of them, are permissible. Our facts are uncertain. We shall need to wear our hypotheses like a loose garment, ready to be put aside as new information becomes available.

But we seem to have reason to believe that the channeling of responses is a reality coextensive with life. The small infant is developing enormous favoritism for his mother's form and appearance as fast as his visual system develops in such a way as to permit differentiation between her and others. Indeed, he begins to crave her specifically. Not only the clinical evidence on early attachments to the mother but also the research of René Spitz suggests that when these attachments have once been formed, no one else can serve as substitute. Thus the eight-month-old child is actually *more* upset by the loss of its mother than is the two-month-old child. The eight-month-old has formed strong attachments; channelings have made the mother literally indispensable. Similarly, throughout life, canalization involves deep cravings and deep hurts when the thing craved cannot be had. Often another *person* is the canalized center of life.

• Self-love as a Form of Channeling

One of the great reasons for personal and social continuity from year to year—for rigidity, if one looks at it in this light—is that we derive satisfaction from being ourselves. Thus far we have spoken of the objects in the environment, the things to eat and drink, the things to listen to, the people who gratify or infuriate us. We have already hinted, however, that while this all goes on we are also developing an interest in our own activities, canalized upon our own action patterns. We must look more closely at this matter of the way in which we are responding to ourselves.

The newborn child loses but little time in discovering that he has hands and feet. He is reaching, touching, experiencing sensations of contact. Along with his reaching, he is experiencing both the external contacts made and the sensations from the muscles. By five or six months of age he takes delight in roll-over and push-up games. Late in the first year he is beginning to recognize his own mirror image. During the second year his first efforts with words begin to reveal that he can refer to himself as a person, just as he can refer to other individuals. He has not only detected the parts but grasped the whole.

Now both on the parts and on the whole he develops very manifest canalizations. Just as he develops a canalization on the mother's breast and voice, so he develops a delight in his own person. As Walt Whitman said, "There is so much of me and all so luscious." Primitive rubbing and manipulation of the body and vigorous defense of the body against injury or shock begin to mean that the world of personal canalizations ceases to be scattered and becomes organized; and the central object of all is his own body. We recall the beautiful story of Narcissus, who fell in love with his own reflection in a pool. Self-love is probably not very sharply defined when it first appears. Indeed, it may be a rather warm, diffuse, tingling sense of "it's good to be alive" or of simple delight in one's existence and activity. As the child discovers the parts of the body, learns that they go together, manipulates, grabs for his toes, learns to recognize his own voice, he comes to delight in this body-self.

During the second and third years, however, as he delights in more and more things which he can do, it becomes more and more an action self. See how fast I can run! But whatever is emphasized by society as an attribute of the self may become an important field for canalizations. As rewards and punishments are offered for being good or being bad, as defined by society, the self becomes still more complex. One thinks of oneself as good or as acceptable or lovable. The self is that which can win affection or applause. Just as the self when it first appeared on the scene was the *physical* self, so now it becomes the *social* self, the self depending upon attributes or traits, things that one can do, things that are acceptable or unacceptable to others, things that win the prestige or status in the group. Instead of, "I am bigger than you," it becomes a question of running faster or shooting straighter or, later on, bringing home better marks on the report card.

At least this is so in the kinds of social organization which we know. It is true of the industrial societies of the Western world, and apparently these values organized around the self have been with the civilized men of the Western world for a far longer time than the era of industrialism represents. In the Old and New Testaments and in the literature of Greece and Rome, the enormous preoccupation with personal worth, with individualized excellence, in terms of skill, knowledge, rectitude of conduct warrant the use of the term *individualism* for this type of society. Children, however, apparently take some time to assimilate fully this intense preoccupation with individual worth. We can watch them at three and four years of age learning the standards of competition for status which prevail among older children and adults.

It would appear that in many of the great Asian civilizations this intense preoccupation with personal worth is less easily found. In most Asian societies the thing to do is to fulfill the obligations of the social position which one inherits, not to become competitively or pre-eminently worthy in one's own personal right. In many preliterate societies, also, the intense status demands that we take for granted are rather poorly developed. We do not have accurate ways of measuring such matters, and any statement should be made cautiously, but it appears that just as all value systems depend upon the organization of the society in which they grow, so the preoccupation with the self as a central canalized object must be regarded as to some degree a function of the individualistic and competitive nature of Western societies. In fact, it is likely that in the increasing intensity of competition that has accompanied the Commercial Revolution and the Industrial Revolution of recent centuries, the individualism of Western man has taken a still more sharply competitive form.

Perhaps this statement is already out of date. Perhaps factors are at work in the modern world which are making people more dependent upon being like others than was the case fifty or a hundred years ago. Perhaps there are pressures, as David Riesman[9] suggests, that tend to make us more and more concerned with what the other fellow is doing and less and less concerned with the sharp outlines of our own individuality. Such issues are raised here to remind the reader that the form of canalization varies with the social order in which it is expressed.

There is much to suggest that there is a favorable moment for the fulfillment of any specific action tendency. In view of the irregularities and complexities in growth, we can recognize that there are individual differences as well as valid generalizations regarding the readiness to satisfy drives in different ways at different periods. We can say, however, that the psychoanalytic material on the enormous intensity of early drive gratification of infant in relation to mother's form, voice, and so on probably describe phenomena of the same general type.

Later, when symbols are used, they serve, of course, to complicate—but also to solidify and give continuity to—early patterns. Abiding value systems are formed while symbols for ways of satisfying wants are held in common by all members of a group; notably, symbols of a strong father and a tender mother. Value, typically, is a *system* of ideas and orientation rather than a single idea. Each society maintains its own system of associated canalizations and hands these forward to its biological and cultural descendants. This offers at least a major clue to the phenomenon of "cultural lag," the fact that various aspects of a social system lag behind those which are undergoing rapid change. Often, for example, an economic innovation, such as an industrial invention or even a region to be exploited, gives rise to new practices almost overnight, whereas the fine arts, religion, morals, even family structure may be slow to adjust to the changes which appear to be required. Compromises are often effected, and rationalizations evolve for a grudging acceptance of those new ideas which are forced by the new technology; but much of the old outlook on life is long maintained.

This type of conservatism, this clinging to that which was precious in one's own childhood, is profoundly intensified and complicated by the fact that one has also formed during childhood an

[9] *The Lonely Crowd,* Yale, 1950.

image of oneself as being a certain kind of person. This image is good. It is a central stabilizing and standardizing factor. It is based, in fact, partly upon the perception of father and mother, who in the long run are good and upon whom we are dependent; indeed, we have no choice, for many reasons, but to form our self-image partly upon the image of them. The image, however, becomes complex; becomes distinctive; becomes something highly personal and precious, more and more internalized and incapable of full communication through words. And as Schilder[10] so brilliantly showed, it becomes (whether consciously or unconsciously) a great centralizing and standardizing center of worth, of value, around which other specific and local values are arranged.

From such a point of view, it appears that since the self is largely made up of images of persons, and things which are here and now standardized in the culture, and since one cannot leave them without leaving oneself, there is an enormous anchor to windward preventing the extravagant dislocations which a rapidly changing society would otherwise induce. Mankind somehow maintains something of its continuity even when uprooted by new gospels or an industrial revolution or the weight of conquest by an alien power.

In perhaps the most dramatic of all total reconstructions of human life occurring within the span of one generation, the Manus people of the Admiralty Islands, as described by Margaret Mead,[11] leaped from the Stone Age to the modern world. Some Manus values are, nevertheless, still preserved. In the same fashion, Herskovitz has shown the maintenance of some elements of African folklore despite the centuries of expatriation, slavery, social upheaval, and physical and educational reconstruction which have been the lot of the West African peoples of slave trade days. In the same way, much that is Greek, much that is Hebrew, functions almost automatically in the technological complexities of Pittsburgh or Oak Ridge.

[10] P. Schilder, *The Image and Appearance of the Human Body*, London, *Psyche Monographs*, 1936.
[11] *New Worlds for Old*, Morrow, 1956.

• *Canalization and Conflict*

What will happen if the individual is canalized upon two conceptions of himself, only one of which he can seriously maintain? He is in the position of a college student who must choose between a medical and a legal career. The issue is, of course, partly the world of satisfactions which the practice of law might offer as contrasted with the world of satisfactions involved in the practice of medicine. Each could be looked at objectively in terms of earnings, prestige, place in society. But at a deeper level each could be looked at in terms of the *kind of self,* the kind of picture of one's own individuality that one has drawn. William James remarked that the young lawyer or medical man had, by thirty, crystallized into a firm pattern which was no longer reversible. Each of two alternatives, "sweet and good," is now available, but once the choice has been made the other will forever become unrealizable. The student knows he is deciding between two ways of life and deciding *between two selves.* The decision is often postponed because of its formidable and threatening character. When once it is made, however, one soon notices a consolidation and crystallization of the values which band together as expressive of the choice made.

Choice means conflict. Canalizations are a terrible nuisance; they are sure to get pitted against one another. There are several goals involved wherever life gets at all complicated. The situation is never quite like that of the ass who starved to death between the two bales of hay which were equally attractive. More often, asses—and men—starve to death because the two bales of hay are very different, because each has desirable attributes which the other does not have. For bales of hay, we can substitute jobs, honors, social positions, whatever is satisfying. Far more common than starving to death between them, however, is the choice of one. There may be ways of finding some of the other satisfactions which have been lost. The medical man may keep up an interest in law or concern himself with "forensic medicine," or may become interested in the legal problems which his friends who decided in favor of law have been trying to solve. Ordinarily, however, it is characteristic of the rejected goals that one is a bit wistful about them. They do not seem to die out happily and completely. That is, as a matter of fact, what we should expect, if the doctrine of the irreversibility of canalizations mentioned above should turn out to be true. We are afraid that it is true. We are afraid that conflicts can be "solved" by making decisions, but not solved in the sense that the rejected goals can lose their lure completely.

Most of these problems are problems of alternative ways of satisfying basic wants and are subject to all the difficulties mentioned above, including the fact that one must choose between two or more different *selves*. Some of these conflicts, however, are not conscious. The individual is not aware that he is pursuing two incompatible goals, or that his decision in favor of one is frustrating the pursuit of another. Suppose he has a picture of himself as one who is ruthlessly honest, yet expects friends to do a little lying in his behalf to get him through a tight spot.

Sexual matters, about which there is such intense feeling, are not basically different here from the others, since in all cases there are wants to be gratified and there are also wants which will be frustrated if the gratification is pursued. Along with this there is the sense of two different kinds of selves. Will one, if one gratifies one set of wants, "kick oneself" because another kind of a self with a particular kind of self-respect has been given up? In all these cases the conflict problem is one of a choice between canalizations and, usually, one of a choice between two self-canalizations, two desired pictures of oneself.

It is, of course, the half-conscious or unconscious aspects of these conflicts that preoccupy most psychoanalytic studies of human difficulties. The very fact that one finds it unbearable to view oneself in a particular light, the very fact that one may want something but not be willing to admit that one wants it makes the conflict especially hard to handle. The person gets all tied up in knots, experiencing a fear or hatred of himself which he cannot understand—a sense of inferiority, inadequacy, or guilt which he is unlikely to be able to work out of unless he can get some understanding guide to help him see what wants he is refusing to admit and what kinds of solutions are realistically available to him. It is in the unconscious canalizations upon paths of life, especially paths which involve a sense of worth or worthlessness in the self, that most of the psychiatric issues take shape.

- *Canalization upon the Self as Perceiver and Thinker*

Side by side with the process of canalization upon the observed self goes the process of canalization upon one's own *personal manner of perceiving and thinking*. One loves the pattern of one's own mental life. This begins with the relative formlessness not only of the emotional and the impulse life, but also of the life of knowing, remembering, thinking, perceiving during the early weeks, months, and years. The earlier studies of Werner[12] and Piaget,[13] the more recent studies by H. A. Witkin and his collaborators,[14] appear to indicate that the cognitive life, the basic ways of perceiving, differentiating, knowing, remembering, imagining are first vague and diffuse, but are shaped and molded as a result of meeting specific drive demands upon the environment —as a result of specific modes of satisfaction in such perceiving, knowing, etc., and of the frustrations which come from perceiving, knowing, remembering, imagining in other ways. We noted earlier how experimental evidence converges with psychoanalytic evidence to indicate that, because much with which we make contact brings bad results, we learn to shut it out, whereas perception of other things brings a personal sense of success and gratification. In the same way, parents and others applaud and support certain *ways of knowing* (mothers in Witkin's study, for example, apparently show disapproving attitudes when the child learns to make certain differentiations), and the children therefore remain less differentiating, more diffuse and global in perceiving. All this apparently leads to certain structuring processes in the basic ways of knowing: one learns to find satisfaction in the particular way in which one's own mind works.

[12] H. Werner, *Comparative Psychology of Mental Development*, Follett, 1950.
[13] J. Piaget, *The Origins of Intelligence in Children*, International Universities Press, 1952.
[14] H. A. Witkin, *et al.*, *Personality and Perception*, Harper, 1954.

We have long had evidence that canalization involves not only the direct *objects* of drives but the forms of mental activity themselves. The present proposal, however, goes much further. It suggests that in any given society the very diffuse latent potentials for the cognitive life, the ways of apprehending, differentiating, taking hold of and giving meaning to the world are themselves subject to the process of channeling or imprinting. This would begin very early, indeed, and receive support or discouragement by the warmth or coldness, the direct or indirect praise or reproof of parents. Later, as one identifies with them, modeling one's thought processes upon theirs, systems of mental activity are molded upon parental norms and likewise assume the negative or defensive forms to which the psychoanalysts give their main attention under the term *defense*.

Perhaps a considerable part of the human mental apparatus is formed in the early years through canalization-like processes, including both positive assimilation—"raking in" the world, so to speak, to one's own familiar style—and certain processes of protective rejection of the unassimilable. Each culture, according to this thesis, would do this massively through two factors: first, the network of interrelated ideas and values that constitutes the culture, and second, the sharing by all persons brought up in the culture or in any given subculture of a system of ways of thinking as well as ways of valuing and of doing.

Thus, as conceived here, the process of canalization can apply to *all* contents and processes in human experience defined in the broadest possible way. There may be canalization upon specific colors, tones, tastes, lines, surfaces, solids, persons, social situations; indeed, upon integrated wholes from very simple to very complex. There may be canalization not only upon content but upon process. One may "love to sing," as well as love specific tones. One may love to solve mathematical problems, or, more broadly, one may love to solve problems in general; or, more broadly still, one may just love to use one's mind. The same with reference to self-canalizations. One may love any specific aspect of oneself, or oneself as a totality or as a performer of an act or as a specialist in a task or skill. The conception of canalization upon process leads into the conception of the early schooling of the mind, taking joy in each step in the deployment of its energies in specific ways rather than in others. In other words, development of modes of experience, whether cognitive, emotional or impulsive, leads to gradual crystallizations of the process of deploying energy in particular ways. One finds oneself comfortably at home in whole areas of life in which such deployment has long been used.

Since cultural arrangements constantly change and enlarge the theater within which intellectual, emotional, and voluntary activities occur, there are new kinds of minds constantly being created. New theaters of action mean new modes of response to the challenge. The potentialities are limited only by the theaters of activity; and the theaters differ from ordinary stagecraft theaters in that they create in their own right new theaters for ever-expanding operations. The mind—the intellectual pattern—of any era is not formed merely by adding more and more components of experience, age by age. It involves a new world of experiencing, opening as new demands and new responses to the challenges are presented. Ultimately the very form and mode of the mind is itself transformed.

Of course, each individual has his own "maturation style," his own form of maturation. The capacity for new experience and for new behavior depends on the delicate rhythms of his own nervous system. Maturational style likewise involves readiness for cathexis upon new contents or processes, readiness for new experiences and the new capacities for action. In time, with growing cathexis on the self, one begins to love one's own personal style. By virtue of the rapid changes that maturation provides, the little child becomes aware of more and more things outside and inside the self, and systems of relationship between *self* and *other* are established. He learns where he belongs, who and what he is. When a predicament is confronted, he resolves it through a system of "coping techniques" which are relative to maturation level but also relative to individual style.

The style is assimilated to each new task; the task draws out certain aspects of the style which are relevant to it. The style, as well as the inner self, draws from the new experience. As Whitman says: "The skies became part of that child." At the same time, assimilating the new may involve giving up something in one's self. And each new adjustment involves some alteration of style as well as of self-image. One is to some degree remade as one incorporates the new and leaves something of oneself behind as one moves on. As Tennyson's *Ulysses* puts it: "I am a part of all that I have met." With maturation, perceptual style as well as motor style becomes more and more crystallized. Not that it ever becomes absolutely rigid; to maintain direction, then, or to maintain "gyroscopic" integrity is to miss essential reality-adjustment problems. But there is some crystallization and stabilization of style.

The primary problem of *altering* a way of thinking is to understand its roots. It is not at all impossible to get access to the complexities and the contradictions in the processes just described. Indeed, where opposed things are valued, the weight may be altered; and when it is realized that a particular step to be taken could actually lead to a goal, this step can itself be invested with the glory which the goal possesses. Even if canalizations are wholly irreversible, the intelligent use of associative and imprinting processes can do much to add new ones, to alter the balance of the total, and to recast individual human nature even in a lifetime. If our main concern is with the educational process, attention to the modifiability of the system of canalizations is a primary task. Practical ways must be found to remove contradictions in the value system and to build additional values to supplement and strengthen those already at work. The first problem is to understand more fully, by investigation and cross-cultural application, the nature of the canalizing processes and the tremendous rigidity which results from them. The second is to study the unlimited potentialities for the growth and redirecting of human nature which they promise when once understood and controlled. We shall return to this problem in Chapter 7.

• *Canalization and Language*

Although animals canalize, human beings exemplify many canalizations that are decidedly more complicated because they involve the use of language. The whole life of tastes and hobbies is greatly complicated by language. We learn to bring together under the same name all sorts of different things, as when a nickname is given to all the Italians or Germans in the same district

and the use of the common name then helps to make them all
seem alike to us. In the little town in which I grew up, there
was an affectionate term for Italians, and there was a derogatory
term for Italians, and either term might be used, depending
upon the situation. When the affectionate term was used, it
seemed to bring into sharp relief all the likable qualities in the
particular individual who kept the fruit stand at the corner, who
was my closest friend among the Italian group. Giving him this
nickname made him one of a group that everyone liked. I did
the same kind of thing later when I encountered my first Nor-
wegian. Having learned that the lifeboat captain, Ole, was Nor-
wegian, and admiring him enormously, I was then able to
romanticize and sentimentalize to the point of making all Norwe-
gians as absolutely delightful as Ole.

This leads into a very large area—the psychology of language—
and the area of the higher thought processes as related to the cod-
ification and standardization of the world that we know. Habits
of naming are, however, more than signals as to the kinds of experience which each group has; language influences experience.
One learns to make more distinctions if one has a larger vocabu-
lary, so that the process is circular; language makes distinctions,
and distinctions make language. Language cuts the world up into
its own patterns and then combines the patterns into ways
which are culturally unique, so that members of different cultural groups observe in trees, in stars, or in religious ceremony
quite different meanings.

While this linguistic process is going on, the process of canalization is making itself felt in respect to the things which are
named. If, therefore, there is canalization upon any given person
or object, all persons or objects which are given that name tend
also to share that canalization. A preliterate man is unlikely to
break up the world into a system of "natural laws" as conceived
by science; he is therefore unlikely to canalize upon the *methods
of science*. Yet, in our own social order, so profoundly devoted to
science, we break the world up into the laws and the methods
of physics, biology, etc. This concept of *natural law* means much
to the scientist; he canalizes upon natural law and scientific
method. As a scientist he would give up almost anything rather
than renounce this method, this way of thinking. Dozens of phe-

nomena in the world of religion, morals, and art reflect the same rule. We can wholeheartedly devote our affections and enthusiasms to classes of persons or objects or activities which are *named* —that is, which are linguistically tied together. Ultimately the system tied together by language is tied by a knot indicating the relevance of these things for the *self*.

• Individuality in Canalization

As already considered, we should expect to find huge differences between individuals in the objects upon which they are canalized, in the intensity of these canalizations, and in the way in which various canalizations are fitted together in the structure of personality. We look through a friend's LP collection, diving for Mozart or Sibelius; or, in an art museum, stop for a long look at the van Goghs or Turners and pass the British portrait painters by; or find on the menu just one item that makes the mouth water when all else is flat and uninteresting.

First, there seem to be constitutional differences in the intensities of the various needs. Some children remain food-centered year after year. They are gobblers and munchers, beggars for candy and ice cream. Others crave little, whether at the table or between meals. They would rather run and jump. Activity is often a more important aspect of life than eating, and excitement or prestige may make food unimportant. We should expect to find the world of canalized wants intense and rich in the former group; and since food and its canalizations are always present, we should expect many other things to be tied into the total pattern, so that almost everything, as with Dickens' "fat boy," leads back to food. With other children, relatively few food tastes are formed, and these are far from intense. There are few associations between the good things of life and the rather trivial moments of eating. We even encounter children who, solemnly treated by the administration of food rewards and of food deprivations for good and bad behavior, simply go ahead and do as they prefer to do, with no interest in the adult whims in such matters.

Some of these individual variations are to be seen in the opening months. But they are certainly greatly complicated by the

attitudes which the parents take, by the frequency and intensity
of the use in the child's life of the various things which are likely
to lead to canalizations, whether of food, of music, of activity, or
of anything else. Children begin to crave more and more those
things which offer them delight. Or, being bored at first, they
may reach a level of perceptual complexity—or motor virtuosity
—at which they begin to discover satisfactions which can be built
into canalized systems of self-fulfillment. They develop their canalizations out of the materials offered by the home and the social environment. We should never expect to be able to draw a
knife blade through the individual to separate that which is hereditary from that which is environmental. Just as constitutional
predispositions must be stressed, so environmental opportunity
must likewise be stressed. Both the specific things that are craved
and the general tendency to crave that particular class of thing—
food, activity, music—must be seen in individual terms.

Another important factor is the intensity of deprivations in the
satisfactions of wants. If there is deprivation of something which
is basically needed to satisfy a strong want, one becomes morbidly
fixated upon that object, craves it passionately; and out of what
was perhaps a weak need develops an intense need. We can see
this happening in the case of food deprivations among persons
in famine areas who are utterly preoccupied with food; we see
another form among children who have been shut up indoors
at a time when craving for the outdoor world was intense. When
the need for competitive success in a peer group has been inflated
to the point where nothing else counts, the individual who fails
to achieve status may be deeply wounded.

By referring to *individuality* in canalization, we have opened
the door to a *quantitative* statement about it. We have written as
if there were always a wide range of things which at first might
satisfy a drive, and as if one of these stimuli had moved into an
especially close relation to the drive. This is a quantitative matter: a question of *degree*. Can we not say that the canalization
process first involves a relative *sensitization*, either in larger or
great degree, toward one kind of satisfier, and a relative desensi-
tization toward others when in competition with it? We may conceive of the original state of the infant as fairly (though not
absolutely) neutral as to ways in which a need can be satisfied.

Babies do not spit out the same things an adult will spit out; there is a preference range, from most preferred to least preferred, among the things that the adult introduces to the infant. We might schematize this in a figure in which X represents the region of greatest original sensitivity and W, Y, and Z represent relatively insensitive zones.

ORIGINAL PREFERENCE

$$\overline{\underline{\overline{\underline{\equiv}}}}\ \overline{\underline{\overline{\underline{\equiv}}}}\ \overline{\underline{=}}\ \overline{=}$$
$$\text{W}\quad\text{X}\quad\text{Y}\quad\text{Z}$$

SHIFT IN PREFERENCE

$$\overline{\underline{=}}\ \overline{\underline{\equiv}}\ \overline{\underline{\overline{\equiv}}}\ \overline{-}$$
$$\text{W}\quad\text{X}\quad\text{Y}\quad\text{Z}$$

The lower figure illustrates the shift in preference, so that now Y, as a result of repeated experiences, is becoming the most sensitive or the most preferred; or the object toward which the individual is moving. Canalization is a question of *shift in the personal preference curve;* and personality consists partly of the collective pattern of such preference-shifts.

The personal preferences tend to become "stuck"—to become rigid. The preference pattern is more like a cast than a jelly; or we might better say that the trend in the individual life is away from a jelly and toward a cast. So, too, in any enduring society, behavior tends away from chaos or happenstance to a code, a norm, an accepted "right" way of living. Without such an accepted way, there is nothing to count upon, to lean upon, to model life upon. But *with* such an accepted way, rigidity, even ossification, arises. It is the very nature of the canalization process to push toward such ossification. It is not the only process in society that does so; but it has great power. One of the most challenging problems facing mankind-discovering-itself is how to provide for the perennial flow of drives with specific channels without making "irrecoverable" investments—getting stuck, becoming rigid, freezing the potentialities in the mold.

Chapter **6:**

Rigidity

One reason for the "stability"—or rigidity—of the "second human nature" has been canalization, especially canalization that interferes with thinking and, most of all, the canalization upon oneself.

Another "stabilizing"—or shackling—force with which humanity must cope is a type of self-reference that results from the process of self-centering—from the fact that things, events, objects, ideas are grasped in terms of the axial center of the universe, which is the self. Like the spider at the center of the web, we are ready to move out in all directions along an intricate and beautiful structure so made that there can be but one structural and dynamic center, and, when disturbing intrusions are sensed, we return to that center.

We are made this way. From an evolutionary point of view, individuals of any species are equipped with organs relevant to their adaptive needs. One selects by very virtue of being an ant, a robin, or a man. In addition to selecting, there is the process of interpreting. Interpretations are relevant to intrinsic biological nature. Individuality in biological make-up can produce corresponding variations in processes of selection, processes of interpretation, and processes involved in action. Each spider is at the center of his own web; each man at the center of a web no less real.

The learning process further limits and shapes the special

orientation of each individual. By virtue of past successes and failures, one learns what has to be attended to in order to achieve success. Sometimes we overshoot the mark, engaging in sheer fantasy or even self-deception. At other times, in order to adapt, one must attend to that which is or has been frustrating. In all these instances, however, one is guided by the consequences of past perceptual habits in all their phases, involving selection, grouping, and interpretation.

This learning process is different for members of different species, different for the two sexes within any one species, different in accordance with the degree of maturity, strength, and endurance and many other physiological attributes. The learning process is, moreover, somewhat stylized as regards both content and form by the social situation in which it is defined. Members of different racial and cultural groups find themselves required to solve different types of problems. Both the things learned and the manner of learning are appropriate to the individual in his situation. From this follows the special stance maintained by members of each specific subgroup. One sees in terms of the requirements of the group—as determined by predisposing conditions and by the specific learning process which has been characteristic of the stance in life which must be maintained by the individual.

We have, then, a series of internal and external conditions defining the special outlook. It is consequently pointless to dream of a process of "leaning over backwards" by which one could achieve a viewpoint without a center, "correcting for one's bias." The best that could be hoped for is to learn flexibly to work from one center to another and to consider alternative stances. One's own basically real stance, however, always remains. A man leaning over backwards is still a man leaning over backwards, not a man with a different bias leaning forward.

Since this is true, the self is, in one deep sense, always "right." But since this self-reference is nursed and coached along in a family pattern, and strong identifications are built with members of the family with whom one sides against other families and with the community when in contact with other communities, there is no likelihood that mankind in society can ever expect to avoid some social overexaggeration of the importance of

one's group—what Eugene Lerner called sociocentrism. We *can*
try to find a point above all the individual and group centering
processes which occur down in the valley of everyday human realities. But just as Einstein found that there was "no privileged
position" guaranteeing objectivity, so we shall find that we ourselves, no matter how we may pursue the abstractions, are destined to bring into the analysis those individual and social centering processes which are a part of our own rearing and outlook. This is simply part of the package to be accepted by the
planner. The more he prates of fine objectivity, the more reason there is to suspect that he is unaware of his own dynamics.
There is, of course, some correction to be had of one man by
another and of one group by another, if there is the will to
learn and if there is such a thing as good will; and it is upon
these, not upon absolute objectivity, that we must depend.

Then, aside from the egocentrism and sociocentrism that stem
from the sturdy reliance on the importance of one's own needs
and the adequacy of one's own perceptions, together with the
self-love which invests with a special halo the ways of seeing
and feeling that are distinctively our own, there is the universal
disparity between a man's *experience* and the thought patterns
to which he wishes creatively to aspire. He wants an objectivity that he will never really achieve. To speak of defining a
thought pattern more complete or more adequate than that to
which one has already struggled through years of confrontation
of difficulties and the quest for solutions is almost a matter of
lifting oneself by one's own bootstraps. *What, are these not
good enough?* We basically feel, *are my best* ideas still grossly
inadequate? And to this the answer is always *yes.*

• *Lopsidedness*

Finally, there is the lopsidedness of man. He has a great deal
of general or abstract intelligence, can discover thousands of exciting things, put them together in new ways, lead himself by
abstractions into science, philosophy, morals, esthetics, and religion. But, along with this goes his pettiness, his pitiful self-deceptions in everyday affairs, his capacity for crudity and meanness,
his frequent willingness to sell out a vast contribution for the

sake of making today's living or avoiding tomorrow's persecution, or his half-conscious belief that what he himself personally does is not of much importance; this means that man is never fulfilled to any great fraction of his potential. Like the classical designs of the steam engine, which even at its theoretical limit cannot reach an efficiency greater than 13 per cent, man is so made that he can hardly expect to reach a very large proportion of what lies implicit within his nature. The problem, then, is partly to help him to build stronger assets, but partly to learn how to free himself from the galling shackles which almost everywhere prevent his using even that which he has.

For it is not enough to say, with the great Pinel, "Let the shackles be stricken off." Our first problem is to discover *where* the shackles lie. Usually we need to discover what purpose the shackles are serving, to learn why it is we cling to them, and to measure their strength against the yearning for new paths.

Or, to put it another way, our lives are cast in a cultural mold because, up to the present, this rather rigid kind of stability is the only one we have discovered. Indeed, until we find a new way, the process that produces rigidity is absolutely essential to the achievement of a stable social order and a stable personal manner of functioning. This is especially evident in the establishment of norms: rules to live by. As Sherif has shown, each individual in a confused and uncertain situation develops a norm, a standardized way of looking at the situation. When he is with others, a collective norm or standardized social outlook is developed. Each of the people in a dark room sees a light move, but before long they are reducing their individual differences and acquiring a "group norm." Norms inevitably become standardized because they have to be lived by.

Now the development of norms—for example, the physical and mental standards for each age level characteristic of our industrial society—has served the goal of helping us to know what to expect; not to be unrealistic in our expectations. They have, however, too often been used to create *new rigidities* which go beyond those required by minimal social standardization and arouse anxieties—for example, in children and parents when a child does not meet the average in all respects. We have then turned a norm into a code or law. An arbitrary average has become a standard. The child is said not to measure up to the group norm or—even more painful for him—not living up to his own norm. Actually, deviation from the average is, of course, as normal as the average itself. Deviation from oneself is utterly normal, and we cripple the potentialities of the child by imposing upon him unrealistic expectancies. Curiosity about the origins of norms and a perspective and a sense of humor regarding them are the most obvious palliatives; respect for individuality in the concrete can perhaps do even more.

It is hardly sufficient to say simply that the shackles consist of encrusted habits—especially of culturally standardized habits and of cultural norms or rules that sustain them. For some cultural arrangements are much more rigid than others, and some are much harder to bear than others. In some African tribes all boys have to have their teeth filed to a point; but that does not make it easy. In the Kachina dance of the Hopi Indians of the Southwest all children have to be whipped by the "spirits," but this is reported to leave a trail of resentment in the growing personality. Cultural rigidities are universal, but qualitatively they differ a good deal.

In other words, some cultures are tougher on man than are others, and every culture is tougher on some children than on others. Following Ruth Benedict's lucid analysis, I think that every social scientist today recognizes that there are differential stresses and strains involved in the various aspects of the child's nature as he comes into contact with various aspects of cultural pressure. Some things hurt more than others. In the same way, there are whole cultural demand systems which are very hard indeed on some children. Take a very evident example: a sensitive, timid, and physically inadequate child reared to withstand the threats and ravages of war, whether he be involved in the carnage itself or not. In the same way, a contemplative or ruminative role demanded in the intellectualizing activities of many societies—let us say, in the elite classical tradition of the Western world—involves very patent strains on the muscularly more active youth which have been testified to in the literature of every kind of escape—from playing hookey, to the hazing practices of Tom Brown at Rugby, to the organized assaults on the schoolteachers so often heard of in American frontier days—as

well as in delinquency and gangdom in preadolescent and adolescent youth today. Cultures can be either enormously gratifying
in what they offer, or enormously frustrating, exacting, indeed,
withering and destroying in their effect on certain persons. The
term *culture-shock*—the shock encountered by exposure to culture—has proved useful in orientation to this situation. It is a
good term, because it sensitizes us to the fact that more than in-
convenience to the child is involved—strain, wear and tear, exacting pressure, even the squeezing of the soul, from which after
awhile no later liberation is spontaneously demanded. "They're
that way naturally," says one who has observed the passivity
wrought by second- and third-class citizenship, dirt, squalor, mis-
ery, ignorance, and consistent frustration in the demand to do a
little better. But from the present viewpoint, the elite in the
terms of society may suffer as much as the submerged tenth; it
is all relative to what the child demands and what the culture
requires.

It is the thesis of this chapter that culture-shock—as with foot-
binding, or the twisting of the tree, or the stunting of those subjected to prolonged malnutrition in the growth period—works
permanent and irreversible consequences. The result would be
that the normal potential creativeness of those subjected to culture-shock of various types is crippled by a process not to be
"unlearned." There is such a thing as being battered down,
either dramatically or just quietly and steadily year by year, until one no longer looks up. It may seem to the reader a little
strange to suggest that proud, wealthy, and powerful societies
are often as likely to work such effects upon their citizens as are
the enslaved and downtrodden, and it would be difficult to prove
the case one way or the other. Yet there is a formula for power
and success, just as there is a formula for every concrete and
consistently achieved result, and this formula, in the case of the
elite classes of an elite society, must be rigid indeed. The classical stereotype of Cato the Censor, the classical stereotype of the
Norman baron, the classical stereotype of the British aristocrat
of the nineteenth century have their roots in the necessity for a
high degree of standardization of outlook and role. When one
asks oneself, for example, about the creative freedom of the
British aristocrat regarding the music which he could not com-

pose, the Shakespeare-like plays which he could not write, one responds almost instinctively that he would not have *wanted* to compose music or write plays and was lucky to have a Sullivan and an Elgar in his Victorian era; lucky that his own norms permitted such ruthless Irishmen as Shaw to upset his equanimity in the manner that none of his own kind could have effected.

• *Industrialism*

But there is a third reason for modern man's rigidity, his failure to extricate himself from the shackles of his own making. This is industrialism. Science and the resulting technology have created a world that more and more rigidly determines the mode of man's life.

Some readers will believe that technology signalizes the liberation from tradition; will, indeed, believe that the process of canalization is impotent to block scientific and technological change; and will insist that science and technology are making for individualism and for intellectual creativeness. Is it not in individualistic America that society has become most flexible, most capable of an experimental attitude, most ready to test the possibilities of new directions? I cannot read history this way. Individualism was vital in a certain period of American history, and it is still presupposed in the folklore. Hence, it might be worth while to look at the origins and special circumstances surrounding the life of American individualism.

The breakdown of feudalism and the manorial system involved the scraping together of capital and the establishment of new enterprises. In Britain, where fortunes were to be made in wool, land was made available for "sheep runs," and those who could command the capital, whether they were lords or yeomen, could get a toehold in climbing the new road to wealth. While the landmarks of the established social order were collapsing, the discovery of the New World opened a vast new theater for conquest, discovery, exploitation, and gain. "The Elizabethan age," said Reginald Robinson, "was an age of great courage, great cruelty, great poetry, and great skullduggery." Dürer painted in his celebrated picture of "Melancholy" the uncertain cast of the eye of the old security as it faced the new insecurity. Soon, however, the tide of goods and gold was moving—for example, in the celebrated three-cornered trade between New England, the West Indies, and Britain—and before long the dominance in the northern colonies was accorded to those able to achieve success in shipping and in banking, supported by a backwoods yeomanry, the farmers (and "minutemen") who served numerically and politically as the foundation for the new American system. In the southern colonies the small, one-man farm was less typical than the plantation. Individualism, whether of New Hampshire farmer, of Boston tradesman, or of Virginia plantation owner, was the watchword. Diversification was still enormous and poverty and wealth still went hand in hand.

After the Revolutionary War, however, down the Ohio River and through the Cumberland Gap flowed tens of thousands ready to fight the Indians and take over what they could of the available freehold. Scattered pioneers from Lake Erie to Kentucky, moving westward at an average pace of three hundred miles per decade and joined constantly by new recruits, soon constituted that relatively standardized simple farm culture, that democratic egalitarian system of which the French observer de Tocqueville remarked, "Everywhere the key is the equality of conditions." Individualism was the basis of the economy, of the politics, and of the new *mores* that were being formed. But the old mores, notably the Calvinist theology, already contained an individualist savor which expressed itself not only in the churches but also in the economic and political life of the day.

These were the men whom David Riesman calls *inner-directed*. These were the men who, if they were to succeed at all, had to maintain within themselves a clear definition of their goal and had to have the resourcefulness and flexibility to find means to such a goal in a strange country where new rules were being made, new interpretations offered. This individualism meant freedom to rise and to fall in the system, and the "equality of conditions" was actually a relative equality of opportunity, not an equality of wealth. This became obvious in the development of huge mercantile and industrial establishments which from the middle of the century on through the Gilded Age dominated the American scene. A certain tendency to respect the individual for what he could do replaced the traditional respect for him as a member of a family. This is, indeed, still felt by Europeans as they encounter Americans everywhere. With certain odd exceptions, such as the Boston Brahmins and the Charleston aristocracy, the American everywhere is known by his individual status—as "the Vice President of the American Refineries Company," the "Secretary of the Intercity Transportation System," or the "Organizer of the Newtown Women's Federation of Church Singers"; as "that banker from Coffeyville," "that mechanic from Sioux Falls," or perhaps at the bottom of the ladder as "that millhand from Springfield." People are categorized by their place in an occupational system.

The old competitiveness, then, is channeled more and more into success in finding a place within the corporate system. The corporate systems compete, combine, compromise, raid one another for employees, and regiment the forms of thought considered appropriate in the individual corporate members to a high degree. Top-level executives are alarmed if middle-level men are insufficiently "company-minded." It follows that, although individualism remains, it finds itself within a corporate structure. There is still room for a great inventor, but he is likely to find the resources, the atmosphere, and the problems waiting for him in Du Pont or Western Electric. There is still a place for a prophet, but he is likely to appear as a member of a strong church. There is a place for a statesman, but he is likely to work his way up through the petty and middle-level politics of one of the established parties. Even if he comes as university president or military hero from some other walk in life, he must learn the ropes of the group within which he is to function, and he must change his color to meet the corporate thinking of his group.

Perhaps by now it will be evident why it is difficult to answer the question whether American life is becoming more authoritarian or more democratic, more group-centered or more individual-centered. The answer would appear to be that with the decline of the frontier and with the development of science and technology, with mass information rather than county newspapers, with nationwide telecasts and academy-award motion pictures, there is a high degree of *standardization of thought* and a high degree of *corporate thinking*.

There is likewise great corporate pressure on leaders, pressure from rank and file on those who define goals and try to drive toward them. It is entirely possible, therefore, for the Frederick Allen[1] picture of increasing prosperity and "leveling up" to be squared with the Riesman[2] picture of mass thinking and with the William H. Whyte[3] picture of institutional thinking. Absolute and arbitrary exploitation by the feudal baron has become difficult or impossible. At the same time, an idea of the absolute freedom of the individual anywhere in the system to escape into his own solitude appears to be equally farfetched.

The implications of all this for the next two or three centuries are not obscure. Barring wholesale destruction of the human family or of the resources upon which its material civilization could make a new beginning, it seems probable that the corporate mode of thinking will continue, that the interlocking directorates and mutual understandings between industries in different areas of productivity will develop further. As we noted earlier, we see no reason to believe that this must *necessarily* entail the domination by the elite of the mass beneath them. On the contrary, it appears to point toward a mass mode of organization in which those at the top *do what the system requires,* as in the "managerial revolution" of Burnham. Insofar as the technologies developed in Eastern Europe, Asia, Africa, and Latin America can follow and integrate themselves with the technologies of North America and Western Europe—and they appear to have no choice—the result will be a world system of corporate science, invention, and technology. This will not necessarily drive out individualism in artistic, religious, and other cultural activities, but the primary controls at each choice point in the evolution of society are likely to be exerted by those in a position to judge the consequences for the developing power and success of the scientific technological scheme.

[1] F. L. Allen, *The Big Change,* Harper, 1952.
[2] D. Riesman, *The Lonely Crowd,* Yale, 1950.
[3] *The Organization Man,* Simon and Schuster, 1956.

• *The Lonely Thinker*

The position of free inquiry becomes at this point extremely hazardous. Granted that it will always be worth while for the larger managers to encourage small corners of individual effort, at least on the part of those who have already made their way as investigators and inventors, the number of such individual thinkers and their lack of resources as compared with the mass facilities of the corporate system would seem to make it rather improbable that the study and formulation of alternatives for social evolution could depend to any very great degree upon such detached individuals.

We come, hence, to the paradox that planning operations worthy of the name can be carried out only by those already deeply committed to the type of system already unfolding. Planning will focus upon more and better modes of realizing the trends already in evidence rather than upon the laying out of genuinely distinct modes of social evolution. Even if the thoughtful individualist should appear who would sketch Utopian modes of social evolution, and even if he should find in the libraries and technical arsenals of his day devices by which to prove the enormous value of taking a different direction, it is difficult to see how he could make himself heard and how such an unaccustomed mode of thought could be made to appear realistic.

The provision of such individual thinkers on a rather large scale—and at many levels, from the independent full-fledged research man to the horde of technical advisers who are given encouragement to work out detail in their own way—will perhaps need to be eked out by devices throughout the educational system and throughout scientific and industrial plants for the establishment of experimental try-outs on a small scale or a pilot basis, and throughout all such scientific and industrial establishments there will have to be devices for encouraging, applauding, and giving open expression to modes of development which are in contrast with those represented by the major stream of development—a sort of "His Majesty's opposition," encouraged and pampered for what it can show.

It might be thought that the pressure for the standardization of thought and action within the individual system could be counterbalanced by individualism in extracurricular activities—that realm of activities which goes on outside of the scientific, technological business world. Leisure time during the last few centuries was relatively scant and was dominated in large part by the struggles, the animosities, and the fatigues generated in the working world—or the comfort which the week's toil and distress had made especially necessary was sought in another world. But within the last few decades the shortening of hours of work has led to a vast amount of leisure. So far, it would appear that this new leisure has been filled with delights and escapist techniques which have offered not a personal fulfillment but a contrast to the working world. Leisure, thus far, has not seemed to lead to individualism or to creativeness so much as to passive pleasures: radio, television, movies, mystery stories; interest in professional rather than personal sports and music. Even the active uses of leisure among the more adventurous focus mainly upon the pursuit of prestige and power: finding and using the right people. But we are shortcutting a complex issue, and we shall return to it in Chapter 7.

• *Education*

Paradoxically, there seems to be rather little hope or concern among most people regarding the role of *education* in this impasse. That part of John Dewey's philosophy which stressed group experience and the utilizing of the school to *prepare for life* has, indeed, made a deep dent. But the use of the school to prepare for a countermove against social rigidity is often regarded as either crackpot or subversive. Education is necessarily bound by the psychological considerations that govern our modern society. Our schools and our other social institutions can mechanically continue the types of living now current; or they can be slowly and blindly forced into changed directions as institutional changes occur.

The by-products of formal education, moreover, are often far more important than the aims deliberately avowed in the schoolroom. It is possible, for example, in one mode of teaching arithmetic to teach *implicitly* the hostility of all against each which is a part of the competitive process. It is possible to teach intellectually a series of religious and moral precepts and to teach emotionally at the same time various laws of the jungle and various types of basic maladaptive response to failure and the sense of inferiority. It is possible to idolize the esthetic values and to make each individual at the same time feel ashamed that he cannot paint, or sing, or write poems as teachers or parents require. The explicit educational process goes clanking along fairly well, turning out people who can master the three R's and read the newspapers and keep accounts. It can, at the same time, produce much frustration that one cannot somehow get the satisfactions out of life that educated people are supposed to get, and that one cannot escape the cycle of grumbling competitiveness which keeping up with the Joneses demands. Such competitiveness is ingrained as a component, indeed a major component, of the educational process. So is the timidity of a status-minded people. So is the "other-directedness" of the men and women of a tightly structured industrial society.

• *Individualism in the Schools*

So the question arises: can the schools reverse the trend to standardization which seems to be suggested both by the nature of canalization and by the history of modern technology?

I once asked a group of young adults whom I had never met before—adults from Sweden, Indonesia, France, Switzerland, Pakistan, Wellesley Hills, Japan, Salt Lake City—if they could tell me where the following school is to be found: In this school, children are found who sit in rows with an adult in front, who are required to learn things which they do not wish to know, and who are forced for the most part to look forward in the room, not at one another or out the windows. They are required to recite—that is, to give back what they have read or been told. When the overwhelming excitement of something that has happened outside of school comes up, and the impulse is to talk about it, they are told that they can take care of that when school is over. When they want to play beyond the brief recess period, they are restrained and may be made to wait or to stay after school, or, if these injunctions are not promptly met, to go and talk to a solemn adult. Their interest in things which are not laid out in the curriculum at the particular time and place is pushed aside as inappropriate and irrelevant. It is the task of the adult to know what the children are to learn. What they are learning all the time outside of school is regarded as an annoyance, a distraction, or even a sign of rebellion against the standard good behavior required of the school. In this way the years from six to fourteen or longer are spent in mastering certain things which are conceived to be necessary for adult life.

Yet the problems of life at large, the problems of family existence, the meaning of the community, the relation of the family to the community, even the relations of fathers and mothers, the relations of parents and children to one another within and outside of the family, are for the most part handled indirectly, or not handled at all, on the ground that these are issues too complex to understand, or are issues for which outside agencies, namely the family and the church, carry the responsibility, except insofar as the school may serve to underscore what has already been taught outside. The elementary school is not only conceived to be isolated from most of the major problems of life which children wish to ask about; the school regards itself as excluded in a formal and systematic way from dealing with these preoccupations of the children. I then asked the adults from Indonesia, Pakistan, Wellesley Hills, and elsewhere, where this school could be. Their reply was: *Everywhere*.

What is this all about?

In Chapter 4 we reached the conclusion that it is characteristic of a culture to get itself standardized into a pattern derived from previous patterns and differentiated from other contemporary patterns which, in order to be stable, have to be relatively firm and inflexible. In Chapter 5 we seemed to find our reason for this in the process of canalization. Perhaps, in view of what has been said here, industrialization is the capstone of the structure.

Some people believe that inflexibility, characteristic of *early* societies, is replaced by flexibility in some *advanced* societies. But others emphasize the fact that many, perhaps all, complex, advanced, well-structured societies become stabilized in a form just as resistant to change as are the early ones. The Roman Empire and the Russian Empire were so inflexible that, instead of yielding at some points to new pressures, they collapsed under attack. And there are serious voices today maintaining that technological society, especially as represented in the United States, is an extreme example of a rigid society which cannot basically adjust to the challenge of needed change, no matter what the threat may be in this atomic age.

If it is true that there is little flexibility to be found in our society, we may as well face the fact now. The rest of this chapter will spell out the reasons why rigidity, even ossification, must characterize our era more and more as time goes on. Later chapters will try to indicate why, both in *historical* terms and in *personal* terms, flexibility and creativeness, if we want them and strive for them, can still be given new life.

- ## Cultural Differentiation Offers No Antidote to Rigidity

The creation of new cultures through a process of differentiation is easy to observe in history—or was until the medieval and early modern periods. At first sight differentiation seems to dominate our own era. But in reality it is on the way out, for there is much today to interfere with it. It is swamped by a new process by which the combination of skill and force has reduced very large areas to a common or similar technological base. Instead of one great empire, such as the Roman, which actually comprised much less than 10 per cent of the globe, we have today the vast and relatively homogeneous area of China, the somewhat less homogeneous, rapidly unifying area of India (and others comparable to it in Pakistan and Indonesia); we have the Soviet system sweeping across one-fifth of the globe; the American system tending more and more to dominate and draw into itself certain reluctant but real allegiances from Western Europe and from Latin America. Scientifically, technologically, and even culturally, despite vigorous protests and counterforces, the Americanization process goes on. It is hardly farfetched to suggest that in another fifty years there will be just a few great technological systems—if we are lucky, only one—in which the borrowing process will have gone much further than today and in which the emphasis upon science and technology will have far out-stripped that which is already evident. Technology *succeeds,* and the success has moved at a whirlwind pace. All technological so-cieties will have to become more and more alike.

Our way of thinking is premised, of course, upon this assump-tion that science and technology, when once fairly started, move at an accelerated pace—a point rather easily documented. Huge national states which were rural and backward a few years ago, notably the Soviet Union and China, are today equally enthusias-tic about industrialization. And, indeed, even the most "nonma-terialistic" of modern entities, such as India, Burma, and Cey-lon, have begun to move vigorously in the same direction. I can-not for my part understand the books on the human future which assume that even one hundred years from now the primitive conditions operative in much of Asia and Latin America will still exist, posing a threat or a problem to technology. Tech-nology does not seem to be that kind of animal. It tears down that which stands in its way.

Nor is there any doubt that technology tends to create stand-ardized, frequently rigid outlooks. Hence arise two huge is-sues: first, the *attitudes* which are to surround science and tech-nology; and second, the *applications* to which science and tech-nology are to be turned. These will call for closer attention.

At a recent conference of industrialists a comment was made that during the depression of 1907 people who lost their capital or their jobs began to protest in an articulate way which had not been possible during the "Gilded Age" after the Civil War; that during the first decade of this century Theodore Roose-velt was in fact exemplifying a trend toward mass control over concentrated power which was new in American history or in-deed in all history. In 1930, the first year in which the great depression struck so many millions of American homes, there was for the first time the experience everywhere in industry that the attitudes of the workers had to be closely studied. Even in a period of widespread unemployment, men who had economic and political power began to realize that the tide had turned. During and after World War II the voices on every assembly line began to be heard. Even though the American people neg-lected the primaries and more than half of them failed to vote in national elections, something had happened which clearly marked the end of the great era of "the public be damned." Control was passing more and more to middle or even lower levels.

The same general trend is evident in two quite different types of studies: first, the study of the changing patterns of power and wealth in American life from the Gilded Age to the present, documented by much economic material and summarized by Frederick Allen in the phrase, "the great change." Allen's data, offered for popular rather than technical reading, are nevertheless sufficient to remind us of the kind of world through which we passed in the buccaneering age of early unbridled exploitation of natural resources; an age in which private banks could draw the savings of common people and explode like a Fourth of July celebration, with the relatively lucky depositors getting perhaps ten cents on the dollar, the rest nothing; an age in which literally millions of unemployed wandered through the country looking for temporary jobs; an age of raw corruption in high places of which the public was not even aware until the muckraking era of Lincoln Steffens and his peers; an age of rapid accumulation of enormous fortunes hardly subject to taxation at all. All this lies within the memory of those still living— living in an era in which 60 to 90 per cent income taxes are exacted on large earnings, in which banks and utilities are watched with a hawk's eye, and in which business in general has come to accept as a matter of course the idea of far-reaching government control. There has been a leveling-up—an increase of real wages, purchasing power, and savings and above all a reduction in the percentage unemployed—which is actually beyond the fantastic dreams of the Utopians of a few decades back: a standardization not in terms of a norm established by the elite but in terms of the requirements of the mass who constitute the individual community.

A more psychological and sociological kind of study, another aspect of this picture by David Riesman, fills out with documentation of the thesis that we have moved rapidly from an era of inner-directedness (self-reliance) to an era of other-directedness (dependence on the group), of eagerness to agree and conform (cf. p. 98), all conforming while at the same time challenging the old, simple, autocratic control from the top. Granting that the issue of control from the top or from the mass is still to be settled, mankind seems to be achieving unity through a sense of abject dependence of man upon man.

Perhaps, indeed, as Roderick Seidenberg[4] suggests, we are *standardizing the world:*

> Organization, dissolving chaos and incoherence in ever-wider arcs of life, moves toward universality; and nowhere has this inherent drift been more compelling in its sweep and more peremptory in its demands than in the expansive claims of the machine and its technology. . . . (p. 27) [Just as a process of crystallization influences an unstable system till the whole mass is crystallized, so the machine can lead towards the mechanization of the social order in which it arises. . . . With the triumph of intelligence] will come a gradual ebbing of historic consciousness, when man may once more enter upon a *state of rigid and continuous stability under the crystallized formulations of intelligence.* [ITALICS MINE] History must then be looked upon as a transitional stage in the evolutionary development of man (p. 52).

> The idea of progress is a tangential conception, born of a high moment in that basic change of direction, and projected forward into the illimitable spaces of wishful thinking . . . (p. 66). For the ideal of individualism shunned by implication the elementary gravitational force of humanity . . . cultural individualism called for the development of the self as an isolated atom, distinct, unique, and valuable only insofar as it might be distinguished and set apart from the social mass . . . (p. 85). The machine, as the most highly crystallized form of organization achieved by man, demands a degree of coordination in the societal relationships of man corresponding to its own high functional development (p. 107).

This way of thinking is basically not out of alignment with the statement that man thinks today more and more in corporate terms, in terms of the group of which he is a member, and consequently that, in an age of huge corporate entities in which everybody works for some huge establishment, thinking is guided by the norms and patterns of the defined group objective rather than by individual taste or idiosyncrasy. As a matter of fact, this appears to be true and to be in accord with what I shall call here the Riesman principle.

[4] *Posthistoric Man: an Inquiry,* University of North Carolina Press, 1950.

I have argued, therefore, that the "second human nature" tends to get more and more rigid and standardized through canalization, through ethnocentricism, *and* through technology, which, accelerating this process, forms *homo technicus.*

The types of rigidity which I have described arise from internal causes, and, however strongly they may be regretted, there is no sense in "blaming" them. Indeed, rigidity is an end phase in a growth process which began with flexibility. Trees, animals, and men through rich exploratory groping find their way into crannies and crevices; yet habits and rules and standardization, even fossilization, may finally supervene. In a very rich study of common factors involved in different kinds of growth —comparing organic evolution with the growth of language and with the growth of value-systems—adherents of "unified science" have suggested that certain basic dynamic principles in development and differentiation, with final adaptation to specific environmental requirements, may be characteristic of all things that live or express life.[5] From this point of view, rigidity is not something to be condemned; rather it is to be studied in terms of the processes by which flexibility was yielded in favor of fixed structure. In many instances fixed structure is an enormous advantage. It is only when the sapling has become hard that it can function as a tree, only when bones have become hard that animals can bear weight and navigate within their habitat, only when customs have become hard that we know where we stand, responding intuitively to custom, code, and law.

From such a point of view it would not follow that this or any other society is characterized by universal rigidity. Some societies may be more rigid than others; in fact, we suspect that a stable economic, social, and political system, as under the Egyptian pharaohs, yielded a higher degree of rigidity and stereotyping in daily life than would be found among, let us say, either pioneers or political revolutionaries. Some rigidity, however, is necessary even to the revolutionary who is to maintain unity of outlook through the stressful period in which his life is at stake; and by virtue of this consolidation of these forces and the final victory, he may become, after his success, even

[5] R. W. Gerard, C. Kluckhohn, and A. Rapoport, "Biological and Cultural Evolution," *Behavioral Science,* Vol. 1, 1956, pp. 1-11.

more rigid than the tottering puppets whom he overthrew. Rigidity, as we are using the term, is the negation of the curiosity-driven search-minded quest for the new in content or in process. And societies which have successfully mastered their major problems may be enormously flexible with respect to issues not yet solved by virtue of the continuing availability of earlier ways of thinking which have not yet become crystallized in the magnificent success of the new standardization of life.

Thus, in a period of highly standardized machine production, there is craving for the enrichment of personal family and community life, often slow to form itself through the lack of leaders and through the job displacement, the horizontal mobility, the vertical mobility, which machine jobs entail. Let there be a crisis, however, within the household or across the street or in the community at large and, with a whirlwind of excitement, the tornado victims or the flood victims—as in Stroudsburg in 1956, or Dallas in 1957—find almost miraculously that there are leaders and effective community channels in church, in club, in business organization, and in the less structured channels of community living through which swift mobilization of aid is possible. Let the processes of industrial standardization give us everywhere effective and cheap implements to simplify our domestic lives, and there spring up, as it were, to fill the spaces, the handicrafts, the amenities in wood, metal, and leather which are everywhere recognized as having a personal value and meaning proportional to the individuality and flexibility that went into the production. Let mass music overwhelm us through hit parades and seven-cents-on-the-record royalties to the great tycoons of swing; there is, as if in a sort of counterpoint, a movement for more and better music education, the development of spontaneous singing and instrumental groups.

This does not mean that the countermovement can keep up with the move toward standardization; far from it. It means simply that considerable areas of freedom for growth still exist, partly because our energies are not wholly utilized in standardization and partly by virtue of our protest against it. If it were not so, the thesis of the present volume would be hopeless. Our job—neither exaggerating nor belittling the large areas of flexible activity which have not at any given time been frozen into order, pattern, and finished structure—is to try to see in perspective where the major areas for fresh creativeness exist; in particular, to discover those areas in which curiosity about the social order, eagerness to understand man's predicament, may be capable of highest development, in order that an educational process attuned to the need for full utilization of such a capacity may do its work while there is time.

We have seen, then, that the rigidities, the intellectual shackles come with life itself: the opaqueness, the obtuseness, the crassness of organic stuff; the difficulty of learning anything; the preference for blood rather than brains and for lazy rather than effective solutions; the proneness to lapse back into the earlier methods of mammalian adjustment; the jerry-built, yet rigid, structure of all human cultures which have shaken down to some sort of working order by incorporating many of the monstrosities and brutalities into the scheme so as somehow to prevent its developing that subtlety, richness, and imagination which sensitive individual thinkers and artists could provide; the inveterate, case-hardened, arrogant assurance of each culture-bound group that it has found the solutions; and the tendency to treat as "enemies of the people" those who see things in another way. Shackles, too, there are, derived from the built-in nature of cultural *assumptions* within the life history of each growing participant in the cultural system; the proneness to socially shared misinterpretations.

How, then, with all this massive system of fetters and manacles which man has forged for himself, can there be self-discovery, self-emancipation from the blind and obdurate system of self-obstruction, the cultural chrysalis within which man has so snugly rolled himself?

The answer may lie in the study of the *process of invention*, the process from stone polisher to firemaker, to animal domesticator, to corn planter, to bronze smelter, which has marked the technical progress of mankind, beginning with pressing problems to be solved, but constantly branching off from the urgencies of an immediate problem to the broader realms of inquiry for the sake of inquiry, the gratification of curiosity, the development of individual creative skills, and, finally, the cultivation of the conception that *creation is in itself satisfying*, richly rewarding, the center of intellectual and cultural life as well as the fountain from which ever more valuable goods and services proceed.

It is the *nature of the creative process* that seems to call for the most intensive study. This is why we differ sharply from all who rely upon the continuation of the essentially blind evolutionary processes of the past. Because time is short, because threats are great, and, above all, because man is man, the explicit recognition of the fetters upon man's mind and the deeper understanding of human directions of growth are the most pressing of the tasks of self-emancipation with which modern man is confronted. In the next three chapters we shall strive to find a way to the bursting of these bonds.

PART III

The Third Human Nature:

Breaking Through the Mold

Chapter 7:

The Freeing of Intelligence*

The problem raised in the last few chapters is how to achieve the maximum utilization by *homo sapiens* of those amazing cerebral hemispheres of his. He has wit enough to make for himself a happy sojourn on this planet and to realize gradually more and more of his creative powers. He has wit enough to study, to understand and to control the predatory impulses of his kind, and to enrich and magnify the impulse to tenderness and good will. Yet he foams and frets, exhorts and moralizes. A visitor observing the Empire of Alexander and returning to earth today might note that intelligence, as the capacity to adapt the environment to one's needs, has been only very ambiguously advanced. He might wonder why man puts only half his mind into the discovery of the solutions he needs for his problem of community living, leaving many critical decisions to the direction of blood rather than brain. Perhaps, he would conclude, brains are not *free* to act in accordance with their potential. Intelligence is fettered by manacles whose design has been imperfectly studied.

Scientific thought, as a full-fledged device for the analysis of nature, has been with us but three centuries. If some modern Job were asked by the Lord, "Canst thou bind the sweet influences of the Pleiades, or loose the bands of Orion?" he might well and modestly reply, "Not yet, but I have measured the dis-

* Based upon presidential address to the American Psychological Association, 1944, published in *Psychol. Bull.*, Vol. 41, 1945.

tance and the magnitude of the Great Nebula in Andromeda and have weighed the invisible companion of Sirius." Indeed, wherever the task is objective and his intelligence free, man has remade the order of his world. Yet on points concerning his own nature, where his impulses have beclouded the process of his thinking, he still relies upon exhorting, moralizing, and argument. He has not, in fact, studied with any great perseverance the very process of thought itself, and he is only dimly aware that the discrepancy between the achievement of science and the achievement of everyday thinking is due to failure to make clear the fetters which bind the thought processes. He has hardly heard Spinoza's precept: "Be not angry, and complain not, but use reason." For how, otherwise, could a species producing the achievements of a Newton, a Darwin, or a Pasteur prove incapable of ordering the relations of men in community, in nation, or in the world pattern of civilization? The towering genius of the great scientist often lapses into childish babblings as he turns to problems in which his personal desires give structure to his thought. When the will to believe or to disbelieve rather than to observe objectively and read the scroll of nature is the guide, the sharpest tool of thought becomes suddenly dull, the greatest of creative impulses falls into the reiteration of petty prejudice.

Simple economic fears, fears of the powers that be, can, of course, muddy the thinking of all men, including those classed as scientists; but the less obvious constraints which we unwittingly impose upon the freedom of our thought deserve much more systematic and deep-probing study. Thought, as we say, is loaded by individual personality trends or we speak of *autistic* thinking: thinking controlled by wishes or drives. We know that the ordered process of thought exhibited in the textbooks differs substantially from the thinking which we ordinarily encounter; but as to the specific dynamics responsible for the difference, and about the manner of freeing ourselves from these impediments, we know little. In our theories the realm of intelligence still remains separated from the realm of impulse, feeling, and motivation. Though we dissect and measure man's intellectual powers, and pry ever deeper into his impulsive life, yet even today, in an era of political bitterness and international frustration, where thinking is loaded with an unbearable freight of anxiety and unconscious distortion through wishes and fears, we have scarcely begun to lay bare and measure those impulsive dynamic relations that lie at the heart of thought.

Psychiatry on the one hand and anthropology on the other have constantly stressed the bondage of thought to obscure, or even unconscious, directing tendencies, and studies of industrial conflict have shown that injured egos and blind stubbornness can daily break the fine thread of understanding which practical self-interest and human reasonableness have tenuously spun between management's and labor's viewpoints. But the deeper dynamics of the ways in which feeling and impulse may influence thought call for more and more study. Here is a supreme opportunity for an integrated psychology to deal with the whole human being.

• *Clues to Wishful Thinking*

We never receive impressions from the *outer* world without getting impressions at the same time from the world *inside* ourselves: the world of sensation from the muscles and vital organs, the world of feeling and of memory. Some of the most important factors are inner tensions, involving biological needs and needs given form as a result of social pressure. In a confused visual presentation, hungry subjects see food or things related to food, such as knives and forks. In one of Sherif's experiments an untrained observer watched a pinpoint of light in a dark room, and stated how far it moved (most people see such a light move even when it does not move). This observer sat near an *experienced* observer, and soon was seeing *as the latter reported seeing*. The need to see as a trained observer did was the chief dynamic factor involved. Perception, like thought, develops as an organized response to a rich pattern or matrix of stimulation in which not only the structure of the environment but also the structure-giving tendencies of the perceiver converge in the determination of the response. The external pattern is, of course, sometimes so rigidly structured that personal factors in *perception* may be minimized; but even here the personal factor is easily detected and measured when *recall* is tested, and it is more salient still in the case of *creative thought* (p. 129).

As far as we know, there are no intellectual responses which are *completely* free from the control of motivation. To be sure, the tension system within the brain may be less conspicuously dependent upon visceral and other internal conditions at one time than at another, and there are many needs which are relatively independent of visceral conditions, depending apparently upon neuromuscular tension systems of a complex order (cf. p. 185). But this does not alter the fact that thinking is an active and directed process in which needs determine both the point of origin and the direction or trend within the thought process.

Intellectual processes are guided by habit, too, and under the term *habit* must be included the naive response to irrelevant cues or thinking by analogy without checking on the soundness of the analogy. Piaget discusses such analogical thinking in children, but these same primitive thought patterns are found abundantly in normal adults. What James Harvey Robinson called the "history of the human mind" is in considerable degree the history of the transmission of socially sanctioned primitivisms. But habit cannot be distinguished sharply from motivated behavior; for habits become ingrained by *serving needs,* and they usually die out, become extinguished, disintegrate, when the drive that underlies them fades away.

The specific steps by which wishes guide the processes of perceiving, remembering, and thinking seem to be these:

First, at a sheer descriptive level, perception, recall, and thought tend to take a direction such as to bring to the individual a situation satisfying to his needs. If he can really remake the *outer situation,* he will learn to achieve this; but if he cannot do so, he can at least remake his way of *viewing* it.

Second, this movement in the direction of need-satisfaction is often unconsciously directed, the individual achieving a wish-fulfilling goal by steps which do not betray to him the origin of the impulse which he follows. This appears to be simply because one of the needs is to keep himself happy regarding his own motivation. In the cases reported by psychoanalysis, the individual reaches his goal, remaining unaware that the pseudological steps taken serve an unconscious need.

Third, the tendency of cognitive processes (perception, memory, thought) to move toward need-satisfaction appears to be a special case of the law that *behavior in general* moves in the direction of need-satisfaction. The experimental psychology of learning defines the elimination of the frustrating aspects and the fixation of the satisfying aspects of behavior processes.

Fourth, as to perceptual dynamics, it would appear that relatively unstructured perceptual situations are given structure in terms of *figure and ground*—figure being that which *stands out* against the "ground"—by virtue of the fact that those elements stand out as figure which have previously been present as aspects of *satisfying* situations. Needs serve to throw some elements of a visual or auditory pattern into the role of figure, so that one sees or hears what one needs to see or hear. This tendency is developed through learning; a designated aspect comes to serve as figure if that aspect appears repeatedly in a satisfying situation. The Rorschach ink-blot test shows the tendency toward one or another perceptual habit in terms of deep dynamics in which the needs of the individual anchor upon one or another aspect of a relatively unstructured field. During the processes of reorganization—"recentering"—which occur in thought, the same process appears; from a complex of elements, those stand out which are aspects of a satisfying pattern, each phase being partially determined by the thinker's needs.

Thought, like perception, is bipolar, the dynamics of figure and ground deriving jointly from the structural properties of the stimulus situation and from the need-patterns of the individual. At times, not only the *wish* but the *fear* may be father to the thought. In many learning situations, perception, memory, and thought derived from fear may be repeated and fixated. The impulse to perceive the nature of the threat is activated by the need to confront it in order to escape; or to deal with the threat. The influence of need upon perception is still very evident.

It may be objected that all such studies have to do with thought encumbered by complications—that, despite such complications, the bare, primordial form of intellect remains as a matrix or substrate: pure intellect *qua* intellect. Now, indeed, if pure intellect is to be found, we should go to the ends of the earth to find it. Pure intellect, free of all personal deviations, would be the pearl of great price, the discovery of which would constitute a master stroke not only for psychology but for civilization. Where, then, is this pure intellect, this Faustian homunculus, this little gem of rationality to which we strive to gain access in our experiments in the psychology of thought? Possible approaches to its discovery might appear to lie in rigidly controlled laboratory research; but here we have found that cultural and personal variables have consistently affected the very structure of the process of thinking. Or we might seek it in early childhood; but here thought occurs as an aspect of a type of global effortful contact with the world in which the non-rational and the egocentric mark the process and the product. Or we might seek it in the works of pure genius; but here the biographer and the historian have consistently pointed to the impress of personality upon even the most logical ordering of scientific relationships. There is, we sadly conclude, no such pearl of great price, no intellect which stands apart from the concrete person's drive-directed efforts at contact with reality. There is no "pure" intelligence at all.

When one looks at the process of thinking in this way, seeing the impress of personal tensions and the resultant personal ways of thinking at every phase in the development of the mind, many of the formal problems relating to intellect take on a very different appearance. Intellect has been conceived on the one hand to lie dormant as a potential within the germ cell, waiting only to be nursed into expression. It has, on the other hand, been conceived to be the impress of a system of social arrangements mediated to the growing individual. But we can learn a great deal from the way in which the growth of the child's mind expresses the arousal of his interests, the development of tastes, and the specific forms taken by the "will to learn"; thus, the child's motives give direction and expression to his intellectual powers. As Richard Sears[1] has put it, "Within rather wide limits the essential factor determining whether the subject's motivational (affective and attitudinal) peculiarities will cause significant deviations of psychometric performance seems to be what the test situation means, consciously or unconsciously, in terms

[1] "Motivational Factors in Aptitude Testing," *Amer. J. Orthopsychiat.,* Vol. 13, 1943, pp. 468-493.

of this particular subject's individual patterning of complexes and desires."

In the light of such observations, it appears likely that in relation to intellectual tasks there are two levels at which personality variables may operate: (1) they may give structure to that which reaches consciousness; (2) they may, through fear, completely prevent the mind from making contact with certain specific materials. Inhibition or blockage, as in the case of reading disabilities, may appear when there is a profound emotional incapacity to give the mind to the material at all. Conversely, we should expect that a positive love of certain stimulus materials would give a better-than-average opportunity for close attention to it, with a likelihood of achieving greater "resolving power" in relation to it. The movement of cognitive processes in the direction of need-satisfaction involves, then, both the figure-ground patterning of given situations and also the crippling or the enhancement of mental functions in accordance with conscious or unconscious drive-patterns.

Perhaps the influence of motivation in directing the processes of thought may play a part in the differential rates of growth among the different *kinds* of intellectual capacities, the mind being progressively sensitized to specific aspects of the environment which take on meaning for the individual. Perhaps when the data permit us to understand the qualitative changes wrought in intellectual functions by various kinds of influences and to measure their amounts, we might go on to ask about their gross aggregate in the form of intelligence quotients. We can hardly expect to understand mentality as a whole until its specific expressions have been accurately observed and measured in the growing individual.

• *Socially Shared Autisms*

I have not meant to imply that all these responses necessarily separate a man from his fellows. On the contrary, it is characteristic of every social group to develop its own socially shared forms of "loaded" perceiving and thinking. There are very clear, consistent, and well-organized pictures of Christian Scientists in the minds of good Roman Catholics, and of Mormons in the minds of good Presbyterians. These pictures have been built up through a great deal of consistent social sharing. Although they are far from personal self-deceptions, they are on the whole more refractory to evidence than are the purely personal forms of self-deception. They do not, however, permit commitment of their possessors to institutions, since none would remain outside; the very collectivity of the autistic frames is regarded as evidence of individual sanity. By and large, more cognitive distortion is achieved through social sharing than through psychotic processes within the individual. By a mechanism which Stefansson[2] has described in the brilliant phrase, "the standardization of error," it is possible for human beings to achieve an amazing clarity of viewpoint which springs not from contact with reality but from the need for protection from surprises and ego injuries. And, in accordance with Sherif's suggestion that the more unstructured the perceptual field given by a situation the greater the role of internal influences, the danger is peculiarly great in relation to matters of social living. The world of social immediacy—frequently the world of the unstructured, the confused, the rapidly changing, the world of uncertain norms and of value conflict—is a world in which need-determined thinking reigns supreme.

Unfortunately, we ourselves have no immunity from this principle. The socially shared views of Americans constitute an example of the sort of thing with which our peacemakers might well be concerned. No casual study of international relations will make clear to an Englishman, a Swiss, a Russian, or a Chinese why we are so certain regarding the essential infallibility of our institutions. We may show much tolerance and say many fine things about other nations, but the glasses through which we look as members of an indoctrinated group are something of which we can never be made really aware, for our defenses are too good. We are only today groping toward techniques by which the shared assumptions of group members may be fully explored.

Thus, it is not merely the lack of precision-measures which makes the social sciences fall short of the mark as full-fledged sciences. Thought works here with relatively unstructured material; it is likely to reflect the wishes and fears of the specialist.

[2] V. Stefansson, *Adventures in Error*, McBride, 1936.

The possible contribution of social psychology to human life can hardly be discussed without recognizing the twofold difficulty that besets us. For, although obstacles stand in our way with regard to controlling this external structure of social reality, we are neglecting the more immediate obstacles—namely, the self-deceptions of individual social scientists. Could social psychology and its kindred social sciences discover a framework in which realities could be ordered with less wishful thinking, we might discover that it is not simply the complexity of the task which makes an acceptable world order so hard to organize. It is doubtful whether world order is really more complicated than the wavicle theory of light—whether discerning the patterns of reality is really more difficult than reducing gravitation and electromagnetism to a common formula. The difficult thing is to get a group of social scientists to mobilize their intellectual powers on the basis of problems as such. How much easier it is, like Luther, to nail our precious beliefs to the door as something to defend.

Psychologists, ingenious at discovering such processes in others, because they remain human, have often exemplified the same basic dynamics of self-deception. Indeed, psychology has often developed a peculiarly rich, subtle, brittle, and dogmatic outlook as to nature and as to human beings and how their minds work. The thought patterns of an epoch and a cultural area, the prevailing mode of viewing life, according to Max Weber's "Sociology of Knowledge," sets the stage for the individual thinking.

The history of hypnotism is a good example of this process as it relates to what the men of a given era can believe. When Mesmer came to Paris in 1778 he presented two problems for a scientific answer—the nature of his cures, and the question of animal magnetism. The scientists of the day seized upon animal magnetism and disposed of it as nonsense. They were not, however, sensitized to the psychological problem of the cures and did little with it. The long struggle of Elliotson in England to get the phenomena of hypnosis under scientific observation led to the same result; the problem of magnetism was handled with dispatch, whereas the problem of the cures, not fitting into the frame of reference, was evaded. When, finally, James Braid made the classical mistake of concluding that hypnosis was largely due to specific *muscular fatigue* and thus found a way of phrasing hypnotic phenomena so that they would not disturb the serenity of medical men, the mistake had its share in leading to the acceptance of hypnosis as fact! Braid later showed that muscular fatigue did *not* explain the results; but in the midst of his positive contributions he had committed the kind of error required to make the phenomena assimilable to the prejudices of existing science, and the trick was done. Hypnosis has been recognized and studied since his time.

If I may permit myself a small prophecy, I would venture that the many independent experiments upon paranormal psychological processes now going on in Britain and America[3] under the strict experimental and statistical controls which are today properly demanded cannot be assimilated, or even noted, by formal psychology until some generous soul, in the manner of Braid, phrases a theory which integrates the results with the existing psychological frame of reference. The new theory will probably be an amiable error, as was Braid's, but when once a substantial group of scientists has begun to study and to repeat the experiments, the theory can, like an afterbirth, quietly shrivel away.

The physicists have discovered a superior way of handling unassimilable ideas, "outrageous hypotheses." They have learned since Faraday's time—with every succeeding year bringing discoveries which simply do not fit into classical physics—to invent mathematical descriptions which simply denote what the evidence reveals, treating events of the older physics as one special class of events comfortably housed within the vast mansions of the new. The local autisms of the physicist have in large measure been washed away by a stream of mathematical symbols. In fact, most physicists do not seem interested in defending any final world view. In the open spaces of mathematical invention there is no such constraint. And oddly, this kind of free thinking yields higher dividends than any scientific effort of the past has ever paid.

[3] G. Murphy, "Trends in the Study of Extrasensory Perception," *Amer. Psychologist*, Vol. 13, 1958, pp. 69-75.

• *Curiosity*

If one accepts the broad conception that thought, like everything else in life, reflects the dynamics of motivation, one might
be tempted to despair, concluding that—if this be so—there is
no truth, there is no science, there is only the realization of satisfactions. Yet this, I think, is a naive conception of human nature
and indeed of animal nature generally. For it is because thought
makes contact with reality that it has appeared in the course of
evolution. Sense organs may not mediate the *ultimate* reality
—whatever that may be—but they do mediate the first reality
with which adjustment is made. Paraphrasing what Marx said to
the idealists, "We do not know what reality is, but we can adapt
it to our needs." There is truth, and there is science, as exemplified by physics and by medicine, which is not only immediately
useful but surely suggests that we are more in touch with reality
than we were three centuries ago. For the sense organs and the
brain are developed as a reality-mediating system of tools; and
the bipolar organization of perception is always anchored partly
upon the structure of an external world with which we must
deal.

But there is an additional factor guaranteeing the integrity
of the scientific enterprise. There is not only a good system of
sense-organs; there is also a powerful positive motivation to make
contact with reality; this motivation is frequently more powerful than any personal drive which might lead to escape from
such adaptation. For creatures like ourselves it is necessary to
keep sense organs and brain in contact with the world, constantly varying the perceptual pattern just as we constantly vary
the motor adjustments, making sure of the utmost use of the
tools of observation by which each pattern is constantly checked
against other information.

This is a way of saying that the curiosity impulse is one of the
most powerful, one of the most difficult to assuage, that man
possesses. It is characteristic of primates to explore about rather
than to stop to digest the convenient banana; and it is characteristic of boy and girl to pry into matters to see what makes

them tick. I suspect, following Holt,[4] that curiosity probably arises from such primordial tendencies as the trend to go on doing what one is already doing ("perseveration") and the establishment of habits in which *a* leads to *b* and *b* leads back to *a* ("circular response"). But whatever the origins, this kind of activity is often enriched and given a large role by the development of intellect. And this impulsion may lead to the structuring of socially verifiable and socially shared experience, for example in the form of the sciences.

As Wertheimer so earnestly insisted, it is the nature of man to lean hard upon the external structure-giving aspects of reality. He *needs* contact with reality even more than he needs escape from it. He can develop such a craving for contact with reality as will sweep away personal autisms and the smug sense of cultural rightness. If this analysis be sound, the curiosity motive would apparently serve, as other drives do, to determine the figure-ground relationships of perceptual patterns. Curiosity would throw some aspects of the stimulus into relief. The curious mind constantly sees new figure-ground possibilities, and this is why, as a probe of reality, it far surpasses the petty limitations of ordinary autism.

Immediately we ask: what aspects of a pattern yield the *true* figure? May not the same pattern of phenomena lend itself to different types of structuring? Yes; a composite phenomenon presented to people with varying types of curiosity will lead them in varying directions. Different cultures and different individuals, dealing with the same perennial phenomena, have made sense of them in different ways. The co-operative venture of science serves in some measure to integrate the individual curiosities of individual scientists.

But curiosity in this sense is not only general. It is also specific. The small child shows not only the will to know but the will to know some things rather than others, the bending of the mind in this way rather than that. These variations in curiosity share in the determination of intellectual limits to be achieved by the individual in the different fields of its application, just as the cultivation of intellect consists largely of the cultivation of the thirst

---

[4] E. B. Holt, *Animal Drive and the Learning Process,* Holt, 1931.

for contact with reality. The individual's personality determines, together with his inherited wit, how far he may go. There is no easily definable limit to the depth to which the individual may immerse himself in material which he loves, no limit to the power of the mind to saturate itself with that which satisfies it. This is no plea against the recognition of constitutional inadequacies, and no plea against the biological improvement of the human stock. We must begin with whatever the stock permits. Rather, then, it is a plea for recognition that not only accidentally acquired tastes but the mind as a whole is molded by that with which it makes contact; for every sensitization of the creative life is quite literally a gain in intelligence.

Such curiosity is highly contagious, and civilization has been built largely by socially transmitted demands for specific kinds of understanding. Modern students of the Greek City State stand amazed at the profundity reached by leisure-time inquirers who sought from their teachers the answer to ultimate philosophical questions. Crude though their science was, limited as was their awareness of the place of man in nature, they had an amazing capacity to perceive and attack problems of great subtlety and complexity. Just as the mind of the artist was molded by a Phidias, the mind of the dramatist by a Sophocles, the mind of the young philosopher was molded by a Protagoras or a Socrates.

This fine whetting of the intellectual blade is a socially continuous process, not simply an individual achievement. In the same fashion, the student of experimental science goes today to a laboratory where a great tradition has been established in order that his mind may take on the mold of those who have built the tradition, just as the ambitious violinist goes to study with those who stand in direct descent from the great Paganini. In this sense, the dynamic mold of intellectual function is the precious achievement of each cultural group, not simply a distortion imposed by cultural limitations; and the molding of the mind in the direction of impelling objectivity and insatiable curiosity into the ways of nature is one of the most priceless gifts which our society could give its children. What we need chiefly to fear is that such curiosity may be narrowly limited to specific subject matter, when the mind during the formative period has known the delights of free inquiry only within one domain. The generalization of curiosity is, however, just as practicable as is the generalization of any other attitude, provided it be not left to chance, but systematically encouraged. The struggle of the mind to keep itself free from every sort of bondage—to remain curious, open, unsatiated in all its relations with nature—is tenfold more difficult than the cultivation of a stable, satisfying point of view, but a thousandfold more precious. (We shall return repeatedly to the problem of the enrichment of human curiosity.)

• *Relaxation*

Thus far, I have praised the active life of curiosity, and have not hesitated to speak of the *struggle* for contact with reality. But there is another approach. We of the West are prone to forget that water quietly freezing can burst a granite that no sledge hammer can crack. There are latent creative powers which wait to move forward to their work when freed from the restless downward pressures of the alert mind; creative powers which spring into being when once the narrow, nervous, preoccupied world of waking activity steps aside in favor of a quiet integration of all that one has experienced; when one is willing to let the mind leave harbor and travel fearlessly over an ocean of new experiences. Under profound relaxation some impulsions wield a benevolent despotism over thought which the whip of concentrated attention cannot control; thinking is still motivated, but motivated with less immediacy in relation to the tasks of the surrounding world. Both the historical record of creative thought and the laboratory report of its appearance today indicate clearly that creative intelligence can spring from the mind which is not strained to its highest pitch, but is utterly at ease.

Indeed the finer instruments in intellectual analysis are better understood when their counterparts are discovered in the humble occurrences of the dream. The conception of a system of cues recreating—"redintegrating"—old patterns, or predisposing toward one rather than another new pattern, has facilitated the application of all the resources of association psychology to the study of thought. Particularly important is the recognition that the world of reverie possesses a richness and a complexity in the light of which the ordered processes of realistic thought become simply a special case.

On one point, we may go even further. We have begun to realize that it is characteristic of fantasy to be more *creative* than is logical thought, in the sense that more cues, and more *unusual* cues, are woven into the composite texture determined by many needs; in the same way the dreams of the night, starting from a complexity of individual determinants, achieve not simply a bizarre, but in many respects a highly creative, end-result. Those interested in Freud's conception of symbolism have at times been tempted to forget the extraordinary light which Chapter 7 in his *Interpretation of Dreams* throws upon the unconscious processes of condensation, synthesis, and goal-fulfillment; there is a tendency to overlook the full implications of the psychology of the dream, particularly if one is concerned solely with the therapeutic problem of the unconscious wishes portrayed in the individual case. More important for psychology as a science is the creative character of the dream itself, realizing a power and an intensity to which waking fantasy is usually alien. In Coleridge's *Kubla Khan,* for example, it was not that the dream revealed fewer of Coleridge's interests or needs; but rather that more of them were free to pool their energies, to integrate their contributions. The dream gives us, as in a natural laboratory, a device for introducing more personal variables and consequently a richer permutation of end-results. It would follow that a more systematic experimental study of the dream might give us a wider view of its creative potentialities, oriented to more aspects of reality than waking life can afford to recognize.

One aspect of our practical Americanism, our surviving frontiersmen's psychology—with its emphasis on wide-awake alertness and its touch of Calvinistic devotion to immediate duty—is a suspicion of all these mental states which seem, according to the standard, not to "get us anywhere"; a general disvaluation of the relaxed, the casual, and the exploratory. The dreamer awakes from an extraordinarily vivid, realistic, challenging dream, an experience which, if encountered in a novel or a play, he would cherish as a new avenue to the meaning of life. "A funny dream," he yawns, and by the time he has his nose in the morning newspaper he has forgotten it. To disvalue the dream is to prove oneself a sensible man.

One state is perhaps still more important, because it can be better controlled—namely, the hypnotic state, in which there has recently been a marked increase in interest. The great utility of hypnosis lies, I believe, in discovering that imaginative richness, that creative power, that capacity to knock down and reassemble the ingredients of life which constitutes independent, unconventional, nonroutinized, original thought. The hypnotic thought may indeed be trivial if the individual experimenter so expects. But because we live under a profound cultural disvaluation of all mental states but that of rapt alertness, the fact that we have here a markedly less constrained and more creative type of intellect has infrequently attracted our attention. Perhaps the experimental use of hypnosis may lay bare the impediments, the blind spots, the personal autisms which encumber the intellectual powers of the subject—may lead to a more focused integration of the associative resources which lie in the background of his mind. Robert White and his collaborators have made this point with surpassing skill. In summarizing experimental evidence that subjects under hypnosis remembered meaningful material much better than they could when awake, they remark: "Relaxation itself, nevertheless, has something to do with the betterment of recall. Most people are accustomed to regard alert, volitionally sustained attention as the best of all possible mental states, so that they are surprised to think that the mind sometimes works better when left a little to itself."

In summary, there is evidence that functional intelligence can be enormously enhanced, first, by the systematic study and removal of individual and socially shared self-deceptions; second, by the cultivation of curiosity; and third, by the art of withdrawal from the pressures of immediate external tasks in order to let the mind work at its own pace and in its own congenial way. We have already stepped over the threshold into the room where creativeness lives. We must next explore that room.

Chapter 8:

Individual Creativeness

To face the appalling realities which arise from the rigidity of technological society has been one of mankind's most pressing and least agreeable responsibilities. The rigidities which arise through the nature of culture are intensified. Nevertheless we have noted some ways in which intelligence can be set free. Let us focus now on those forms of intelligence that we can call *creative*.

• *Stages in the Creative Process*

Something is known about creative thought—about its historical and psychological conditions and about ways to stimulate it. Research on the process of creative thinking provides a few clear principles. From Lowes' exquisite study of Coleridge's poetic conception of *Kubla Khan*[1] to Rossman's patient analysis of hundreds of inventions in the files of the patent office,[2] there is general agreement that acts of creativeness, great or small, arise in a context typically involving four phases.

First, there is the long immersion of the sensitive mind in some specific medium which gives delight and fulfillment, whether it be the world of color, tone, movement, space,

[1] J. L. Lowes, *The Road to Xanadu*, Houghton Mifflin, 1927.
[2] J. Rossman, *The Psychology of the Inventor*. Inventors Publishing Co., 1931.

time, the world of force and organization, the world of words, of images, of social relationships, or the world of contemplation or of mastery. Through the tentative gropings of the mind in its early formative states, steeping itself in the sensory or the intellectual riches of this world, one falls in love, as did Newton, with space or force; or, as did Blake, with line or color; or, as did Mozart, with tone and rhythm. Minds both great and small are first marked out for the pathway of creativeness through the fact that they are sensitive to something in this challenging and fascinating world.

The second phase in creativeness appears when this sensitivity, this demand upon the world for contact and assimilation, leads to the acquisition of storehouses full of experiences which consolidate themselves, just as all learning processes do, into "higher units" or structured patterns or ordered experience. To be sensitive to tones means that soon there are melodies and soon thereafter harmonized patterns, as experienced in the part-singing of the school chorus or the barbershop quartet or the glee club. In the same way there are the color combinations and linear combinations of the world of pencil, crayon, and brush. There are the organized patterns of temporal and spatial relationships that go into mechanics. There is the world of social relationships, privileges, and obligations. Now, since all these things cannot be kept in consciousness at a single moment, they are organized unconsciously into systems upon which we may draw as we need them—living storehouses of ready, yet adaptable and flexible, information and experience. New stimulation, new love of such experience, "incubates" them, makes them grow warm or even brings them to a "flash point" of readiness so that a new spark will precipitate a chain reaction of glowing creativity.

For it is from these great storehouses, based upon years of accumulation and incubation, that the third phase, the "sudden inspiration" of the composer, the dramatist, or the scientist, derives. This inspiration or illumination is our *third* stage in creative thinking. Archimedes leaps from the bathtub shouting, "I have it!" The chemist, Kekulé, sees in a dream the components of the benzine ring ranging themselves in his fantasy to satisfy his long struggle to understand the problem of their organization. Such creative acts are the necessary derivatives from the two preceding phases, the phases of sensitivity and of organization. Insights, illuminations, large or small, come to all of us in all spheres of life. They depend for their very existence upon environmental encouragement of the child's sensitivities and the protection of his freedom to accumulate, and to keep warm through "incubation," the living storehouses of experience upon which most illuminations depend.

The *fourth* step which always emerges in the process of creating is the "hammering-out," or the sifting and testing, the critical evaluating and perfecting of the work done. After the "fine frenzy," the "quiet eye"; after "composing with fury," "correcting with phlegm"—and, especially, correcting with socially responsible judgment. The creative teacher, for example, can represent the mature evaluative judgment of the social order. He can help the creator to create if he can share the creator's struggle.

These are the stages in the history of the *individual creative act*. But what about their relation to the growth of the person in whom they appear; what are the stages in personal growth that are relevant to the capacity to go again and again through the stages of creativeness?

• *Factors in the Growth of Creativeness*

In Walter de la Mare's extraordinary collection of early memories of those who later became creative men, there is much evidence of the importance of an intimate and stimulating mother-child relationship. It seems legitimate to conjecture that the warm response of the mother may in the experience of many children give quicker life to the imaginative fire, or her prohibitions may mark off areas through which exploration becomes less and less feasible and ultimately less and less interesting. This accords, in a curious way, with the recent unpublished data of H. A. Witkin about the role of "growth-hindering" mothers in blocking the development of finer perceptual differentiation. It is almost as if clinging to the restricting mother had entailed an unconscious attitude that there are some distinctions not to be made, some explorations not to be permitted, some realities not to be broken down and seen in all their sharpness.

The culture, too, can serve as an inhibiting agency, in which whole areas and regions of childhood experience are opened to stimulation or are marked by a mind-binding process much like the foot-binding process of traditional China. The Tennessee hill children are very credibly reported to lack curiosity and creativeness, in large part because there is not a very wide range of experiences available and because most of those that are available are accepted as a matter of course, calling neither for deep probing nor for a quest to discover what lies over the hills. A high degree of community isolation and narrowness of outlook may nevertheless be associated with very rich exploitation of creative possibilities, as in the villages of Bali, or of India, or of Brittany, in which handicrafts are early experienced as the most real and important of a boy's activities. Apprenticeship to a master may encourage, from early childhood through the years of maturity, an uninterrupted avidity for the full exploitation of each possibility—with esthetic, economic, and prestige values all being intimately fused. A family within such a community may make the utmost use of the community tradition and may, through a combination of genetic and environmental factors, reach the great pitch seen from time to time in the local brilliance of a family of composers or sword-makers, potters or toy-makers.

This recognition of sensory and motor readiness and the skills which spring from them, of the urgency of the need for fresh experience, and of the capacity to direct energy into channels not blocked by family, community, or culture implies that creativity can in a sense be regarded as the normal expression of humanity. In each individual and in each cultural group there are laid down traces, structured or crystallized residues, of all that has been created; and of all the urges that lack fulfillment waiting to find new structured incarnation. That which has been done in the past—the past of the group or the past of the individual—can be conserved, provided the energy maintains itself, provided the love of new experience and of the specific material which a new vista offers is kept. If the energy is too great to pour itself into existing channels, there is, inevitably, a spilling over; and this spilling over will take a structured rather than a chaotic form insofar as the habit of looking for structure is ingrained and waiting for the task; insofar as one is *open* to structured reality.

The new channel into which such energy is to be directed may depend upon the cast of mind at the time. Often, if many moods and many ways of creating are native to the person, the expression may be one of embellishment, decoration; the solution of a problem; the facing of a new reality; the making of a fresh contact with something in oneself (an infantile reservoir) or with the vast sweep of a Utopia; the rescoring of a folk tune or the creation of a sonata. All this depends much more on time and place, the documentary cues from without and within, than upon any ultimate social "market" waiting for a product. It is, after all, realization of self that actualizes the potential that keeps hand and brain at work. Whatever incompleteness or *frustration* gnaws at the heart may give fire or fury to the effort—but *fulfillment,* rather than frustration, may also lead on to finer fulfillments. If the organized skills and the passion for experience are there, then, paradoxically, both defeat and victory may lead on to new victory.

The fine frenzy of the creative impulse is obviously correlated with the pitch of life's energies themselves. In all the arts except those in which long years of experience or steady sober judgment are paramount, the period of early manhood has always been dominant in the record of great creativeness. Even when a man such as Beethoven or Verdi has been able to maintain the pitch of creative passion for decades, we recognize in the greatest works something of the first flush of manhood.

Since the height of general powers and of sexual maturing go hand in hand, it is a question of judgment whether one should regard the creative energies as a direct outflowing of the energies involved in sexual maturing. Perhaps no such sharp distinction is valid, since the general growth is derivative partly from the endocrine factors of sex, and the endocrine factors of sex are clearly derivative to some degree from general maturing. The point is nevertheless of some importance with reference to the wide individual differences in the continuity of creativeness. One cannot help feeling that the sudden damping of the creative fires in the case of Wordsworth in his late thirties and the slower damping in the case of Burns may have been directly related to the course of physiological aging. From such a point of view, physiological aging need bring no decline in powers if there is sufficient external stimulation to keep the day-by-day energy level high. The stimulation pouring into the nervous centers "does not know" whether it comes from inside the body or outside. It is the availability of the energy, not its ultimate derivation, that would be important for the maintenance of the flame.

• *"Creating" vs. "Combining"*

It is clear from all this that creating is much more than sheer "combining." Most of us still use "association psychology" in everyday life; we may be tempted to believe that creating consists mainly of associating or connecting things together. A creative mind would thus combine two ideas and make a third idea. Later, we begin to wonder how so vast a structure as a man's mind can be built by a process of sheer connecting. It is certainly true that Mozart had, by the age of five, connected many lovely tones, one with another; but it is hard to see how he could have written the piano compositions which we have from his hand at that period through blind trial and error, randomly connecting tens of thousands of tone combinations and then selecting those that he liked. He surely did nothing of the sort. Indeed, the problem of childhood creativeness often involves just this issue: the intuitive *integration* of far more than could ever have been associated on a piecemeal basis; and this has led to many efforts to conceive of other theories which will explain the nature of the creative act.

There is, for example, the conception of Platonic *goodness of structure* intuitively grasped at the moment. The clue would lie in a basic *tendency to good structure*. This can hardly be the full solution, however, when we recognize that with a few simple musical materials, the tones of a few instruments, and a few principles regarding rhythm, there exists a working infinity of possibilities, all of which have a high degree of form. As a matter of fact, this is what characterizes the capacity of the composer to "improvise on a theme" and to go on with this rich and fascinating task almost indefinitely, even as other composers can develop the same simple materials in thousands of other ways. It is indeed true that there are definite limits to the number of combinations that are acceptable, satisfying, and real as music; but the fact remains that the number is far greater than can be accounted for by the sheer quest of good form. If we look more closely, we see that the creative mind is looking not just for a specific example of good form as such, but for good form that is relevant to the specific task in hand, *i.e.,* to the whole structure (whether of science or of art) that has already been built; and (especially in art) to the *mood,* the feeling quality that prevails throughout the work. In anxiety states our fantasies and our dreams are like the macabre images of Poe's stories; to the rage-sensitized thinker, the hateful aspects of man and world become overwhelming. To the erotically or esthetically minded, the images miraculously suit the mood. Mood is the key to the vast system of connections. It is mood that creates receptiveness, *openness,* to each new challenge.[3]

Let us see what happens when relevance and mood get left out. There is a story, probably apocryphal, about the Dramatics Workshop at Yale. The young playwright must produce a dramatic sketch each day. The problem was solved by setting up four wooden rollers. The first of these bore, pasted closely together, common adjectives, such as *good, bad, rich, poor.* The second born commonplace nouns: *man, woman, president, lawyer, stevedore, actress.* The third described common actions: *runs, fights, calls, loves.* The last included modifying or supplementary terms: adverbs which might modify the verbs, nouns which might act as objects of the verbs, etc. The task now was to give each of the four wooden rollers a tremendous spin. The end result took the form: adjective, noun, verb, and supplementary term. We might come out with something mildly ridiculous but decidedly useful to the panting inventor. "Wise actress runs happily." "Poor soldier goes twice." The slightly schizophrenic nature of many of the word combinations need not bother the creator. Many of his dreams, if he be honest, are inclined in this direction, even without benefit of spinning spools. Even if nothing else come of this, he develops as he spins (so the story goes) certain selective

[3] This is, of course, an ancient idea; among the moderns it has been especially well developed by James, Freud, and Bleuler.

habits, ways of looking for combinations which had never occurred before. These selective habits depend partly upon realistic possibilities or relevance, partly upon *mood*.

Now suppose we wish to convert our quadruple spinning spool
into a thinking machine, what should we do? Let us start with
our first list, our adjectives. We have, let us say, a hundred adjectives and a hundred possible nouns. We want to go beyond
the random connection of any given noun with any given preceding adjective; we have, let us say, a hundred adjectives in
search of a noun. But if we have used the machine many times,
selective wear and tear will produce uneven or biased selections,
just as a book opens more easily at the place at which we stopped
reading last night. We can easily build into our machine a factor
that will give here the traditional factors of association psychology:
recency, frequency, and vividness. Note the need for the additional factors: realistic possibilities and mood. If, for example,
"rich merchant" has been a combination used a good many
times, whereas rich spider, if it ever appeared, has not been used,
a suitably devised machine will tend, when the adjective is "rich,"
to select merchant rather than spider. When these factors have
been taken account of, there remains, let us say, some differential in favor of a few over others. Rich merchant and rich prince
are about equally good, but if one is writing for modern readers, rich merchant has better possibilities. The full range of possibilities of the story has been cut down somewhat by the audi-
ence to whom it is to be directed. However, choices get frozen
into machine preference. But now, just as "rich," so to speak,
selects "merchant," so "rich merchant" selects from among the
possible verbs in terms of what has actually been found workable in the past. When the choice is between "buys" and
"screams," "buys" will prevail, whereas if it had been "frightened spinster" appearing in the first two columns, "screams"
would have been selected as a more appropriate verb. Here,
again, recency, frequency, and vividness appear; likewise relevance and mood. And in the same fashion, whether the merchant
buys slyly, happily, boastfully, stupidly, sorrowfully, and so on
depend partly on these factors. "Sorrowful barrister" must be
followed by "withdraws" rather than "fights."

Elaborate this crude paradigm, granting that it can never be made complex enough to serve.[4] It suggests that the associative process must be dominated by realistic selection and by a mood process, a prevailing feeling tone, before it is anything like a creative process.

Now we seem to have come to the point at which we can answer the question: How is it that we can get to any given goal by startig at any given point? We need on the one hand certain mental furniture in terms of experiences. They have to be built through a certain amount of repetition; they have to be kept bright. Above all, they must be looking for something; they must be sensitized to a cue; they must be resonant with the feeling tone of the outcome. A somber mood produces a slow cadence. The emotional value of the slow cadence can be picked up by a child or even an animal. Moods reach out like radar and find their counterparts. *The mood gives direction to the movement to the goal.*

• William James and "Impartial Redintegration"

There is always, however, the question of why we sometimes fail to reach such goals. The problem is to discover the blocks and blinds that impede the flow of this creative facility which lies implicit within us. Perhaps we have said too little about the key process of selection. Association is often *too* rich, and goals and patterns too numerous. What prevents the factors of recency, frequency, and vividness from activating many or all systems at once? And if, indeed, there are many thoughts compatible in mood with any given thought, is it not likely that many lines of association will all be called into play at once? This is what William James called "impartial redintegration." Do we not confront here a magnificent extrapolation of the problem that faced Buridan's ass, caught between the two bales of hay, equally large, attractive, and distant from his nose? Is there not the possibility that we shall think a little of everything rather than something specific, or the possibility that we may develop a sort of generalized lockjaw of mutual inhibitions, being unable to move at all?

[4] The machine suggested here is much simpler than the very ingenious machine contrived by Ashby in *Design for a Brain* (Wiley, 1952), which exhibits a quasi-purposive consistency in reaching its goals.

R. S. Woodworth, embellishing James, tells how Abe Sanderson set off from Salem to go around Cape Horn to the Orient. Two years later, sitting on a cracker barrel, he described his adventure. He spent the morning describing the weather from the day in which the schooner put out from Salem. No detail of cloud or wind was left out. This was all right among mariners, but after lunch he was asked if he couldn't get on with the trip. He described the wharf and the tugs, until after much urging, he got as far, by nightfall, as the captain's selection of the moment at which to cast off. By Christmas he had completed the description of the round of activities in the schooner sufficiently to describe the hatchways down which he made his way each evening to his bunk. It is, in fact, a world of "impartial redintegration" that comes before us as we think of the possibility of widening or enriching the range of the mind's grasp. Without selection there is no mind at all.

Man has often tried to stimulate creativeness—by drugs, by ritual, by autosuggestion—and produced only a sort of "impartial redintegration." In the terrain which he would explore, the trees have fallen so densely across his path that he has doubled back, losing the trail, unaware that there was a *beyond* to which he might somehow have cut his way. There are two safeguards: to maintain the direction, by selecting always in terms of relevance, and to maintain the mood of the adventure.

Thus the process of combination into high units under the joint pressure of relevance and mood offers a first step toward a theory. It will serve us, at least, as far as ordinary tune-making is concerned. A Beethoven quartet, however, cannot be constructed by these principles alone. Even when the formula is evident to the musicologist, he cannot make the necessary manipulations. There is often a sort of a "skip-to-the-moon" by which a new and resplendent integration is achieved without passing through the intermediate forms.

There may well be some further clues, similar perhaps to those short cuts which we all use in getting from here to there without necessarily traversing all the hypothetical pathways that exist between one point and another. Given, for example, (*a*) a certain *mood* which greatly reduces the possibilities, and given (*b*) the limitation to certain instruments (let us say, violin, cello, and piano) which greatly reduces the possibilities that can be expressed in representing that mood, and given (*c*) the general form of the art style to be used (let us say the sonata), and given (*d*) the time and place, the cultural atmosphere of the creation, we can, in a very considerable degree, define what Beethoven will and will not do.

Sometimes we can tell what Beethoven will *not* do but not what he *will* do. But affirmations, too, are often directly suggested by this type of approach. They show the kinds of rhythms, the kinds of tonal combinations which are inevitably appropriate with this form. If, now, we grant that there is a very much higher degree of integration in the composer's mind than that which is available to most of us, we can compare the composer to the architect or the engineer who sees the possibilities for a certain kind of building and, thinking dynamically in terms of what that location, that material, that cubic footage, etc., will permit, has gone a large part of the way toward envisaging the structured total which the building is to be.

Creativeness, then, is perhaps not the absolutely insoluble problem that it may at first sight appear to be. But since the higher units that are used in this process are themselves built up from simpler units below, a large integration calls for more material than can be held in consciousness at one time; a large part of the material used at any given time is therefore beyond the fringe of consciousness. Much of the material "wells up from the unconscious"; or, if we prefer, the associative trends operate unconsciously until a product appears in consciousness.

When we have gone as far as this, some will say that we have come within sight of port. Yes, some kind of port. We have noted the fluid hierarchy of creative structure. But we still seem to encounter a gap between the lesser and the greater creative achievements. Let us, for example, contrast Schubert's "Unfinished Symphony" with his simpler creations, such as the ballet music in "Rosamunde." We can, as a matter of fact, find in Schubert many besetting ideas which reappear in combinations over and over again—in the "Moment Musicale," for example, in "Rosamunde," in the quintets, and elsewhere—just as we find in Beethoven or Shakespeare the repetitive catch-phrase, perhaps unconsciously used, which may move a transition off dead center onto a new creative mood, or which may represent, as the psychoanalyst suggests, some early fixation with which the composer has never fully come to terms. But when these materials have all been codified and explained, there remains the startling creation that seems to go beyond the material in hand. These creations go beyond the sensory modality of the creative act itself. Music, for example, being ordinarily a matter of hearing, moves other senses into action, especially those from within the body. The Schubert "Unfinished Symphony" leaps into a multimodal type of expression in which acoustical values and the proprioceptive values (from the muscles) are joined by those reverberating materials from the viscera which we call interoceptive—joined, indeed, by complex memory materials from large segments of our personal autobiography. As Charles Dana Gibson said, "words that laugh and cry" may bring back not just the ideas but the whole of a personal response.

It is likely, in the same manner, that there are heights of integrative activity which express the whole of the person's response to the world rather than chains of association limited to the formal art process. Just as we receive from the universe in integrated fashion much more than that which the separate senses have to say (as from our own inner interoceptive and proprioceptive mechanisms we may make at any moment a new unity), so in the creative act we may include much that is in our sensory world, in our cognitive world, in our affective and impulsive world—a single, unified representation of what we make out of the universe itself.

• *The Habit of Creating*

Many studies of the creative effort have stressed the long accumulation of organized information or skill and the sudden fulfillment of a goal in a flash of creative insight. They have, however, found a place likewise for the *habit of creation,* the fact that these insights come more and more frequently to those who have had them and have worked them through into adequate expressions of the creative drive. The habit of creativity may persist even in periods not so fully dominated by the white heat of creative frenzy. Rossman's records of inventors—

indeed, even the single narrative of the life of Benjamin Franklin—should remind us that creativeness may become a habit of perceiving, ruminating, catching a point through analysis, rearranging, trying out. Some of this undoubtedly is constitutional, but the records of the inventors seem to offer convincing evidence that *learning to create* is as dominant a fact in the sphere of practical things as it is in poetry and music.

Since learning to create, like all learning, is intimately dependent on a personal context, we cannot speak of creativeness as isolated from the rest of life, once a beginning is made. In every mind there are widening regions of creativeness if once the spark has been allowed to generate the fire. We can speak, therefore, of the development of a personality "slanted" toward creativeness and maintaining this slant—and slanting more and more determinedly—unless pushed violently back into some other slant through adverse circumstances.

Hence arises the question: how far, in the individual case, can the habit of creating be expected to move? Can it even leap from one field of endeavor to another? Can training in literary creativeness generalize to creativeness in science? It is not sufficient to reply that there have been in all eras certain widely gifted persons who have contributed, as did Leonardo, to mechanics and anatomy, to painting and to the theory of knowledge. The generalization goes much further; in an era that is really generous and open toward a reconsideration of all fundamentals, as was the Periclean age in Athens, or the Romantic era in early nineteenth-century Germany, each area of inquiry may actually break down to some degree the barriers into other areas, however unrelated, and there may literally be an *era of inquiry*.

Such an era, as a matter of fact, certainly existed early in the nineteenth century in many points, both in Europe and in America. Indeed, if we may accept the luminous pages of Van Wyck Brooks as they open for us the story of early nineteenth-century American life in the age of Jefferson and Irving, we may believe that American education was in fact beginning to open in just such a way to all the sunlight of the newer human wisdom that came as the age of enlightenment led on into the age of democracy. Soon came Emerson, Thoreau, Whitman. Creativeness can transcend an art form and become a quality of life.

Chapter 9:

The Creative Eras

Having noted some of the components in the psychology of the creative thinker, let us now try to examine the characteristics of the creative era.

As we look at history, we note that cultural change moves more and more rapidly as time goes on. A period of a hundred thousand years marked but slight gains in the fashioning of stone implements. When polished stone implements appeared, more could be done in ten thousand years than in the preceding hundred-thousand-year span. When the age of metals began, there was a still broader cultural base, a wider variety of cultural techniques upon which to operate—and much could be done in five hundred years (a ridiculously short time span for paleolithic or even for neolithic man). With the mastery of metallurgy came many new skills which affected the industrial and martial arts, the class and power structures, and the ways of coping both with the material and with the ideal problems which beset mankind. Thus it was in the age of bronze and the age of metallic currency that the rapid evolution of Greek and Indian philosophy occurred; this may have played a part, as well, in setting the stage for the great religious systems which took shape in China, India, and the Mediterranean. The historian Lynn White reminds us that Heraclitus was teaching that everything can be "converted into gold," and gold into everything, at the same moment in history in which he was proclaiming that everything is interchangeable; that man is the "measure" of all things; that all things "flow"; and that the law of circulation is the law of life and social structures.

Thus, without insisting upon single causal factors, we may note the accelerated construction of a "culture base" in Greece, say from the Trojan War, about 1000 B.C., to Alexander, about 330 B.C.; and in India, say from the Mahenjodaro period, 3000 B.C., to Buddha, 500 B.C.

• Cycles of Creativeness

Creative impulses come in waves. The West-European Renaissance, from the late medieval period onward, was at first largely a renewal of the ancient quests—an acceleration of the development of the old skills augmented by geographical discovery, inventions borrowed from the East or newly made, accumulation of liquid capital and of banking facilities, the reduction of the population through plagues and through the steady siphoning off of masses toward the new world in the process of empire building, and many other overlapping movements. Here, again, *acceleration of the tempo* of social change is evident. Hornell Hart has made clear, in a series of quantitative studies, that any type of specific inventions that one cares to choose—whether that affecting the range of a missile or that affecting the number of persons that can be reached by a recorded word—moves onward at an accelerated pace; as much as would have been developed in a hundred years at the beginning of the Renaissance period is now developed in ten years. It is, in fact, the application of this last principle that has frightened many with respect to the development of pure and applied science; the development of nuclear fuels and ways of using them is moving so fast that it may well mean that humanity will have insufficient time to think out a mode of self-preservation against such colossal means of destruction.

But all that we need insist upon here is the reality of geometrical increase in the pace of social change, both with respect to material achievements themselves and with respect to the intellectual and esthetic phenomena which attend, precede, and follow. Certainly in the fields of mathematics, the physical sciences, the biological sciences, the social sciences, this type of acceleration can be well documented from at least the sixteenth century onward. But with respect to creativeness in the arts we see not only a broad trend over centuries, as revealed in the sciences, but also a series of *spasms of creativeness,* as in the painting of the fifteenth and sixteenth centuries in Italy, the sixteenth and seventeenth century in the Low countries; the lyric and Romantic poetry of the late eighteenth and early nineteenth centuries in Britain and Germany; the symphonic music of Vienna from Haydn through Beethoven and Schubert.

In every one of these periods of rapid cultural acceleration, there is, of course, some interdependence among the various styles of human expression. We take it as a matter of course that Velasquez and Cervantes appear in the same period in Spanish history. Even between artistic and scientific waves of creativeness there is often a close affiliation. We take it as a matter of course that the Netherlands which produced the great physicist Huygens and the great microscopist Leeuwenhoek was the Netherlands which produced Terborch, Vermeer, and Rembrandt. On the other hand, we do not insist that British music in the nineteenth century should equal in brilliance the scientific achievements of Darwin and Lord Kelvin, or that the France of Pasteur should produce great architecture. Just as we do not expect anyone, not even Leonardo, to be a genius in *every* sphere of human activity, so we do not really expect any cultural epoch to advance on an even front to the shattering of all historical standards in all regions of human endeavor at once.

Perhaps enough has been said to suggest that there are definite laws relating to the acceleration of both specific and general cultural achievements; that there are some types of acceleration which can be shown to maintain themselves for long periods whereas with others there are periods of intense creativeness followed by long fallow periods—and again by creation anew. Are we in a position to say that we understand the dynamics of such cultural flowering?

There must, of course, be savings, capital, surplus value; there must be leisure; there must be an individual or an oligarchy or a social class that cares more about discovery of the new than about conquest as such, or magnificence in display, or the un-limited snobbery of forced adulation imposed upon slaves and flatterers. There must be intellectual curiosity, or delight in new aspects of color and tone, or some other enrichment of experience. Most monarchs show off; but some are aware that things more worthy of display can be discovered. Those intellectual and esthetic cravings to which we have already given so much attention must be combined with leisure, purchasing power, and interpersonal power in a manner permitting the evolution of specific creative activities.

All this can plainly be seen in the great Athenian empire which, as the Beards pointed out, received tribute from a thousand Mediterranean cities. The treasure chests groaned with the wealth from the olives and dates that supported the Athenian leisure class at which Aeschylus hurled his stately rhythms and in the midst of which the quiet old man, Socrates, could stand all day in the marketplace, with wealthy and unemployed youth, drawing out from them questions about the ultimate meaning of human life. In the same way, Italy, Spain, Britain, Germany showed their vast creativeness in periods when the wealth, the leisure, the sensitization of both monarch and people converged in a flash of brief but eternal magnificence.

But this offers no explanation of the decline, the loss of vitality, the long stagnant periods which have again and again supervened. One can very properly say that the Peloponnesian War destroyed the morale of the Greeks. But the Great Wall of China and the Himalayan mountain barrier protecting India gave those lands long and relatively quiet periods for experimentation with painting and sculpture which rose to great heights—but again quietly declined into cultural valleys between the great heights not through destruction of the economic opportunity or the loss of a leisure class but through more subtle factors of morale. Nehru, indeed, shows clearly that India underwent (more or less contemporaneously with the decline of Buddhism, and not necessarily as its cause or effect) a slow moral and cultural deterioration and was, long before the British invasion, a relatively vulnerable society.

This is not the sort of volume which can effectively deal with the complex problems of the rise and wane of civilization, problems which have vexed historians from Thucydides to Spengler. Our purpose is simply to ask *whether human potentialities and their release can be studied in terms of the attitudes of the creative periods.* I think that much can be done in short-range terms, in terms within which a movement can be caught, so to speak, *at its work* and, decade by decade, analyzed in terms of increasing productiveness and the establishment of richer and richer areas of expression. I believe that Hornell Hart's and much similar material shows that the principles of extrapolation are sound within specific areas of activity; and that similar methods, such as those used by economists in "time-trend" studies, permit us to predict, for relatively short periods, what may be achieved in one form of cultural expression, such as music or lyric poetry.

The limitations of the method are, however, suggested by the fact that a towering genius may appear at about the time that decline is to be expected in the curve, and he may give it a secondary burst, as, indeed, Descartes's sharp dualism of mind and body did to a declining scholastic philosophy—a point that has led philosophers to refer to Descartes as a "postscript to medieval thought" rather than as a founder of modern philosophy. In general, however, "delaying actions" of this sort are hard to find and, when the light has gone out of the eyes of a gigantic era, one must wait for a new breed of giants to arise.

The most evident fact about the great periods is that they depend on a "culture base," a level of cultural achievement which has been maintained for centuries or millennia; but then rather suddenly the culture begins to experience an exaltation, rising at an accelerated pace to a peak of brilliant creativeness. Italian painting against a background of Byzantine art moved rapidly into the magnificence of Botticelli and Michelangelo. From medieval science, we find the onrush from Copernicus and Galileo to the twentieth century. Sometimes several branches of human endeavor show these bursts of creativeness simultaneously, as we note in the science, medicine, and painting of the seventeenth-century Netherlands.

• *"Challenge and Response"*

But who or what sets the movement going? Is there some way of defining the character of that spark which initiates a great era, providing a dynamic which would give an understanding of *new potentials?* Among the attempts of modern times are those of Toynbee, with his conception of "challenge and response." He strove to establish a scientific control by comparing *pairs* of historical epochs which seemed, so to speak, equally ready to make such creative contributions. But, of each pair, one possessed and the other lacked effective challenge—or one was incapable of making effective response. He compared, as it were, those societies that had the creative spark with those that had not.

For our present purposes there is one point of genuine importance in Toynbee's approach—namely, the implied emphasis upon the conception of "progressive mastery" in response to challenges long developed by students of the arts. The artist, this thesis maintains, faces a problem to be solved—say, the painter's problem of the creation of the appearance of the third dimension on a two-dimensional surface. There is a focusing of effort, a high degree of ego involvement in response to the challenge; a delight in mastery of technical difficulties; and a glow of satisfaction in success. New love and new creativeness appear at each phase. As the master wrestles with new problems, so do his pupils. Progressive mastery by the individual artist or by the school that he leads is the key to creativeness.

Such a view would exploit several of the conceptions we have used, such as "activity drives," "ego involvement," "canalization upon the task," and "canalization upon the self." If, from such a point of view, the individual confronts a series of tasks to be mastered and gains increasing skill and an increasing love of such tasks and their solution, and if at the same time there is a new preoccupation with such tasks within the society which has nourished them—so that pupils flock to learn and to contribute to the development of still greater possibilities—the movement can proceed more and more swiftly until the inherent possibilities of growth have been realized. Italian painting could thus move forward from the Byzantine era until the era of the Venetians, when the essential problems of classical painting, except those of aerial perspective, had been solved. With these solutions, the great era in Italian painting would come to an end, except as a sheer continuation of that which had once been discovered. From this point of view, "progressive mastery" can continue to complete mastery. Then the movement goes stale.

As we have already noted, it is necessary to do justice to the economic aspect of the problem, insofar as leisure and preferably a patron or benefactor must be available—at least until a community has been so sensitized to the new work that mass support rather than personal support is available. The "great periods" have regularly been periods of patronage through a great power or through mass understanding and support. Such an "economic" component could be readily assimilated to the thesis which has been sketched. Some degree of autonomy, of course, rather than mass coercion, is essential to the very nature of the task, and some form of political experimentation usually serves as background. But wealth does not directly *produce* creativeness. The thesis offered is that challenge and response leading into progressive mastery and depending upon *canalization, ego involvement,* and the *reciprocity of master and pupil* is the heart of the "great period," whether in creative ecstasy or in steady devoted craftsmanship.

Implicit in this view of the creative periods is the conception that cultural discovery "rolls up like a snowball" for the same reason that individual acquisition of tastes and skills rolls up like a snowball—that is, through the development of higher units in the learning process, and through canalization upon the new units as they are discovered and exploited. It is this that James Harvey Robinson had in mind when he noted that new patterns of thought tend to carry themselves further and further from the original raw material that went into their being: "There can be indefinitely more 'mind' accumulated as time goes on, now that we have the trick."

• Periods and Ideas

What has been said can be said in a more psychological way. Most of the great periods can be characterized by a word or phrase representing the great *ideas* which they sought to realize.

The ideas expressed what men were already doing but made them more conscious, gave them a more explicit aim. Even the ages of bronze and iron, simple as their technology was, were dominated by the economic, military, social, and political consequences of a new idea regarding the flexibility and malleability of the material things of the world, an idea expressed in the metallurgy of the period. This cast its stamp upon a whole civilization, its pure and practical arts, its humble daily toil, its magnificent engines of production, or war, or agriculture, or architecture. As the pace of life moves faster, one can discover in the mercantile age of the Mionian kings of the Mediterranean, in the fig-gathering and oil-producing era of the Athenian empire, the transition to a more complex idea. The new civilization which arose from the interaction of the Achaeans with the dark-skinned Minoans, 1500 to 1000 B.C., represented an age that loved the beauty of *order*, "cosmos," whether in bronze, marble, poetry, drama, or philosophy.

As Nietzsche showed in *The Birth of Tragedy,* the ordered and disciplined beauty of Apollo found a way to make peace with the wild and exotic fury of Dionysius. The quest of beauty was set free as never before from the majesty of power and regal immortality. Then, in the succeeding centuries of the downfall of the city-state, the rise of Christianity within the slowly dying Roman Empire put the seal of meaning upon *reality beyond the veil,* and for a thousand years through the slow crystallization of theology and the final massive and heroic beauty of Gothic architecture and stained glass, the idea of man's *salvation and fulfillment* through the atonement became ever more fully expressed. Henry Adams, in *Mont Saint Michel and Chartres,* summed up well the thirteenth-century adoration of the Virgin as a symbol of the adoration of a Divine generative power which gives sustenance, forgiveness, and new life to all who seek it. The rediscovery, in the fourteenth and fifteenth centuries, of the world of classical antiquities gave back with renewed joy the Greek quest for beauty and order, and the new rationalism of the Church fathers had to contend with rationalism of the naturalistic order to which the Greek philosophers had aspired.

A dominant idea thus provided in each case an explicit meaning for the creativeness of the age. There had been lovers of sensuous beauty and of form and order in all times and places, but until the Greek conception of the body as expression of order and beauty had taken hold, the artists of the Western world could not make bodies beautiful. They could make aspiring, struggling, suffering, primally magnificent bodies as vehicles temporarily housing the soul, and from which the soul ultimately would fly to its true home, but it took a new conception of the body to make possible a world of creative arts dealing with the body. High creativeness could not arise from sensory material; it had to arise from ideas, the highest cognitive level, the apex of human understanding.

In exactly the same way, although men in all ages enjoyed melodious sounds, it was not while "oaten stop" and the rhythm of castanets bespoke the simple sensory and motor joys of the world of sound that music could lead to creativeness in our modern sense. Creativeness could come to fulfillment only when a music-fulfilled life became a goal, an ideal representing what is human. It was with this conception of music, arising in the late medieval period and carried forward through the period of Bach, Haydn, and Mozart, that the art of tone and rhythm could become worthy of the great work in which the creative mind must lose itself if it is to function at all. Creativeness must fulfill the idea of a period if it is to represent that period and if the essence of its relation to that period is to be understood.

Perhaps it is for this reason that we vaguely bewail the lack of creativeness in the schools of today. This is a lament not heard in periods and in lands where something vitally new is being sought by the thoughtful men of the era. If the thought is there, the creativeness in all the aspects of the society that are free to move will be forthcoming. The disillusioned youth of the period in the midst of the Depression and of the period immediately after World War II could be preached at without limit about the need for less apathy, more vision, more creativeness; but if they did not believe very deeply in the society in which they lived, if they did not see where it might be going, if there was no great idea on whose wings they could fly, there was a place only for the petty arts of ornamentation, the arts concerned with decorative detail (car bodies, costume jewelry), the glosses on the meaning of life.

Many are still bewildered. If so, an education ready to focus on the positive goals which are being discovered in our own society can infuse creativeness into the schools. It may be that our own uncertainty here at home regarding the possibility of implementing our democratic beliefs will keep us behind the leaders of the world caravan. Perhaps, however, the overwhelming responsibility placed upon us for world peace and world order in the coming decades will be the very idea that will give us an open sky of achievement and an immeasurably demanding task. At dozens of points in history, political renascence and world responsibility have guided the vital and creative arts. If we can stimulate creative curiosity within the intellectual framework of the idea of the oneness of the human family and the ways of realizing it, we may start a spiral leading to political, then cultural, then again political initiative and creativeness, as in the American Revolution, but on an ever greater scale.

• *New Dimensions*

When once a new idea has been expressed and has taken root— an idea such as "individualism" or "liberty" or "equality" or "the brotherhood of man" or "a classless society"—it is difficult to see how mankind could ever have lived without it. It acts like a "new dimension" in thought. This matter of new dimensions is in more than a metaphorical sense fundamental to all speculation about the ways in which we may transcend the realm of our present thinking, and I should like to expand it—first in a literal-minded way—for a few pages.

Repeatedly in the history of the Western world this discovery of a "new dimension" has been literally the discovery of the third dimension itself, the third dimension of space. The flat land of the ancient world was broken by the imagination of the astronomer, Aristarchus, who even measured the diameter of the earth. The generations sighed and forgot, but Ptolemy rediscovered the terrestrial sphere and made it central in a system of spheres of which the ancients had dreamed. Of all the incredible things about Columbus, the most incredible thing was that he convinced men to believe that there might actually be a third dimension in the gently curving surface of the earth bending down before and below him in all directons; instead of falling off the edge, one might fall slowly into another world given by a third dimension.

Curiously enough, the date 1492 marks almost exactly the date at which the painters of the high renaissance in Italy were also exploiting the discovery of the third dimension. The thirteenth century had painted in the flat. Gently folded hands, turning necks, and sparkling eyes led on past 1400 to arms which actually reached toward you out of the canvas, shadows which cut across rising slopes, divine and human forms which advanced and receded; and with Masaccio there were actually tangible or tactile values. This discovery of the third dimension went on to the frantic exaggerations of the Venetians. The third dimension had not only been discovered; it had been idolized, almost deified. The seventeenth century went on to study with the microscope the manifest three-dimensionality of the plane beneath the lens, and ideas about the structure of waves developed through the microscopists and the mathematicians until a solid geometry of the third dimension had been reached which would apply even to the new physics, the new sidereal universe of Laplace. With the nineteenth century the surfaces themselves became curved and, so to speak, thrown into three-dimensional form, as with Riemann, and it was but a step to think of fourth and fifth dimensions whirling ballet-like in all imaginable and unimaginable trajectories where the eye fails and the imagination grows dizzy.

Geography, through the map maker's art carrying out what Copernicus and Columbus had been saying, and the arts of transportation which used the new dimension—the elevators in the mine shafts, later in buildings, the balloons and lighter-than-air machines and, finally, the machines of Darius Green, the Wright Brothers, and their spiritual descendants—made it seem natural that whatever man can discover and conceptualize he can command and traverse.

And it was not in the least accidental that Sigmund Freud, aware of spatial dimensions in the most intense and intimate way, began speaking of up and down and found himself forced into the use of surfaces and solids, as in his celebrated sketch of the relations of id, ego, and superego. He more than once made clear that the various dimensions of the conscious, pre-conscious, and unconscious systems deployed in time involve also dimensionality with respect to clarity of articulation. The mind was not crudely represented as four-dimensional; rather, with the introduction of metapsychology, it was recognized that every mental process entailed "structural" relations. There were, so to speak, systems of dimensions, not merely frozen three-dimensional charts to be apprehended; and there was a flow, a gyration, a struggle of aims or of vectors within each system.

Of course, through all modern psychology, especially since the up-and-down thinking of Herbart at the beginning of the nineteenth century, the concept of subconsciousness and superconsciousness, of depths and heights, had been toyed with, and the spatial, mechanical, and energetic analogies from physics ran riot all over psychology. With Freud, therefore, we seem to have not so much the elaboration of the familiar spatial dimensions as the recognition that it is convenient to push spatial analogies very far while also using "economic" and "dynamic" principles; useful to look for analogies that can be visualized; above all important to recognize that there are always as many dimensions to be imagined as there are classes of phenomena calling for separate treatment—flying, as it were, at right angles, one to another. Multidimensionality, then, was intrinsic to the psychoanalytic conception itself.

The idea that more dimensions can always be added is in keeping with the conception of unlimited possibilities to which we already referred in speaking of the mariners of Columbus' time. There are always new dimensions to be added, always new systems of realities at right angles to that which is known. Indeed, if there is any central plea with which this book could be said to identify itself, it is a plea for the adding of dimensions as rapidly as areas of experience appear which cannot, however forcibly, be squeezed into the dimensions that we know. It is through the recognition of the third dimension and its spiritual successors that curiosity has been able to feed upon the stuff on which its life depends, breaking through into new realities, giving itself life for further adventures, and giving humanity, in the meantime, the visions of reality which no exploitation of given systems could ever afford.

It is this recognition of new dimensons that is forced upon us in the study of people of other cultures, including the members of past and present societies. The men of primitive societies, no longer just "savages," become people with other eyes, other ears, other worlds. In the same way, we have discovered the worlds of those subjected to physical and psychological conditions different from our own; the world of "men under stress," and the "psychotic," at root much like the rest of us; and indeed the world of the child which, though it lay just around the corner, we had forgotten. "The world of our present consciousness," said James, "is only one out of many worlds of consciousness that exist." Other new worlds—physical and social—keep coming into existence, ready to act upon man. We are beginning to recognize a few; the more important thing is to recognize the infinity of the quest. Without new dimensions comes *satiation*.

The term "idea" and the term "dimension" as developed here refer in fact to a new perspective; not to a rational or intellectual perspective alone, but to a way of grasping with all our being a new world of meaning, value, and fulfillment. Essential in the vision are many components not purely cognitive—namely, feeling patterns which have developed as structures to which men are devoted: the songs, the political aspirations, the religious, philosophical, and artistic values which have glowed at white heat when ideas in their ever-increasing consolidation became more and more commanding to the life of feeling and impulse. Sometimes the resulting structural wholes have such stability and such appeal (Hebrew Scriptures, Greek sculpture, Chinese painting) that they may continue even through the long barren periods between eras of creativeness. Sometimes, however, they fade to a point at which a new prophet, a new philosopher, a new poet, a new political leader may give them life only through a new interpretation and a new accent appropriate to the times.

• *Limitlessness*

It is not asserted that there are never any limits at all. But James Harvey Robinson's idea of the indefinitely spacious world of the mind leads naturally to the conception that there is no limit to the complexity and the power of such intellectual structures to be achieved. Robinson thus bypasses the intrinsic limitations in the flexibility, the learning power, the achievement level of mankind; he seems to assume that with *any* human nervous system one can push to *any* level of complexity and function. This is out of line with what one observes in human learning—in particular with evidence as to what can be learned by children at various levels of development. It is not just a question of time required. There are some things which are intrinsically too difficult at any given level. The idea of unlimited development of the intellectual capacities makes sense only if higher units can be so organized that each new synthesis demands no more basic intellectual power than one can mobilize. The nature of our limits is an experimental problem, not one which can be solved theoretically. The same would have to be said regarding the limitlessness of human capacity for esthetic feeling, esthetic creativeness, or, for that matter, the power to love or to exercise self-control.

We are far, however, from actually reaching the limits which can now be conceived in such areas—far, indeed, from any landmarks which would suggest the beginning of a need to slow our pace. Let us speculate a bit as to the degree to which man can hope to cultivate his creative powers. The potentialities of favorable organization in the brain are breath-taking. Hebb's concept of "cell assembly"—the physiological basis for the assembly of psychological patterns—is useful. Sherrington came near to establishing this point, in neurophysiological terms, by showing that *every nerve cell is potentially linked with every other nerve cell.* Under conditions of general sensitization resulting from strychnine, it is possible to elicit *any* response as a result of applying *any* stimulus. In fact, we find under the microscope the converging and diverging channels, the networks and articulations, which make possible this type of convergence upon the "final common path." From such a point of view one can reach any goal one likes, starting from any point—provided that there is direction. It is partly from this conception that psychoanalysis has developed its notion of "overdetermination." Reversing the image and looking backward rather than forward, one may trace any act to an infinitude of preconditioning circumstances, or may appropriately label the distinctive drives, images, or infantile residues from which a given response emanates.

The full implications of this thought, that from any point we may reach any goal, are certainly staggering. This suggests the freedom of the mariner upon the face of the sea, or of the aircraft navigator through the air or ultimately through the interstellar spaces. We can go anywhere we like. Every conceivable combination of ideas is possible. Every situation permits an infinitude of responses through the compounding of responses implicit within us. If any challenge be worthy of the time and effort required to meet it, it can be met.

There remain then, these two fundamental conditions: first, the limits of the physically possible; second, the limits of our strength and skill. Mankind may not turn back time or make internal contradiction into logical plausibility; may not set going biological and social forces which produce changes in human nature within time spans which are out of keeping with the physical limits of change. We can, however, go far indeed, and we must demand always that proof be given that the impossible is truly impossible. The alchemist was not essentially wrong in hoping that gold could be made from lead. He was wrong simply with reference to the time, knowledge, and physical scope required.

Often in contemplating the amazing range of power set free in a person who is once liberated from false assumptions, arrogant rigidities, or bland complacency, one is amazed to see how far the untethered mind can roam. Most of us while asleep produce dreams far beyond our ordinary capacity for subtlety and range, whether we happen to accept the psychoanalytic conception of dreaming or not. The complexity of the dream process permits a condensation and enrichment of thought, often a great richness of conception, which has astonished the thoughtful men of all ages. And even under artificial conditions of imaginative liberation, such as those of hypnosis, delirium, mescal intoxication, extreme fatigue and hunger, and a thousand other conditions of relaxation of control, we begin to realize the rate at which the capital of our potential may compound; the rate at which new connections may be formed.

Is there any possibility, despite the difficulties already suggested, that our own era might learn something from all this; might catch the creative spirit; might fulfill itself; might become a creative era in its own right?

Chapter IO:

Creativeness in Our Own Era

There are many forces at work in our society that block and limit creativeness: the rigidity of an industrial-technological system; the sheer complexity of the world to which adjustment must be made; the fact that so much is new, all at once; the fears that hedge in the freedom of teaching and of learning; the lack of a dominant new idea to symbolize a path to be followed; and the "atomic" fears that we shall have to consider in Chapter 12. Other great periods have faced great obstacles and a few have transcended them. There is perhaps some justification for optimism in the fact that there is at least an increasing understanding today of the nature of the creative drive. Can we assist in clarifying the nature of the task of home and school, artist and scientist, in freeing the creative impulse in the child—assist in defining the directions in which our own society might move to realize its own creative potentials?

The task cannot be easy. As one reads the modern studies of creativeness and of ways of stimulating it in the schools, one must ask oneself: are we really facing honestly the massive obstacles which an industrial-technological society imposes in the form of the need to do as others do; are we recognizing the monolithic solidity of today's standardized ways of living—of group methods, especially group methods of setting the stage for thinking? The first half of the chapter will be given to the character of this group process as it relates to the standardization of thought and the ways of using it in the service of creativeness; the last half to the methods still available for the cultivation of individual creativeness within our industrial society.

- ### Group Thinking

We move in a world in which we are squeezed in upon one another like sardines, with house lots of a tenth of an acre, apartments with window boxes for gardens, subway standing room determined by the "compressibility of the human body." Time, like space, is squeezed, so that we resent five minutes' "waste of time." We buy space and time as we advertise; actually, we buy one another's attention. Newspaper, radio, television take a good share of what there is. Togetherness is a primary reality, both in terms of a genuine cordiality of fellow feeling and also in terms of the sheer pressure of man on man. We may think of this as a new thing in the world; but where most of the people of the world live—Europe, Asia, Africa—it has long been chronic, and we are just catching up. With the physical togetherness goes the loss of privacy in solitary thoughts and the legitimate demand of neighbors and workers that we share the problem of neighborhood and work in which all of us have our existence. Since we live through a group process, many of our pressing problems are group problems. This makes the individualists among us squirm, but there is still a reality here to be faced: the group character, the corporate character, of the thinking process. There was a corporate character in the thinking of the "creative eras," too. Can we use this corporate character and find strength in it, rather than simply protest against it?

The most prominent aspect of corporate creativeness is the fact that in every era many works of art, or science, are essentially like "cathedrals" in which no one man dominates and many play some part; this collective way of working more and more characterizes ourselves. A sort of architecture of thought emerges, dependent, of course, upon a *system* and upon *structural soundness* all the way through. Yet in a sense it is impersonal.

Let us look more closely at scientific creativeness. Those who love the role and the personality of the scientist may become uneasy at the thought we have learned to accept today—that scientific discovery is in fact rather impersonal. When once the ways of science have been discovered, the individual variations may produce a sort of orchestration without essentially altering the proliferation of scientific thought. When once the structure of science has reached a given level, each discovery is made at almost the same time in many parts of the world. Almost every young scientist knows the problem of getting his work finished so as to get the credit which comes from original discovery, knowing that a similar discovery is about to be made at other research centers.

The role of the very exceptional scientific figure is, of course, of a different character, and we can show by Galileo, Harvey, Newton, Darwin, or Einstein that it took a huge push to raise the block to its resting place at the top of the structure. Even so, it has become common in recent decades to derive the history of modern physics from a list of names which certainly could not be shorter than twenty and would ordinarily run to forty or fifty, limited to the great seminal figures who carried us beyond the essentially mechanical world system of the year 1800 to the electromagnetic-quantum-relativist world of the mid-twentieth century. In chemistry, the list beginning with Lavoisier and including all the scientists through to the leading figures in the stabilization of organic chemistry, and in biology the list of figures who created a new conception of the evolutionary process, from the time of Charles Darwin to the age of the study of genes and their mutations, would show again that it is rare today for a single figure to contribute anything radically unique. The new levels are like the levels of an engineer's sharp grading up a slope, with turning points of higher grade here and there as the switchbacks ascend the steepest parts. The giant steps are for the pioneers; the gently or steeply graded slope for the caravan which follows.

Most of this holds for the arts, for the professions, and for business. The gradual recognition of the progressive orderliness and the impersonality of professionalized and technical thinking, the corporate nature of the modern thought process, was what Harlow Person described as the "institutional mind." Most thinking that makes a difference in the evolution of society, the thinking done in huge industrial and financial establishments, the thinking done in engineering organizations, the thinking done by government, is done by very complex and beautifully organized "institutional minds." The newspaper writer knows this when he says, "The Pentagon expects that by next September" or "It has become evident within the last few weeks that General Motors is going to agree to. . . ." At the very heart of modern life these decisions are made within a complex power structure, prestige structure, dependency structure, in which we know little about the top and middle-level leaders and their sensitivity to one another's pressures. We know even less about the form of their life, the structure of their interpersonal world, the ways in which everything from their newspapers, their clubs, their wives, their secretaries, their appointment books, down to their specific confrontation of a balance sheet or an inventory enters into their thinking. Consciously or unconsciously, when each individual's interaction with other individuals has to be assessed, gross mistakes are made in each interpersonal assessment; but gain, power, and prestige are to be had by making few rather than many mistakes, and by working smoothly rather than clumsily within this vast network of interpersonal institutional thinking.

It is easy to damn all this. But he who is concerned with human potentialities must be concerned not only with the potentiality of the individual—biological or social—and the way in which this potentiality comes to terms with the potentiality of every other individual but also and always with the nature of the structural and functional wholes which are thus involved, which constitute the actual environment within which each person breathes and realizes his own individuality. Human potentiality is a potentiality of institutional achievements; creative thinking derives not simply from Steinmetz or Urey, but from General Electric or the Navy Department or the CIO. One of the reasons, in fact, for the relatively inadequate efforts of labor and agriculture as compared with business lies their poorer organization, the atomized nature of thinking as contrasted with institutionalized and structuralized group activities through which the higher structures achieve clarity and skill in their quest for power. Ultimately, the thinking becomes separated from the individual; in a sense, the thinking is governed by the *nature of the task itself*.

If the reader can assent at least to the general tenor of the conception that any task generates its own way of thinking, it would be tempting to believe that there are no limits at all to the kinds of group processes which might fulfill the creative need, and the kinds of intellectual, affective, and recreative processes in which a group might find itself at work. There would be literally a freeing of the mind from the original roots provided by perceptual and cognitive structure, the roots provided by the affective and impulse life, and the roots which lie in the concatenation of experience and impulse through processes of association. Man might ultimately emerge into a state almost of Godhead, in which his original evolutionary nature and indeed his membership in a specific cultural tradition might be altogether transcended in a new biology-free and culture-free capacity. We can discover, in the work of Gordon Allport, S. E. Asch, and others of today, this conception that man ultimately discovers a realm not directly anchored upon anything that is built into his original humanness.

I am myself sorely tempted to pursue the thought to this far point. That I cannot do so is partly a matter of my belief that the life of feeling and of thought is still anchored upon the kinds of sense functions and the rich variety of drives (p. 69) which mankind possesses in the early years. If creativeness in the group is to be set free, it must first be born in the satisfactions of early creative experience in home and school; it must be nurtured at the intensely intimate level of the personal discovery of sensory values, meanings, pursuit of curiosity, delight in uniformities and laws, just as we suggested in Chapter 8.

All this calls for more, rather than less, attention in an industrial society and a group-centered way of life. Indeed, the ability to use creatively the facilities of group organization will depend on the cultivation of a love not only for things, tones, colors but also of "social discovery," as E. C. Lindeman called it. The fresh discovery of social meanings and of *ways of using group organization* can still be a major invention of today; a major creative step toward the fuller understanding of human nature. We always thought we understood the nature of group life; but new kinds of group life exist and, through blundering in laboratory or clinic or diplomatic conference, we learn how large a world of group creativeness there is waiting to be discovered. To stimulate individual creativeness in children is just half the story; to teach boys and girls, young men and women, ways of discovering and using the new group structures of today in the sense of finding creative solutions for shared problems is coming to be recognized as a major challenge for social research and education.

Here lies the importance of "group dynamics," "small group research," group therapy, and the thousand new skills which are being born today that salute the new ways of understanding the group process. Education and industry alike are daily discovering new kinds of man-to-man relationships.

- *Social Support for Individual Creativeness*

Our path turns back now to the individual.

Can we be more precise regarding what it is that parent, teacher, and society can do to nourish the creative roots in early experience?

Let us face the difficulties squarely.

The first problem that confronts parent and teacher is how to avoid overcontrol; how to allow the first generous outpouring of mind and heart to have its way. We know relatively little about how to encourage but all too much about how to impede. We find a thousand devices for regularizing, stabilizing, restraining, or even for poking fun at the earliest exploratory efforts of children who are transported by a great challenge or a great discovery. Whatever stray creativeness gets through the sieve of our adult system of approvals and disapprovals of children's behavior is likely to be knocked down by classmates who, through their own earlier subjection to restraints or ridicule, have learned that to poetize, to daub, to speculate, or to dream is just a "waste of time."

The same fate would likewise attend the efforts of the young child in the direction of science were it not for the fact that in our moment of technical mastery Western society has been willing to give freedom to boys, at least, in their first scientific efforts, and in some environments permits sheer dabbling in the ham world of electronics or the homemade laboratory of chemistry. Even here, however, where creative thought seems to be encouraged, it is, unfortunately, the acquisition of the standardized skills of the culture rather than the encouragement of true freedom of inquiry that provides security and status.

It is the responsibility and privilege of the teacher to encourage, to give freedom, to swing wide the gates wherever the child's or adolescent's mind wants to explore, to make contact, to know, to grasp, to assimilate the new. This involves three steps. First comes encouragement of the child's sheer *sensitiveness* to the charm, the challenge, the mystery of this wonderful world and protection of the warm response to sensory, motor, and cognitive challenge. Second, aid to the formation of strong canalizations on sensory, motor, and cognitive content and the forming of positive canalizations upon the *self as creator*. Third, the freedom to move from infantile, direct wish-fulfilling fantasies (Freud's "primary process thinking") to a controlled and ordered thinking in which cravings are fulfilled by dealing with reality ("secondary process"). The amount of coercion exercised by extreme reality will usually be greater in the sciences than in the arts.

• The Early Emotional Roots

Among the many psychoanalytically oriented suggestions as to the nature of this transition to reality orientation, let us note here just one:

L. K. Frank[1] has recently developed the thesis ("tactilism") that during the opening years of life our being is organized to an extraordinary degree around the things that we can *feel through our skins*. The first childhood experiences are experiences of contact, support, communication through primitive give-and-take. Slowly the self begins to be shaped in terms of differentiation from the world outside; the outer world is a world of seeing and hearing, organized in opposition to the warm inwardness of our primitive tactual and within-the-skin world. The obvious dependence of little children upon the love and support of those about them is paralleled by many studies of animal infants which likewise can be carried through a crisis by "gentling," by rocking, soothing, physical contact. Thus, stress situations can be handled without permanent damage, it would appear, only insofar as children or young animals can consolidate a world within themselves

[1] "Tactile Communication," *Genet. Psychol. Monogr.*, Vol. 56, 1957, pp. 209-255.

by making contact with the pillars of strength, their parents or companions, whom they can touch.

As through eye and ear the outer world takes shape, the more intimate world learns to adjust itself to the law and order outside. The "primary process" activity, the free flow of fantasy governed from within, must slowly learn to respect *order*, especially time and space arrangement given by eye and ear, must learn to respect the abstractions and the logic of an outer world. The beginning of the "latency" period (at about five years) is actually the end of the way for the first tactile order of experience, as the order given by external requirements and sanctions drills into the child from about five to adolescence the necessary sequences, the inexorable logic, of a world shared externally with others.

In this new mastery of the outer world, there is much response to the coercion of reality; but, if the tactual world has provided strength, there is real readiness to use and delight in the firm structure of the outer world. As Elizabeth Barnes puts it, there are often "areas of virtuosity," as in the skills of ball-bouncing, stamp-collecting, or specialized fact-gathering with which children often astonish their elders. Here, before it has been spoiled by years of drudgery and drill, lies the consummation of the warm enthusiasm which survives from the tactile period. Children rush into the free-moving world of outer things and events, the world of sight and hearing, the world of symbols and of concepts, the world of the social order, of religion, philosophy, right and wrong, and all those overwhelming and preoccupying concerns, so distinctively human, which mark the emancipation from infantile dependence. It is only, however, because infantile dependence originally provided the warmth and solidity, the base from which to move forward, that the latency period and the secondary process could have their will.

One of the great problems of the release of human potentialities is the wise and creative use of this great burst of fresh enthusiasm which sweeps like wildfire through the minds of those boys and girls who want to know, to control, who want to get hold of meanings, who want to grow in and through this strange, exciting, challenging environment. It is the prolongation of infancy, as John Fiske[2] said, that permits mankind this span of years for

[2] *The Meaning of Infancy*, Houghton Mifflin, 1909.

the enrichment of the creative potentials before the responsibilities of adulthood have arrived. One of the greatest problems of the release of human potentials consists, therefore, in the study of the ways in which the fires of infancy can be gently transferred to the new furnaces of high creativeness, preserving the primitive intensities of the first vital responses but channeling them into the infinitely diverse realms in which discovery and creativeness may flourish.

We ordinarily think of children as learning to use tools and skills to reach their goals. But so far as we can see, virtually every activity of which the human sense organs, muscles, and nervous system are capable becomes a joy in itself (cf. p. 82); nothing is left as a sheer tool or instrument to be handled mechanically in the service of goals. All the tools become creations of delight not only because they lead toward great goals but because in themselves they yield more and more sensory and manipulative pleasure. The world of colors, of numbers, of words, of ideas, can be a world of intense gratification. And perhaps the measure of freedom to release such potentials, to move in such directions, is the measure with which the adequacy of our schools should be gauged. In all this tumultuous period where children reach out to discover and to bring the world into themselves, it is tragic to be concerned simply with drilling into them standardized information and skills—skills often picked up incidentally in adolescence much more easily if creative discovery has been fostered in the first years of the latency period.

All of this means, we are told, that creativeness depends on "environmental stimulation." Actually, however, this is a misleading way to summarize the social functions involved in creativeness. There are two reasons why the school and the teacher are of especial importance. In the first place, illuminations come when they are ready to come in terms of the readiness of the mind. Particularly important is the *mood* of searching in which the imperfectly organized material leaps, if it can, into its own integration. The possibility of integration depends upon the inner logic of the material and upon the inner logic of the human personality in relation to the structure of the material. A standardized group process, in school or elsewhere, cannot provide a maximal opportunity for an intensely individualistic construction. On the contrary, it is typically the Archimedes of the bathtub, the distracted and absent-minded Newton, the eccentric and angry Beethoven to whom, often in the least appropriate moment, the sudden inspiration comes. A certain willingness to allow for chaos and irrelevance, a certain freedom from every type of social regimentation is essential for free movement.

At the same time there is a paradoxical counterpart of this principle of the solitary creator which may at first sight seem to be a direct opposite of what has just been said. These illuminations come as a result of years or even decades of highly social experience. The great periods of human creativeness are notoriously circumscribed in time and place, and dependent upon the living example of a series of heroic figures with whom each newcomer comes to terms. Whether one thinks of the dramatic poet of Athens in the fifth century before Christ or the Italian and Dutch painters of the Renaissance or the composers in early nineteenth-century Vienna, one finds periods in which there is accomplished within a few years more than a thousand years could ordinarily produce through the warmth of interstimulation of a like-minded and like-souled generation of men, each inspiring his comrades and followers to a new achievement.

Special facilities for the recognition and encouragement of highly creative persons need to be provided within the very structure of our educational system, so that one may seek out and make the most of the inspiring leadership of others who have already begun to blaze a trail. When the world of economics, politics, religion, and social values is struggling to defend itself against chaos as it is today, it is not enough to urge the student to think creatively; he must be encouraged to associate with freely creative peers in fellowship with daring and inspired teachers. If it is only great painters who can inspire those who are striving to paint, it is only with great thinkers that students can learn to think creatively. This may sound obvious, but do we not practice exactly the opposite, expecting our students to attempt individually to solve the herculean social problems of today? One learns such creativeness in any human field of endeavor only by first sharing with others, in the company of those who have already known the struggle to think out the meaning of inspiration. First, support, a hand to hold; then a few steps alone; then a race against time to see how much a short life can yield.

• *Personal Growth in a Creative Society*

This means that it may be necessary to encourage a long period of groping and gloating, messing and manipulating, to permit a fuller sensory gratification and a wider range of associations between gratifying sensory materials in any given modality. In the case of the child interested in color, line, surface, shadow, form, and movement—as he plays, for example, with paints and crayons—it may be necessary to do much more than help him to make simple juxtapositions by way of color contrast or the reinforcement of color values, one after another. It may be necessary to help the child to form richer associations between chromatic and kinesthetic materials, to steep himself more fully, more luxuriously in the world to which his first glimpses invite him.

It may be necessary at the same time to encourage free movement, allowing him to get down and lie on his tummy as on a Saturday morning at the art museum, or to dance about, or to watch the dancing activities of other children, seeing the way in which an art form more complex than that of painting may come into existence. He may, for example, begin to see the relations of the moving human body to color as a dancer or a creator of plays and pageants might see them. According to the thesis already developed, he must richly experience, richly interweave, richly integrate, while the mind glows in earnest contact with these delights and grows ready to make its own higher integrations. He may, in the same way, acquire words which serve to complicate and to interrelate the various types of experiences, so that his poetry, derived from such experience, may both breathe what the other modalities have to offer and, in turn, act upon them.

Indeed, this sight of polychromatic, polymodal experience of delight, involving more and more of the whole human organism, discovers again for us what the Greeks discovered—the radiant love of the sensory beauty of the world—and in particular of the designs in the stars, trees, waves, animal and human forms— which constitute that feeling for life and for the intimacy of man and nature which we call Greek. It was exactly that which made up the Apollonian as against the less organized, more primitive and impulsive dynamic of the Dionysian in that great contrast between the ordered and the chaotic to which Friedrich Nietzsche devoted the magnificent pages of *The Birth of Tragedy*.

In the medieval period the slicing process by which man's cognitive functions were more or less separated from his affective functions was expressed in a scholastic philosophy which often stamped his impulses with the mark of Cain. The Roundhead armies that chopped the heads from medieval sculpture were doing more than "attacking idolatry"; they were attacking the guilt that stemmed from free expression. The fear of that loveliness that springs from the Greek feeling for wholeness succeeded for a long time in convincing us that, in order to teach any given sphere of artistic activity, we must in the first instance deal only with the specific content and form which relates to that limited process. In teaching sculpture from such a viewpoint, for example, one must teach space, surface, and—to a limited degree— movement; to a still more limited degree, the innervation of muscles in maintaining posture or activity. But much of the true context is missing. The suggestion offered here is that understanding Homer or Sappho might have much to do with the grasp of Greek sculpture, because it is by these intersensory, these trans-sensory experiences that the use of line, surface, and form in Greek sculpture can actually be grasped.

This brings us now to the thesis, hinted above, that the inhibition of human functions through fear of the goals toward which they are directed, or through fear of the very functions themselves, can have much more than a limited restraining effect, much more than a stylizing or freezing effect on the human capacity to deal with the fluidity and the creativeness of life. There is always the possibility of a critical *interference with the integrative process by which the many free components in a free personality flow together at the time of the first great explorations in life.* This fear, whether it be the fear of a punishing father or of a rigid social order, a fear of some unnamable absolute or of a despotic control in the universe, may interfere basically with being creative.

• *Discipline*

Some will doubtless consider this a plea for unlimited and uncontrolled expressiveness, or for the conversion of every impulse into act; impetuosity held up as an ideal. Are we not in fact pleading that almost any interference with function in a specific situation may overshoot its mark and interfere massively with the given function itself or, indeed, with many functions? A troubled reader may well feel: "Is there not a need for discipline in facing the reality with which man must cope, and a need for discipline to accept those rituals, restraints, and interdependent checks and balances which make up any society, with norms which all must understand and respect if each one is to have a life worth living? You must remember that for your Greeks the first principle was cosmos, *order,* and order is heaven's first law."

The problem is one of balance. Extreme laissez-faire indulgence, or uncontrolled or undisciplined expressiveness actually results in an *overaccentuation* of any specific impulse that is at work at any particular moment and plays a role diametrically opposed to the one for which we are pleading—namely, the integrative role of a multi-expressive integration of human potentials. Any sensory response which is, in its physiological nature, manifold can be oversimplified and made arbitrarily narrow by the sheer process of accentuating it, the process of excluding all other sensory appeals. But it is also true that when there is interference with gratification one develops that passionate intensity to recover it to which the Freudians have paid tribute in their discussion of the "oral dependent" character type. Clara Davis' experiments show that there is no great danger in letting the small child temporarily "overeat" a particular type of healthful food, provided only that there are available to him all the foods that he needs at his age and growth level. The little child may eat too many bananas one week, too much meat another week—but balance it out in the course of six months and you find that he will eat a balanced diet. In the same way, the danger of overdriving any particular human need at any point in early childhood is equalled by the danger that obliteration or blockage of expression in one area may cause a wild overemphasis upon that area, or the danger that the integrations between many satisfactions which life itself would easily afford may be lost through the damming or clogging of communication between the various activities.

Creativeness may, indeed, consist partly of that readiness for new canalizations upon content and form which we have already considered. It may depend largely upon the general capacity for formation of canalizations. This might be like the mobility or "lability" of cathexes in the psychoanalytic system. In particular, that type of readiness for new attachments to which we have given the name *curiosity*—that capacity to respond vibrantly to new content, new relationships, new processes, new persons, and new aspects of oneself—that readiness for *discovery* may itself be a central element in all creativeness. It may be that what I have called progressive mastery consists of the capacity to keep alive this precious freshness of response, this capacity to deploy energy in the form of cathexis or canalization at such points as give new meaningful structure, new relations of person to world. Insofar as responses are merely iterative, they involve the restamping of old patterns; insofar as they are responses to the relations waiting to be discovered, they may properly be called creative. Insofar as they are meaningful in terms of what one already is, they involve the projection of oneself into the future.

- *Personal and Social Incompleteness as the Mainspring of Creativeness*

Creativeness springs from the unrealized portions of individuality as well as from the unrealized potentials of the medium used. No one has seen more clearly than G. H. Mead the distinction between the realized individuality which can be observed and contemplated, the *me,* and, on the other hand, the integrated, ongoing activity of the self focused upon life and its objects and tasks in such fashion that the creative "I" is constantly a surprise to the "me." *The "I" that is responsible for effective changes in the world comes into awareness only as the act is completed and can be contemplated.* "However carefully we plan the future it always is different from that which we can previse. . . . It is only after the act has taken place that we can catch it in our memory and place it in terms of that which we have done."[3] Sometimes someone else can tell a man something about himself that he is not aware of. He is never sure about himself, and his conduct astonishes himself as much as it astonishes other people. "We get a great deal of our enjoyment of romance, of moving pictures, of art, in setting free, at least in imagination, capacities which belong to ourselves, or which we want to belong to ourselves."

The artist, in particular, brings into existence that which is a fulfillment both of his own unfinished and never-to-be-finished individuality, of which he is aware only after the event, and of that which is potential within the group, as he moves towards its half-formed goals and aspirations. Creative leaders of all sorts —and in particular religious, moral, and ideal leaders—fulfill that which is implicit but not explicit in the ideal demands of a society. Because the formulations are not explicit, these leaders are often persecuted or destroyed, but because they express that which belongs to the active, but not yet consciously grasped, component in the society, their self-realization becomes in time a self-realization for others and for the collective life of the group. Often, moreover, in the community of the artists or the religious brotherhood there is the liberation of a flood of potential interpersonal responses; the awakening of a love which never before found expression. In Mead's words, "This breakdown of barriers is something that arouses a flood of emotions, because it sets free an indefinite number of possible contacts to other people which have been checked, held repressed." The creativeness of childhood is in large measure a function of the primitive and unorganized nature of the "me," the fact that the differentiated world and the differentiated empirical self are as yet waiting to come into being.

It does not follow, therefore, that an industrial society *must* progressively rob man of his creative freedom. On the contrary, progressive differentiation or even mechanization of the outer world may provide larger leisure and an explicit urge for a counterpoise in the form of areas relatively free of structure. In general, we have been unimaginative about the provision of such counterpoises, allowing the mechanization of leisure time activi-

[3] G. H. Mead, *Mind, Self, and Society*, University of Chicago Press, 1934, pp. 203-204.

ties and amusements to deprive us of the urge to make something fresh and vital out of the open spaces. The groups that got together to sing and to square-dance in the *Middletown* of 1890 have long since become preoccupied either with the passive satisfactions of television or with the formally arranged meetings of service clubs and other arranged affairs. "Other-directedness" applies to leisure as much as to work and duty. What is defective, however, is primarily the planning function. One can plan for emancipation from an overcontrol of planning. In particular, planning for freedom can supersede planning for the mechanization of leisure.

Is there too much planning? It would hardly seem so, for we are further ahead in those areas where we have allowed intelligent and flexible planning its way. Take, for example, as a contrast with the stereotyped school described above (p. 101), what is already done, through careful planning, for handicapped children. The deaf or the polio-stricken child, for example, gets, as a result of specialized planning, a wide variety of incentives and assistance, gratifications and challenges, which offer a strange contrast to the rather passive and mechanized routines demanded for ordinary normal children. There is real virtuosity today in work for the deaf, and in many aspects of work for the blind. We carry out, in other words, brilliant repair work on the damaged members of our community against a rather sleazy backdrop of general fumbling with the creative potentials of our normal children. A polio-stricken child can be led on to make the maximal use of his physical equipment, but the intellectual, social, esthetic, and moral equipment of the normal child is to a very large degree cast into a lock-step form, routines explicitly taking the place of originality, and formal achievement levels taking the place of the unstructured and imaginative components of growth.

The sick or crippled child has offered a *challenge* and brought a *response;* he has inspired in us a mood, a spirit, a faith, an attitude. The thought of the challenged and inspired teacher has moved forward in response to him. The normal child is taken for granted. There are buildings and chairs for him. As for the work of the school, there are content and skills to be imparted; that is about all. If "Johnny can't read," there is trouble for the teacher.

But to develop creative potentialities, teacher is too busy. The least that can be added is that the inspired handling of handicapped children be established as a goal or standard for normal children; that normal children be accepted as sources of excitement, challenge, unlimited opportunity in creative teaching and creative parenthood.

Planning seldom overshoots the mark. Much more often, it falls far short of what is known about human needs. Architects are foresighted in planning for the use of solar heat, and housing projects are providing maximal sun and air for people of modest incomes. But human beings, especially children, need to do more than breathe; activity drives are compelling and most city housing projects offer little or nothing for childhood exploratory and manipulative needs. A first step here is for city planners to consult not only engineers but those concerned with childhood needs, in order to build environments in which personalities, as well as bodies, can grow. Small hard-surfaced playgrounds and a few swings and slides are no substitute for places to dig, make tunnels, castles, and roads, or work out fantasies which are the childhood precursors of later creativity. Some unstructured space is essential for growth, not just for prevention of delinquency. What may be said of architecture may be said of our culture as a whole: it has a long way to go in thinking out ways of releasing and stimulating the creative potentials.

For even though we work within the pavilion of a tightly controlled group process, we can nevertheless give greater and greater support for the growth of individual potentialities. Indeed, if the spirit of discovery, so central in science and technology, can be made dominant in our attitudes to human nature itself and to the individual child, our scientific-technological age may achieve as much creativeness in dealing with the development of its own potentialities as it has achieved in studying the potentialities lying hidden in the world of physics and chemistry.

Chapter II:

The Yen to Discovery*

The second human nature arose when the raw stuff of the first human nature underwent transformation through culture. A crystallization resulted, a process of living within cultural requirements. But a new thing happened: culture led to the discovery and development of intellectual tools—powerdriven by the craving for understanding—which gave man a world capable in some ways of transcending culture through new ways of observing, new contact with reality. Against the obvious pressures toward standardization and rigidity, there is a huge counterthrust based on wonder about the world, embodied especially in science. We are changing by virtue of what we discover and by virtue of the fact that we are engaged in a voyage of discovery. Let us turn now to a closer look at these *processes of discovery*.

- *Sensory Experience and the Extension of Human Nature*

Our own discoveries make the world richer in its offerings to our experience. We are living in a new world, and we are becoming different people. A study of color names in English literature since Chaucer shows not only that we have become aware of richer and richer differentiations in hues, tints, and shades but

* Another version of this material appeared in the *J. Individual Psychol.*, Vol. 13, 1957, pp. 125-133.

that, through the development of industrial chemistry, we are capable of giving ourselves a virtually limitless range of *new color experiences* never available to man before.

Along with the new products with which technology surrounds us and the incredibly rich combinations of new ingredients worked into man's creative fantasy of things that never were on sea or land goes the almost unlimited extension of experience through the invention of *accessory sense organs*. The world that the science of Aristotle's day comprised was the world of the naked eye. The simple hand lens of Archimedes later magnified this world and in time broke it into tiny particles, each of which had new meaning. With Leeuwenhoek's microscope, in the seventeenth century, one could see what we now know as bacteria. The compound microscope, the oil-immersion microscope, the electronic microscope, have diversified the world, have shown an unknown and, in the profoundest sense, inhuman realm, a realm in which some of the basic structural laws, the basic temporal sequences are different from those of the naked-eye world. And the lattice-work structure which X-ray examination yields—the world of physical chemistry in which we may actually apprehend the migration of elements through ultramicroscopic sieves which let some particles pass and strain out others—gives us a world at least as strange as the underwater world of a William Beebe. Man makes for himself a new world to live in, a world in which the primary tool is no longer the eye but the compound eye of which the microscope is a part.

In the same fashion the telescope and, more particularly, the spectroscope extend the eye beyond the world upon which the naked eye makes its report. The telescope's world is not only immensely big; it is a world conceivable only in terms of light-years, the curvature of space, the displacement of black bands in the spectrum which tell of unimaginable velocities of expansion and contraction, the world of giants and dwarfs among the stars, each obeying a cosmic law so different from that of the simple world about us that the mathematician has had to invent new hyperspaces, new time-space structures, in order to comprehend and predict the comings and goings of galaxies and nebulae.

Man has appropriately begun to modify his philosophies to take account of these new worlds in which he has begun to live.

Eddington has suggested that on a geometric scale man's body is midway between the electron and the knowable universe, for his body contains 10^{29} electrical particles, and the number of particles within his body multiplied by 10^{29} would comprise the number of particles in the knowable universe. As he was for Heraclitus, man remains "the measure of all things." He no longer sees himself as man; he sees himself as a bit of cosmic stuff. He has turned in upon himself like a convolvulus, a chambered nautilus looking in with a cosmic eye upon the soft little form which, though building stately mansions "with a dome more vast," is instantly turned into a new iridescent chemical pattern to be succeeded by other patterns, part of the cosmic time-space structure. Man has thus learned to accept both the brevity, the relativity, and the dependency of his own existence upon a peculiar set of segmental laws of time and space, which are only special cases of more general time-space laws which he attempts to apprehend.

As apprehender, he has tried with desperate intensity to transcend his humanness. Remembering what Kant said about the impossibility of transcending the laws which make up his being as knower, feeler, and willer, he has nevertheless attempted a new stance, a new place, like that of Archimedes, from which to move the world and himself. He has attempted to see what manner of creature a man would be when living no longer in terms of an acre of ground and a span of threescore years and ten. He conceives himself to be a representative particle of the cosmic stuff, to be understood in terms of the perspectives of a cosmos which he believes he is beginning to glimpse. Man's conception of man is indeed still a conception based upon seeing and hearing, touching, smelling, and tasting—a world of warms and colds, pains and aches, and the despairs and ecstasies which come from the reverberations of his physical being—but instead of being limited to those characteristic human ways of observing which come with the bodily package which we call his anatomy, it is the world as known by his *extended* sense organs, the world of spectroscopes and radar, of "chemical atmospheres" and radioactivity, that constitute the structures into whose spaces his fingers grope.

With these new senses which he has constructed, man does queer things. He gives to the world such meaning as he can, both through science and through science fiction—that strange art of carrying wild fantasy into the most sober reflections. Often he fails through assuming simply *more and more of whatever we already know,* failing to make the great leap into that which new senses, new modes of experiences, new ways of feeling might bring mankind. Science fiction, extrapolating always from the wars of today to the wars of tomorrow and from the halting diagnostic skills of today to the supposed unerring medical omniscience of a few decades hence, leaps from the faint and fitful paranormal phenomena of today to the world of infallible mind-reading or the unlimited control of another's thoughts—or the unlimited skill of the duelers who, while trying to read another's thoughts, set up effective shields and barriers to the thought-reading activities of others.[1]

Actually, what a dull world this whole world of extrapolation is! How poor a substitute for the actual re-creation of human nature which the last few centuries and in particular the last few decades has actually given mankind! Emerson remarked that if the brilliance of the starry heavens were to be seen just once, man would forever talk of the magnificence of such a spectacle. If there were but one new scientific revelation of man and his relation to the world, rather than a continuing succession of revelations, it might jolt us into some semblance of the appreciation of the vast change which comes over us as we see ourselves through the new instruments.

• The Nature of the Impulse Toward Discovery

The world to which our extended sense introduces us is potentially exciting; it is a come-on to discovery. We reach out toward new experiences, lovingly gloat over them, turn an eagle eye toward fine differentiation among them, modes of grouping and ordering them; put them into hierarchies and systems; look always for new experiences, and new modes of organization. Let us now attempt to understand the basis for this craving for new experience. It is tempting to use the label "curiosity drive." But to speak of "curiosity" is too little and too much; too little because

[1] A. Bester, *The Demolished Man,* Shasta, 1954.

an idle glance at the sports page is also "curiosity"; too much because it simply slaps a name upon what has not been analyzed or understood.

To begin with, this craving certainly seems related to some of our visceral needs. Yet we found, in Chapter 3, that mankind's interests are not dependent on his viscera in any simple and clear way. In contrast to his animal brethren, he is potentially in love with the sky, the earth, and the sea, and all that flies, runs, or crawls upon or within them. He loves to dissect, to analyze, to reconstruct, to create, to fathom, to understand, to grasp both sensory values and abstract relationships[2] in virtually everything that exists or can be imagined to exist. Although we recognized a visceral component, we seemed to find a place for the (Platonic) view that we find universal or abstract or general law or order in what our senses apprehend and that we are carried beyond the realm of the senses to the realm of beauty in which generalization, or capacity for the universal, is expressed. But there is also a place for still a third factor, a nonspecific definition of human interests which makes the human constitution capable of almost unlimited resonance, beating in tune with much which acts upon it. This will give us a threefold basis for the craving to know and understand: (1) the visceral drives; (2) the love of order; (3) resonance to the nature and structure of that which surrounds us. All of these components appear in the first human nature, but they are reworked and enriched by culture until in their turn, as we shall see, they begin to transform both the first and the second human natures.

Pointing to the visceral components is the fact that clinical data, notably the data of psychoanalysis and ethnology, underscore the reality of veiled instinctual satisfactions from the rhythms of wind and water; man finds in the things about him apt reminders of his own primitive needs and action tendencies.

[2] D. E. Berlyne has made vivid the distinction between the need for *perceptive contact* and the need for *understanding*—"epistemic" curiosity ("A Theory of Human Curiosity," *Brit. J. Psychol.*, Vol. 45, 1954, pp. 180-191). This restatement of a well known traditional distinction may also be useful, in some degree, in differentiating art and science: Both art and science utilize both of these kinds of curiosity, art emphasizing the perceptual, science the epistemic. But both contain many other ingredients as well (cf. Arnheim, p. 180 and p. 291.

The second view, which emphasizes man's quest of order and form, finds no great quarrel with this first view, but instead of emphasizing the instinctual tendencies rooted in the viscera emphasizes especially the goodness of form which arises from the rhythms of action and, as in the magnificent synthesis by Rudolf Arnheim,[3] finds the balance, symmetry, and rhythm of the neuro-muscular activity in which the whole body is involved a primary cue to the goodness and order to which all the arts aspire.

The last of these views, the *nonspecific* doctrine, can claim no such lofty interpretations. Like an Epicurean at the Stoics' meeting, it begs only to be allowed to utter very simple and pedestrian realities. It points empirically to the fact that the more complex the central nervous system, as we go from simpler to higher animals, the more there is of the response to anything and everything as exciting and interesting—the more sharply the world of spatial and temporal relationships stand out, as contrasted with simple physical satisfactions, and the greater the fascination with movement and order, whether what is sought is perfection or simply the earthly things which act upon the body. For, from this third point of view, there is a potential excitement about sheer reality in itself and about our capacity to respond to it; human potentialities are realized wherever sense organs, muscle, and brain are at work, and wherever the impact of a real thing upon these sensitive and hungry tissues of ours can make itself felt, engendering a hunger which often demands more of the stuff which gave it birth. As Walt Whitman had it, poetry belongs "to real things, and to real things only." One wants more and more of the world itself, not because it is the best of all possible worlds but because it is there; not because it is ideal but because it is real; not because it contains unlimited hidden meanings—though, indeed, as we shall see, it does contain them—but because in its own right it is exciting, moving, satisfying, yet always prompting to new modes of contact, always giving birth to new hungers. If so, our urge to new experience must be a tremendously potent, though largely latent, component in human nature.

From the position to which we have now come, all three of the doctrines just stated seem relevant and useful. It may turn out

[3] *Art and Visual Experience: a Psychology of the Creative Eye*, University of California Press, 1954.

that there are contradictions between them and therefore that refinements and choices must be made. It may also turn out that the three doctrines are all directly to be derived from the evolutionary view of human beings and from empirical materials on the development of infants and children, and that the problem is one of integration of empirical findings in such a way as to give full scope to the reasonable applications of all three conceptions.

Let us ask, for example, what part a scientific understanding of rhythmic movement would play in our enjoyment of a fine ballet, of a graceful woman's walk? There is not the slightest doubt that there are, both in the broad and in the more narrowly defined sense, erotic components in response to bodily grace. Indeed, in the beautiful rhythms of courtship behavior of birds and insects, as in nature's direct and primitive use of color in arousing strong feeling, it is hardly possible to doubt that the esthetic has an intimate relation to the erotic. Nor can there be the slightest doubt that deformity, old age, imperfect sexual differentiation, strained and awkward modes of movement, can all interfere with the broadly sensuous and, more specifically, erotic components in the response to the ballet and to the graceful walk. There is, then, clearly some reason for saying that the response to grace in posture and movement is to some degree directly erotic and to some degree a "sublimated" response; and if so, it seems likely that a scientific quest of rhythm, the delight in orderly temporal patterns, contains such elements.

At the same time, there is a huge difference between what might be called a direct or gross erotic appeal and a more complex one involved in the art form of the ballet or the rhythmic pattern of walking to which the term "grace" could be applied. As the Platonists have pointed out, there are simplicities, balances, principles of order or form, which to some degree can be generalized. They can be found not only in the woman's walk but in the fanning movements of a butterfly's wings, or indeed in the movements of the walking beam of a ship, or the path of a baseball into the bleachers. Here there is a mathematical pattern to which even the Pythagoreans had access—the sort of thing to which they pointed in their insistence that number was the key to beauty. It is the realization of numerically ordered line, surface, and temporal units that expresses the Pythagorean view of beauty as form. To some degree the erotic may be viewed not as the *source* but as a *subtype* of the human need for form. As always, human nature is both general and specific.

But the story is not yet fully told. What can the *nonspecific* theory offer that is as good as this? What can it set side by side with Homer's Helen of Troy or Goethe's Faustian dream of the eternal feminine? It can offer only a very simple thing—the conception supported by humble, daily, empirical observations that there is almost nothing at all that does not appeal to eye or ear or nose or sense of balance or need to understand or an impulse to get more of (cf. p. 60, sensory needs). Babies are interested in virtually everything and only through burns, bumps, or dire consequences learn to give up some of their imperious demands upon the world. Despite this early interest, many things lose their appeal in childhood, as by regimentation and the removal of intrinsic satisfactions in favor of so-called extrinsic rewards, one makes the school world boring. In childhood virtually everything for which our senses and understanding are ready is exciting. Watch children as they respond, for example, to nature-study *before* they learn that it's sissified to be interested in birds and bugs. Or watch their interest in the world of creative activity, from making boats to making pictures, *until* they learn forms of social disapproval or the rules which define taboo on such activities, or a sense that these things belong to another kind of people, that they are ego-alien, outside of us, out of bounds to us.[4]

To the argument that most of the early interests to which we have pointed arise from association with something pleasant, the best answer is that many of these things in the world around us patently *lose* their primal interest, year by year, and this despite the role of canalization working in the opposite direction. For many people there have to be more and more sauces and spices added to everyday foods to make them interesting, and in the

---

[4] This conception that human wants are directly related to the positive outgoing nature of man, and not only to his visceral tensions has grown with me for so many years that I cannot properly acknowledge my indebtedness. Among biologists I have learned much from L. von Bertalanffy; among psychiatrists, from Lawrence S. Kubie and Karl A. Menninger; among psychologists, from Solomon Diamond, Lois Barclay Murphy, and Robert S. Woodworth.

same way, there must often be a liberal dose of excitement or slapstick or the bizarre or the savagely sadistic to give interest to jaded tastes. Frequently, we contrive to deprive human nature of many pristine delights that come from sensory and conceptual grasp of the world.

Considering how much delight in discovery there can be in human life—in people, in hobbies, in leisure, in the decorative arts, in reading, in thinking and looking—one can only wonder why many human beings settle down to a narrow area of satisfactions in which instinctual gratifications with a prominent representation of narcissistic or self-love activities, keeping up with the Joneses, and primitive power satisfactions, embellish the competitive industrial scene. Often there seems hardly enough gratification to balance the vague apprehensions regarding the encroachments of others upon one's privileged position, and the normal fears of illness and accident, losing a job, growing old, and, of course, destruction through war.

Despite such defeats, it seems to me that the interests of mankind *can* flow outward into everything that exists or could exist, unless and until a rebuff of some sort is encountered. It may be rebuff through anguish arising from specific discoveries, or through social disapproval, or through the fact that the social situation causes preoccupation with this area to lead to poor results. Or the individual may discover that he has found all there is to be discovered at his level of operation and with the opportunities for study available to him and hence simply settles down to boredom. The limit is set, then, not by the subject matter or by his mind but by a complex sociocultural totality which says, for example, that he must accept a narrow repetitive task and work within it. The third human nature, the craving for sensory and motor contact and for understanding and manipulating the world emerges wherever it is not nailed down or hemmed in. And health does not consist in the absence of these—or other—normal human cravings. As Florence Clothier[5] says, man needs the capacity to be *disturbed*.

A homely illustration will serve. A child discovers sooner or later the delights of manipulating words in the manner which we

---

[5] At the meetings of the American Psychoanalytic Association, 1957.

call poetry. But after a few years he becomes ashamed as a result of ridicule and hides his poetic efforts at the time when greatest creativeness might well be available—namely, in the pre-adolescent and early adolescent years. Or, if it is the manipulation of tones or colors that gives him greatest satisfaction, he goes on until some teacher tells him that in comparison with others he has no talent, and again the intrinsic satisfaction of the materials of this world are bypassed in favor of the secondary rewards of any social approbation which can be found. Human potentialities can be released only within a specific life space which expresses the world of a given individual at a given time, and the world can be and usually is ordered in such fashion that negative feelings are powerfully aligned against the positive feelings which most simple things at first possess.

It is easy, then, to put together the three conceptions that have been defined and to say that man naturally and primitively finds everywhere in nature that which is relevant to his instinctual needs; that which is relevant to the order, rhythm, and motion potential of his own body, as the Platonists made clear long ago; and finally, in the interstices between these two great realms of activity, that which is a ceaseless flow of sheer outward response to, and joy in, the world of things and the world of relationships among things. Since this last world is not anchored to the body in any narrow and specific way, it offers almost unlimited potentials. Instead of trying to explain man's love of the smell of the sea, we might do well to think of the humanness of responding to the sheer impact of the world itself. Far indeed from indicating that this would make all objects equally interesting, it would provide that those which had a Platonic formal stimulus value would have some advantage over those which had a sensory appeal and nothing more; and it would make clear that when all three factors are involved, the instinctual, the formal, and the sensory—as exemplified, for example, in the moving tide of great music or poetry, where instinct, form, and sense are all blended—we would have the most stirring, the most enduring, the most dependable sources of profound arousal.

• *Pythagoras' Number-Theory and Human Rhythms*

From this vantage point one might well ask whether the three interpretations of human delight in the stuff of which life is made are really so fundamentally different. We have already noted that a major clue is offered by ideas that were formulated by the Pythagoreans and developed by the Platonists; and we can now develop this more systematically. The Pythagoreans taught that *number* is the key to order and rhythm and ultimately to all beauty, as in music and poetry. The rhythms of a dance or the contours of a vase seem to be made of essentially the same basic stuff as are the rhythms of life which are evident in our deepest physiological and instinctual cravings and fulfillments. Even the humblest manifestations of life, as in amoeba or our own red blood cells, are expressions of ordered rhythmic cycles of activity, as is true also of the larger cosmic trends, quaintly conceived by the ancients as the "harmony of the spheres." [6]

As we pass, moreover, to the broad dispositions which we have called "nonspecific," it is clear that they are similarly rooted in profound physiological rhythms—of a different sort—to which recent biological research has offered an extraordinary key. It has become evident that the patterned and rhythmic activities of the central nervous system are often responses to the patterned and rhythmic activities of the environment; extraordinary things happen when one is "in beat with" the world. Biology has been learning in the last few decades that many rhythms of physical and chemical structure become rhythms within the living system; *e.g.*, waves of depolarization, action currents in the nerve cells, such as those picked up by the electroencephalogram. The rhythmic beating of nerve cells and other tissues in resonance to forms of wave activity impressed upon them give us not only the feeling that man is, so to speak, numerically or numberwise made of the stuff of which his environment is made, but that he is extraordinarily sensitive to modulations of these numbers. If, for ex-

[6] There's not the smallest orb which thou behold'st
But in his motion like an angel sings,
Still quiring to the young-eyed cherubins—
The Merchant of Venice

ample, a subject submits himself to "photic driving," sitting near an instrument which emits flashes at intervals, he may reveal his own breaking point, the point at which the rhythm induces a convulsion. If, for example, the number is 16, he may rapidly lose consciousness as this number of flashes is presented in the standard time interval. Seventeen and 15, however, are safe numbers for him. It is not until we get to 32, or other multiples of 16, that he breaks. This might remind you of the bridge that can be shaken to pieces by a regiment marching at a given tempo, or the piano wire or even the glass tumbler that is thrown into a frenzy of sympathetic vibration by a tone which "has its number." There are general human rhythms and individuality in rhythms; both are selectively responsive to *outer* rhythms.

The human nervous system possesses, then, curious and profound hungers for many objects which are neither meat nor drink, neither satisfiers of oxygen need, nor of sex need, nor of maternal need, nor any other more obvious visceral demand. The extraordinary power of music suddenly makes more sense than ever before when one realizes that, as has become clear in the last few years, the basic rhythms of music are to a very large degree basic rhythms of the vital system itself. A considerable part undoubtedly is directly dependent upon the visceral rhythms, such as those of the heart and respiratory system, but a great deal more, apparently, depends upon the way in which nerve, muscle, and other tissues are made, the resonances inherent in their construction. In a physical and physiological analysis of music, De Quénetain[7] reminds us of the old struggle to define the response to music in terms of some very fundamental capacities for rhythmic response and the interaction of different rhythms within the living system. There is provision for a kind of affective language, a language of resonances, which is very much deeper than the language of words.

As Susanne Langer[8] has beautifully expressed the matter (though not emphasizing these matters of number), the fundamental human capacity for response to ordered sound represents a kind of universal human communication system, of which lan-

[7] Tanneguy de Quénetain, "Origines et aboutissements du pouvoir de la musique," *Realités*, No. 141, 1957, pp. 86-117.

[8] *Philosophy in a New Key*, Harvard University Press, 1951.

guage is a refinement and an elaboration but of which it can
never be a complete expression. Language remains a refined and
specialized aspect of a very much broader and deeper general capacity for "emotional" resonance. One can even say that music
"means" something that cannot be "symbolized" in words, if one
is willing to give up the sharp denotation and the "deictic" or
pointing role of speech and can recognize a capacity to feel deeply
one with the substance of the world or with that special class of
material substance of which one's neighbors happen to be made.
The "pure" music which, in contrast to "program" music, speaks
to us deeply of unnamable things is not, from this point of view,
talking meaninglessly. Quite above and beyond its capacity to
arouse our martial or tender or lonely or despairing or ecstatic
moods, it has a capacity to bring us into touch with certain resonances, certain rhythmic structures, which are inherent in the
world. These resonances are as deeply in the world as are the
electromagnetic waves that pass through our rooms or through
our bodies all the time, of which we are ordinarily not aware
until special instruments are devised that enable our bodies to
tune in on them.

It is through the sensory mechanisms of the ear, of course, as
well as the skin and muscles, that rhythm is conveyed, and it is
often necessary for the wide range of environmental rhythms to
be stepped down or converted into rhythms which our bodies can
pick up through these various senses. The fundamental issue,
however, is the fact that, in addition to these, we are discovering
peculiar properties (as in the case of "photic driving") which
represent basic rhythms of the body and are not ordinarily
triggered into action by such waves. It remains to be seen how
far we may go in catching and trapping wave forms which will
convey moving or illuminating or broadening experiences—whatever you wish to call them—new ways of responding meaning-
fully as well as affectively to the world. It would appear, however, that there are vastly more rhythms about us than we have
guessed; that we respond potentially to a far greater number of
them than we had realized; and that we can be enabled through
scientific discovery to respond to still more and more of them.

We have, then, discovered a few of the environmental rhythms
(light, sound, etc.) to which we are by nature biologically res-

onant; a few to which we are nonresponsive (*e.g.*, X-ray); a few more to which our bodies are at present sensitive without our knowing it (*e.g.*, action of cosmic rays on germ-cells); a few to which we become sensitive when special equipment is used ("photic driving"). We are on the threshold of discovering an unguessable number of new rhythms, extensions of the experience capacity and the activity capacity of human nature.

All these kinds of responses, like the extensions of the sensory system, are ways of realizing more fully the human potentialities which have lain dormant since man became man. From this point of view, music is not simply the exploitation of a simple auditory sensitivity long useful from an evolutionary point of view; it is the deepening and enrichment of a basic capacity for rhythm and resonance, the end of which we cannot begin to guess. It proves, as so many other instances of human liberation have proved, to be at the same time a discovery of how man can be more fully man as he is and the creation of much that is equally human, but never was human before, simply because it never could exist before. New ways of acting upon man result in new kinds of humanness. Cycles of new humanness are laid bare by probing more deeply into the latent structure which was never suspected before.

In all these matters of rhythm, moreover, we find huge individual differences. The love of things conceptual may (as in the case of Gauss in his attic, working on the theory of probability) dominate the instinctual and the sensory. For some people in some situations the sheer love of the sea, or even the love of the smell of the sea, may be so great as to overpower any contribution from the instinctual or conceptual components. Human nature is multiple and composite; but whereas we are hardly likely to forget the instinctual or the conceptual components in man's demands upon the world, it is the raw universal sensory response, together with the raw love of grasping, understanding, and immersing oneself in this world, that is in the greatest danger of being forgotten.

This implies that the internal rhythms are subject to the command of the external rhythms. As the biophysicist Selig Hecht would say, "The organism does not adapt itself to the environment; the environment adapts the organism to itself." This is, however, an incomplete rendering of the story. Every organ of the body is part of the "environment" of every other organ. The rich reciprocities of the inner environment involve mutual tuning and adjustment. It has become evident from recent work that one group of cells modulates or controls the rhythms of another. Indeed, what L. K. Frank has called "organic integration" consists of this type of inner attunement. The inner attunement goes with the attunement by the outer environment, and we have a "harmony of the spheres" in miniature.

But this inner attunement means much more than attunement of the living system to its world, and of the various parts to one another. It likewise provides basic protection from destruction. The reason lies in the fact that there are countless rhythms, countless forms of energy modulations, existing at large in the environment, some of which are benign, some destructive. We are like little fortresses which by their own internal rhythm prevent disruption by outer rhythms. We are like gyroscopes, able to withstand a push which is incompatible with our own basic postures and rhythms. The problems of the adaptability of man to changing social, biological, and physical environments is partly the problem of the capacity to protect the essential inner rhythms while assimilating those outer rhythms which sustain life and permit new regions of existence and experience. Just as each individual is especially vulnerable to certain rhythms, so each individual may be able to maintain counter-rhythms which constitute defense against disruption.

It is apparent, of course, that those most vulnerable are sometimes those who possess the greatest strength in the very respect in which vulnerability appears; for example, that those most sensitive to the rhythms of tone may, like Sidney Lanier, find it too beautiful to bear. Fortunately, the converse of this statement is likewise probably valid: the discovery of regions of special vulnerability may well help us to discover regions of special sensitivity. Of one thing we may be sure: the life rhythms recently discovered by physical analysis of the senses and physical analysis of the rhythms of the central nervous system, notably by the electro-encephalogram, point to an extraordinary range of interesting human variations in response to environmental impact. We have an extraordinary range of internal forms of control by which the various portions of the living system can, in attunement with one another, thwart the disrupting influence of alien rhythms and move in the direction of assimilation and utilization of those which are in basic harmony with inner potentials.

From all this it follows that sensory extrapolation of human interests goes hand in hand with extension of the human sense organs, already considered. Indeed, it is to a large degree because of man's potential for rich sensory experience that he has craved the sensory extensions. Economic gain can always help the process along, but it was not the economic factor that led to the sensory extensions, and it is not the economic factor that makes modern men—and, in particular, children—eager for new experience.

• Motor Experience and the Extension of Human Nature

Side by side with all the *sensory* extensions go *motor* extensions. Tools are the first such extensions. In our study of paleolithic, neolithic, Bronze Age, and Iron Age men, we recognize that it is not only men that made the tools but tools that made the men. Our own tools are remaking us. Ordinarily, however, we limit our attention to the things that we make rather than to the thought forms that the new objects impose upon us (in particular the retroflex effect of the sheer making process upon the maker).

We assume now that almost anything can be made. It is a maker's world. We no longer find blasphemy but simple realism in the comment of the little Dutch boy who, very skeptical about God, was asked to look through the microscope and see what wonderfully delicate snowflakes God had made. His comment was, "That's not so hard in the winter." Men and children too, learn constantly how things are made, and they make things with less and less primeval wonder, until the very making process itself is no longer wonderful but built into their souls. The aboriginal population which, as Margaret Mead tells us, a few decades ago found ghosts and spirits inside the machines which the white man brought, today repairs and builds the machines with the same gusto as that which the white man himself shows. And the making process can become either boring when simplified to the point where it is too fully understood (as in the assembly line), or it can, through a sense of progressive mastery (as in a dramatic workshop), provide a constant renewal of delight in each day's discoveries.

The cultural anthropologists, the historians, the historical sociologists have given us wonderful ideas to work and play with as they have taught us the endless variety of human institutions and the almost limitless malleability, flexibility, adaptability of the human young when encountering the footbinding or mindbinding, the skill-inspiring or philosophy-inculcating habits of varied human groups or of classes and guilds within the groups.

They have, however, made the molding of the mind somewhat too easy. They have often suggested that there is no special bent in one direction or another; that mankind is equally ready for almost *any* kind of contortionist adaptation. This has gone too far; has denied the instinctual readinesses and what we have called the platonic dispositions to move more massively in some directions than in others. It has, however, been valuable in reminding us that there is much to be discovered in *any* social order; that there is much which, just because it is a real thing somewhere to be encountered, can have its human appeal. To *discover,* whether the process be sensory, motor, or intellectual, is fulfilling, and it is this fulfillment which the emerging third human nature everywhere craves. It tends toward richer and richer satisfaction, as we understand more fully through "cognitive mastery" and as we control more fully through action.

We may well push beyond this point and ask ourselves the question: What are the biological and cultural biases which limit our capacity for imagining *new societies?* Working against such capacities to conceive the new, what are the old thought forms? What are the special conditions governing the "sociology of knowledge" which guide mankind into the presumption that societies *must* take certain forms rather than others? What, on the other hand, are the kinds of societies that men *might discover;* what are the sensory and conceptual—or, indeed, instinctual —satisfactions in inventing (as in the game of chess) new rules, new orders, new potential deployments of men with reference to one another, with reference to their physical and their cultural environment, with reference to the cosmic totality which they face? Certainly we shall recognize the deeply ingrained cultural assumptions, the unconscious and axiomatic assumptions which even the most radical of men like to make regarding the longevity of the existing kinds of human societies. They led even a Buddha to assume that there will always be unsatisfiable wants, that there will always be temptations which must be renounced, that there will always be a way of light to be followed in contrast to a way of darkness. Karl Marx assumed that, no matter how changed a society might be, there would always be certain invariant attributes of hand, brain, or heart constituting the raw human nature (cf. Lenin's belief that competitiveness would remain, and even increase, in a classless society). Most prophets assume that even in a new social order, the fundamental human traits will persist; the relations of man and woman, the relations of adult and child, the relations of brothers in blood and brothers in function will remain intact; will remain essentially the familiar relations which prehistoric men knew, which Chinese, Indian, Incan, and Mediterranean men have always known. After all, the time perspectives have been such that it would have been preposterous to expect otherwise. The science fiction which looks ahead fifty million years still represents the relations of human beings as essentially the same as they are today, in that kind of unconscious extrapolation of the self-evident which it is the task of books such as this to challenge.

From the present point of view, man, who extends his sensory equipment to see the infinitely small or the infinitely great and who extends his motor equipment to manipulate, through shafts of light or guided missiles, that which moves far beyond his grasp, is only in limited degree the same man that will cast the social orders of the future and extend his control techniques to mold them more to the heart's desire. If mankind can invent, in the manner of Luther Burbank, new citrus fruits and leafy greens for the table of tomorrow, he can likewise invent social orders which presuppose *not* the human nature that we know but the human nature which both biological and social evolution may *create;* can lay down, as it were, in the manner of the mathematician, the poet, or the prophet, potential relationships of human beings, potential schemata of human relationships which realize the latent potentials that never have been realized and never could be realized within the thought forms of the past or the present. He can literally imagine into existence unknown relations of man and men. It is indeed true that these schemata can depart in no detail from what is *fixed* as human nature; but the theme of our story has been the *meagerness* of what is known to be intrinsically and necessarily fixed. We deal always with a world of intangibles and shadows which strangely mold themselves somehow into solid realities and pass away into shadows again. There is no fixed human nature, no fixed social order, except within the short time span and the local conditions of the neolithic and postneolithic societies that we happen to know, superimposed upon which is the martial technique of the West, followed by the commercial, industrial, and technological skills which this martial society hit upon in the great Mediterranean era. And the danger that we shall stick too closely to the pattern that we happen to know, in our attempt to extrapolate into the future, is far greater than the risk that we shall wildly imagine impossible human beings and impossible relations among them.

The last few chapters have described the transformation of the first human nature into the second human nature; the cultural hardening of the second human nature, with its rigid system poorly adapted to the demands of a rapidly changing world; and the recent emergence of a third human nature, embodying an attitude toward culture which is bound to question and challenge, break down and re-create human life.

• *The Setting in Today's Crisis*

If there were a vast canvas on which to paint the slow conquest of rigidity by creativeness, all might be well. The time, however, as measured by the rapidity with which man could destroy himself, is short indeed. If the opportunity to use intelligence for the redirection of human development is to be ours, some psychological aspects of this crisis period must first be considered, and a reason given for believing that peace, world order, and intelligent control of social development are possible. This is the first task.

Thereafter, in the remaining chapters, an effort will be made to show how the three human natures can be expected to integrate or coalesce into one, and to show some of the attributes of the man-to-man and man-to-cosmos patterns which can be expected to emerge.

PART IV

Self-directed Change

Chapter **12:**

The Long Haul

Three human natures have been sketched, the second arising
from the first, and the third arising from the second. The
third, whose essence is the quest for understanding, begins to
promise to leaven and to transform the first and second, and to
effect a genuine synthesis with them.

It would be pleasant if we could proceed at once with a study
of the ways in which this integration can be achieved. But the
same scientific trends which are producing a potentially new humanity have produced an appalling crisis, or system of crises; and
any study which seeks realism must face this fact. The political
and international aspects of this crisis must first be considered
(the present chapter); then the aspects which arise from human
biology (Chapter 13). The tentative answers which then emerge
in Chapter 14 will point our way to Part V, in which a conception
of conscious and deliberate planning of the human future will be
spelled out in terms of a conception of the indissoluble oneness of
man and man, and of man and cosmos.

• The Three-fold Crisis

In the midst of a lovely dream there may come a resounding
crash. We awake from the dream about man's social and personal potentialities to face three realities which can blight all his
hopes: (1) Huge international power systems are locked in a

struggle which may at any moment precipitate the indescribable destructiveness of World War III. (2) Behind these international power systems, the everyday fact of the Frankenstein monster, the political or governmental system, is controlling us more than we can control it. (3) Biological changes in man's fitness for his environment and increasing inadequacy in meeting his future environment may soon deny to man even the precarious quest for progress that this planet has allowed him.

The men and women of this century face these issues at the very moment at which they begin to discover the almost limitless potentialities of the human future. If they and their descendants are to move toward the fulfillment of those vast capacities which they hope can be theirs, they must grimly think through and work through these issues now. As William L. Laurence[1] puts it, ". . . international collaboration in the maintenance and control of peaceful atomic plants could provide a precedent for extension of inspection to nuclear weapons production. Thus the peacetime atom in the long run may help to make the wartime atom, in a way, obsolete." A dream far better than most atomic dreams. But can we allow ourselves such dreams?

Many of those who trouble to study such books as this one will feel that mapping the human choices is an easy intellectualistic blueprinting of unknowable and uncontrollable futures; that, like the Utopias of the past, those of the present can have no real relation to the trends of history. Some feel that such trends "just happen"; or that they spring automatically from the occasional genius of a great leader; or that they arise from deeply unpredictable changes in economic techniques with reference to which no processes in society can exert a controlling influence; or that their origin is beyond the comprehension or control of mankind. Such despair is understandable.

The only answer one can make is to point to the many instances in which thinking about humanity's future and humanity's choices has actually made a difference. One may recall More and Machiavelli, Locke and Montesquieu, Jefferson and Marx, not to speak of those who, like Harriet Beecher Stowe, have formalized specific issues and produced immediate action with a

---

[1] *The New York Times Magazine,* Oct. 27, 1957, p. 84.

vengeance, or those who, like Charles Darwin and William James, have influenced the political atmosphere of their age. Books as the makers and distributors of ideas are not obsolete. This book may well fail in its aim, but it is one of an ancient line, and a line which will continue. Humanity cannot afford to belittle its only weapon in such a crisis: the weapon of sustained dispassionate thought as to its place in the cosmos and the devices by which the perils which surround it may be overcome.

Such thinking must take into account both the various long-range goals of centuries and the short-range goals which may make possible the later discovery of a path toward the long-range goals. Unless one decides to freeze humanity into some permanent and unalterable form of perfection, there will, of course, be no "ultimate" goal. But there will be steps which must be taken in various orders, no step to be taken except when a preparation has been made, with "business as usual during alterations."

An obvious instance of the difficulty of combining the short- and the long-range modes of thought appears in those solutions to the problem of the "cold war," which are sought in terms of devices which will keep one side ahead of the other *for such and such a number of years.* It is indeed possible that mounting threats on both sides may become so awful that neither side dares attack (though military history seems to give little support to such an idea). The problem, however, is how such a stage of concentration upon the capacity to exert a massive destructive threat can carry us on to a period of threat reduction, and what sort of plan is really being cultivated as to the mode of living *after* the threat and counterthreat have been reduced or put aside.

One even wonders, as one studies political utterances, whether among political leaders *any thinking beyond the next ten or twenty or fifty years is being done;* whether there is, in fact, a serious belief that there *is any solution at all.* It would be foolish to belittle any serious plan which may exist in the minds of the great political leaders of either side, or indeed of any contemporary nation; but it is difficult to make sure whether there is, in fact, *even the recognition that a tentative long-range plan is necessary.* If, within fifty or one hundred years, there will be placed not only in the hands of two great powers but in the hands of many the capacity for more and more appalling technical destructiveness, one would think that the human family might well be intent upon thinking through more than the devices for artful momentary escape—if such escape does, in fact, exist—and might well try to find some sort of basic human future building in which all men can share. This, indeed, is a theme without which any discussion of long-range human potentialities is meaningless.

World War III or even IV or V might conceivably come and go and still leave humanity energy and resources enough to go on slugging at itself; but through that era, despite the incredible devastation, such tentative and feeble beginnings as are represented by books like this must still be nursed and kept alive and new thinking must be done. For, unless humanity destroys itself utterly, there will have to be plans conceived in terms of the whole human family already pressing ever more closely upon itself, so to speak, and capable of existing on this planet only if some ways and means are discovered for an orchestrated planning of humanity's future. Clearly, these must be both *short-range* and *long-range* thinking, with emphasis upon the dominant role of science and its implications.

• *The Short-range View*

What, then, are some of the possibilities for this century: the choices which immediately face humanity? Some of the immediate possibilities can be outlined briefly.

First, the rate of industrialization may continue to accelerate in the United States (and with some forward movement in other Western countries), with increasing uncertainty or demoralization on the part of Soviet and Chinese leaders as they watch the caravan get beyond them. The result: compromises and capitulations—*e.g.*, in such matters as atomic weapons inspection, and in the matter of guarantees which will convince the American military leaders that there need no longer be global fear that Asia or Africa or the rest of Europe will fall into the Communist camp. Thereafter may come a gradual copying of Western ideas—technological and political—and the end of the Soviet system. This would be conquest by technical advance. (We *might* have to admit to the possibility that the Soviet system might win this duel!)

A second possibility is an arms stalemate for a considerable number of years, a large amount of the total income of the greater nations being thrown directly or indirectly into weapons and defenses, until an accident or critical test of strength in some remote portion of the earth leads to a stance being taken on both sides from which there can be no retreat, only a spread of war. Sooner or later, atomic weapons and missiles are brought into the affair, and a "knockout blow" attempted. With enough deep, unbombable hide-outs (and air strips) on both sides, war might go on until nothing but human and other rubble exists.

A third possibility lies in elaborating some ideas formulated by Leo Szilard,[2] one of the pioneer nuclear physicists involved in the development of the American atomic bomb of the Hiroshima era. Szilard points out that both the United States and the Soviet Union are now in control of sufficient nuclear fuel and heavy bombers to destroy one another's cities. It is likely that both have developed systems of underground air strips and of refueling in air which make it possible, even if their own surface bases are destroyed, to go on delivering savage and unanswerable attacks at the cities of the other country. Widely scattered air strips could, it is assumed, make possible a fairly adequate hide-out for undestroyed planes and permit renewed take-offs for the completion of a distant mission. This may mean that neither country can knock out the other. The sneak attack has become less and less important. Even if the timing of each attack were unforeseen by the opposing side, it could not *end* an atomic war.

The result, Szilard suggests, is likely to be a system of bargaining attitudes in which each country can say to the other: "You have destroyed two of my cities, and if you will stop now and agree to rebuild, it would be worth your while far more than if you let me go ahead and destroy two or more of your own." He points out that we might rapidly come to the point at which each side would give notice to the other to evacuate its citizens from certain cities and could quite coldly and without much fear of resistance knock off, as in a clay-pigeon shooting party, whatever cities it chose to destroy, knowing full well that its own cities would be destroyed in the same summary fashion.

[2] "Disarmament and the Problem of Peace," *Bulletin of the Atomic Scientists*, Vol. 11, 1955, pp. 297-307.

These are among the reasons which Szilard offers as suggesting that very possibly *potential atomic war* has come to stay. It is obvious (though usually forgotten) that even after destruction of all bombs and stockpiles, *a country with technical knowledge can reconstruct its full arsenal in a couple of years.* Szilard goes on to discuss a series of feasible disarmament steps to be taken in a certain order, which would provide that each country *can* feel reasonably safe *at each stage in the disarmament* until ultimately everybody feels safer through the achievement of a large part of the program. Smaller countries, or countries not possessing the same concentrated power of destruction, could go along in their own way, knowing all the time that they were relatively safe from atomic destruction if the two great powers themselves were safe in the manner suggested.

Arguments such as these show clearly how the entire conception of the ability of the human race to maintain itself upon the face of the earth has altered in the last few years. It is entirely possible, of course, that a mistake may occur; that tactical use of atomic weapons may spill over somewhere in a major threat and that a decision may thus be made which could catapult us into the holocaust of World War III with the unlimited use of atomic weapons. Hence the urgency of such a series of disarmament steps as Szilard outlines. It is, however, possible that the knowledge of unlimited destructiveness will, if mankind can be rational enough, lead to a long period of forced live-and-let-live philosophies. From this might follow a broad plan for universal weapons inspection. We cannot possibly guess the types of weapons, especially the types of missiles, that human ingenuity might contrive; nor can we guess the social and intercultural patterns which might develop if humanity genuinely recognized the danger and organized itself around the central desperate point of trying to forestall it.

In spite of the ideas noted by Szilard, a fourth likelihood remains—that there would be a long period of garrison life, a continued struggle at the spots of resistance, to find a way to destroy what is left on the other side: a form of atomic guerilla warfare. From a Jeffersonian point of view, the prospects are not very pleasing. The Indian philosopher Radhakrishnan remarked to me: "If war comes, the Soviet Union will be defeated, and Com-

munism will engulf the world." That is to say, a new kind of
man, a very desperate man, trying to salvage what is left and begin again, will be different from any man which has existed. But
he will inevitably, through the crushing blows to which democratic organization has yielded in such a war, be more like the
disciplined Communists of today than like the free-thinking,
rather lax and easy-going independent devotees of the democratic systems. He will be rather less able to think his way
through in the terms of science, in the terms of a study of the
predicaments which he faces and the ways to meet them. He will
be more of an authoritarian, simply because his existence will depend upon coherent and disciplined leadership and followership.
In times of such stress, there is just too much danger of lone
wolves. The historical record of catastrophe is one in which the
looters and the extravagant individualists have simply had to be
held in check.

But gains, both within the Western system and within the
Communist world, may be so considerable along economic lines
within two or three decades that a fifth possibility emerges—a
genuine willingness on the part of the leadership of both communities to allow the two systems to compete for the good will
and the acceptance of the remaining communities in the world,
with the consequence that after a few decades there is actually a
heavy preponderance of power on one side or the other and consequently a reversion to what we have indicated above as our first
possibility.

If the less terrifying of these prospects give a period of a half
century or more for joint or global world planning, it is conceivable that the industrial man will find himself very much the
same animal everywhere, that political forms will accommodate
to his changing nature and that without war there may be an integrated scientific technological world society. The sharpness of
existing contrasts may disappear and human groups already
sharply differentiated may lose the sense of strangeness, one from
another. We might become like some bees I know.

A friend of mine who keeps bees in Connecticut tells me that
beekeeping is worth while only if you have a big swarm. Small
swarms will fight and destroy one another. To meet this contin-
gency the standard procedure is to select a large hive and put a

sheet of newspaper vertically down the middle, introducing one swarm of bees on one side, one swarm on the other. The bees, of course, hear those of the opposite camp buzzing on the other side of the paper, and in order to get at them they begin to chew holes in the paper. As they do so, the little holes permit the odor to pass from the A group to the B, and from the B group to the A. By the time the holes are large enough for the bees to crawl through to get at each other, the odors have spread back and forth and are completely mixed. Everybody smells alike. You then take the newspaper out and you have one happy swarm.

Our concern is not with prophesies. No one is nearly wise enough to predict with any confidence which of these possibilities or what other possibilities may become an actuality. But it is probable that our actual choices are few. If we cannot maintain democratic control over the scientific and technological processes, if we cannot escape rigidity and thought control even under such favorable conditions as those of the moment, we certainly cannot do so as the cold war becomes hot. If we cannot maintain a social system in which free science can flourish and the results of the scientist's brain can be made available for the common man, our system cannot successfully compete with those in which science is state-controlled. The maintenance of force and the threat of force is undoubtedly necessary in a crisis period, such as that through which we passed during and at the end of World War II. But the question of the permanence of the crisis and the question of what this will do to science and technology—what will be the form of science, the thought forms developed by it, the mode of its application, the kind of good that it makes available for humanity—all these are questions that will soon be decided through the operation of our educational and political systems. Let us look more closely, then, at the choices that will be forced upon us by the rapid implication of the world in a single industrial system.

• *The Long-range View*

Assuming that short-range problems *can* be solved through the stabilization of a warless world of a sort, we may look ahead to some of the long-range possibilities from which a choice will be made before the end of this century. These are necessarily conceived within the framework considered above—*i.e.*, assuming that there is an ordered society in which there is still a chance to plan, a world society which, whether politically unified or not, is individually and culturally unified. Here there seem to be three possibilities.

The first possibility is an international authoritarian system based upon a world hierarchical concentration of power and the channeling of human sentiment through gratifications of power and prestige. Such a system can undoubtedly work pretty well for a while, except insofar as those disgruntled in the establishment will, of course, plan "palace revolutions" with the most destructive devices available. It is difficult to see how those at the middle and below the middle can have access to the technique of government or the means of communication sufficient to organize a counterrevolution. Autocracies with such hierarchically organized power have been the primary mode of human existence until recent centuries. The experience with Fascism in this century in Italy, Spain, Germany, the Dominican Republic, and elsewhere, and with essentially Fascist control in the Soviet Union (subject to a hierarchy of power and prestige, and subject to the eternal threat of palace revolutions) exemplify the principle "Uneasy lies the head that wears a crown." They can still offer bread, circuses, and much more for the mass, but the mass can have only a rather limited degree of understanding or choice as to where it is going.

In such a scheme, in the world of Authoritaria, since prestige and power are of the essence of state control, it is hardly thinkable that science and the arts could acquire a flavor essentially different from that of the guiding elite. There might, indeed, be lone-wolf artisans who would carve their initials and comic strips upon bits of stone which they think will not be noticed by passers-by or by the great Moguls at the top (as H. J. Muller[3] describes them in the structure of St. Sophia at Istanbul). There would be a place for songsters, mavericks, and hoboes who might give picturesqueness to the total scene. It is difficult to see how science and the arts can have any major independent dy-

---

[3] *The Uses of the Past: Profiles of Former Societies,* Oxford, 1952.

namic if they must accord with or even personally please those responsible for the status system as a whole.

A second possibility would be expressed in a world system having a high degree of centralization of scientific investigation, technology, and the arts, with carefully studied rules for the preservation of soft spots—local areas of individual freedom of the scientist to conduct experiments which have no place in anyone's federally conceived plan; a place for artisans to invent everything from brush strokes and ceramic casting to automobile body design and to private model space ships, provided that no damage to the society as a whole is involved. This is a sort of loose-jointed Authoritaria.

Here we would have something like the old-fashioned bicycle in which the huge wheel moved ahead and the little wheel was notoriously prone to do less perfect following than was expected and did on occasion (as in rounding a curve) have some slight controlling effect on the manner of guiding the big wheel. Big wheels in all periods are guided by little wheels more than they like to acknowledge. This might be called a sort of state control with built-in allowance for maverick tendencies. The larger the area for maverick tendencies, the greater the role of the creative and the practical arts is likely to be. As a matter of fact, most of Western Europe since the collapse of the medieval system has been a fair exemplification of just this, except that the science and technology moved toward their central position only slowly. Actually there was, under the papacy, under the Hanoverians in England, under the Hapsburgs in Austria, exactly this sort of encouragement of individuality coexisting with a centralized state control. Many poets and composers starved in garrets, but many found their ways into the interstices of a not too absolutely monolithic state. And more and more, with the shaking loose from the feudal tradition, there has been a tendency to give larger place to competing devices in craftsmanship, from pottery to poetry. The coercion exercised by centralized control is still only a question of capital available to the patrons, seldom one of absolute dictatorial decree.

But in the matter of both capital and dictatorial decree, the safety valve of such a system lies manifestly in the provision of areas adequately nourished and encouraged, in which persons

with sentiments and competences may offer something interesting and novel, from a whim to an epic, from a perpetual-motion
machine to a philosophy of nature, which will nourish the
soul of man and perhaps prevent the development of those colossal blind spots which any monolithic system inevitably entails.

A third possibility is a world state, or system of states, based
upon free competition of ideas in the sciences, in the arts, and
elsewhere, and free competition, so to speak, between the various institutions of society. Imagine a world society in which there
is an effort exerted by those who want finer painting, those
who want better private helicopters, those who want a freer
and more flexible political system within which to navigate toward power, those who wish simply more leisure to spend as
they jolly well please. Can there be such a competition among
wants, such a free-for-all struggle of the various tastes, so to
speak, as to the ways in which the new productivity and leisure
are to be used? This will appear to the reader to be possible
only if he believes that there is no special momentum or inner
logic by which the scientific and technological trend of today
must move on to become dominant over all other aspects of contemporary life. We might call this a society anarchic in spirit
and in institutional organization, though politically centralized,
a sort of Idea Anarchy.

Some thoughtful people believe in a fourth possibility: the
ant-hill possibility. The tendency of men in a technological age
to form larger and larger aggregations and to lose individuality
in the process may produce a gregarious, group-centered type of
society *without requiring any higher control from the top.* Spec-
ters of such loss of individuality in a group-centered type of life
arise as we read of "Suburbia" and the men and women created
by middle-class conformity.[4] World society may, indeed, develop
into a leaderless machine-like system, no one really making
any individual decision but all taking their cues from one another. Yet it would take a great deal of historical research to
establish the fact that such a movement toward ant-hill "interdependence" is anything more than a phase in a cycle. It must
be granted that science and technology will probably commit

[4] W. H. Whyte, *The Organization Man,* Simon and Schuster, 1956.

man permanently to group living in many phases of his work and of his avocational existence; and we must grant likewise that his need for companionship will be one of the needs that will be satisfied in such a life. But if man has many other needs as well, including the need to channel his own cravings and impulses and to make his own discoveries, it is difficult to see how one can safely assert that the pendulum must forever go on swinging in the group-centered direction unless some Power does the swinging. If stabilized by political power (whether authoritarian or democratic), a great deal of group-centeredness can be maintained; however, it will find its level as a resultant of the tussle of many forces. For these reasons, the ant-hill possibility will not be included here.

• *The Choice Among the Possibilities*

The reasons why independent states, each with destructive weapons, cannot long endure have already been given. It would even be possible to believe in "the withering away of the state" and the disappearance of state control as such if it were possible to believe that destructive weapons, as they exist in the hands of a large number of persons in an atomic age, could be safely left to individual caprice. Weapons, we must remember, can be quickly made out of raw material by unsupervised modern scientists. The generalized risk if many persons have access to them reminds one of the "sharps room" in a mental hospital, in which scissors, knives, and the like, are kept, with the recognition that one cannot take risks with destructive tools, however useful these may be most of the time for most persons. The lust for power and an occasional urge of a purely sadistic sort would make world control too hazardous a toy to allow to anyone without a highly disciplined state control. A world system there must be.

If, moreover, we got along for a while without a state, the sheer urge for personal power might well bring the return of a hierarchical power system, unless the agencies for the prevention of such a possibility remain continuously active. It is, of course, possible that all persons would become so fully absorbed in and devoted to their mode of life that they would never think of any other mode of relationship with their fellows, any more than they would think of a new individualistic style in sports or hair-do. I cannot read history this way. It is, of course, possible that most people most of the time will become thoughtlessly habituated to a mode of life; but to imagine that the raw and primitive satisfactions from power and prestige which we see everywhere in the human family can be so absolutely extirpated (or to imagine that such as we see are solely the results of a particular cultural direction which has accidentally operated in all human societies) is more than I can assume. Even if most of the drive for power and prestige is traceable to the huge emphasis on these factors in the societies which we have studied most closely, this is a very different thing from assuming their absolute destruction among all human beings of all cultural groups now and forever. Typically, the role of culture is to strengthen and qualitatively alter the basic cravings of mankind and to direct them to new objects so that their mode of expression differs from society to society but not to create a passion out of nothing and not to destroy absolutely the first human nature. The power need and the prestige need are notoriously insatiable, unless they are faced rigorously and controlled by the participation of many—in other words, unless these satisfactions are widely shared rather than concentrated in a few.

Such satisfactions would be provided for in our second alternative—loose-jointed Authoritaria. Can this possibility be made to work? One promising sign is that advanced individualism has, as we have noted (p. 162), been moving into a strange new psychology, away from the autocracy of early laissez faire and the barbarism of the Gilded Age into a sort of "the public be pleased" position. The worker-consumer, though still weak and confused, is trying to stand on his own feet. Perhaps with gradual shortening of hours and the development of more and more organized leisure and resources through commercial, private, and government-sponsored recreational and educational facilities, there may be modes of individual thinking which are satisfying and ultimately capable of offering some sense of perspective (or even sense of humor) with respect to the scientific and managerial world which takes up the hours of gainful employment. It is only through an education of children which will prepare them for genuine enjoyment of this kind of thoughtful and free utilization of their free time, and only through this kind of adult education which can keep individuals (as in the Danish Folk Schools) sensitized to the values most precious in their own civilization, that an adequate counterpoise to the concentration of corporate power and momentum can be contrived.

And it is possible that many of the cultural systems of the world, such as those of India, Burma, Indonesia, Egypt, Central Africa, will hold out against the trend which we have been defining—will prove capable of maintaining—through music, through the drama, and through handicrafts—a type of cultural richness and even a type of individualism for which the major trend cannot find a place. Yet it seems to me that if these various other parts of the world are caught in a system of world trade and a system of scientific and technological exchange, both of goods and of ideas, they are bound to be assimilated into the central system.

On the other hand, there will probably remain, as provided for in our second possibility, large areas of cultural freedom involving the arts, religion, philosophy, and literature which are only loosely attached to the scientific and technological momentum as such. In these areas it is entirely probable that rich developments—in fact, often richer than those in the primary, corporate system—may flourish and may leaven the development of the latter.

None of this, however, is offered with the suggestion that the *weak*—whether man or idea or factor or capital—can compete individually with the *strong;* for if by strength we refer only to that which wins its way, this would be nonsense. We assume a broad tendency for the stronger to win in competition with the weaker, and in time to become even stronger through the conquest. "To him that hath shall be given, and from him that hath not shall be taken even that which he hath." The assumption is the principle of dominance; the principle that when countervailing forces meet, they cannot for long remain in suspense, but the one will dominate the other and even utilize the strength of the weaker to lead to aggrandizement of its own superior strength. As William Graham Sumner put it, "the strong will grow stronger." It is believed that science, technology, and the corporate form of organization represent strength in this sense.

But, here, *institutional* strength rather than individual strength is involved. Institutional minds will be victorious over private minds, and the individual will strive just insofar as the system can provide those recesses for thought and expression, those organized and encouraged forms of indivudalistic training and expression to which a little attention was given above.

A student of Turner's studies of the influence of the disappearance of the frontier, or of W. P. Webb's book on the influence of *The Great Plains* upon those who migrated to it, or of the impersonal Juggernaut character of the Industrial Revolution, its acquisition of momentum and its crushing of all who stood in its way, might well believe that it is utterly fatuous to attempt at this time to suggest any sort of countertrends, checks and balances, ameliorating or complicating circumstances. Communities today often can and do delegate planning and implementing powers. This is done all the way from the use of consultants in city planning to the series of five-year plans of the U.S.S.R. *Planning* has become a respectable word, and democratic processes involving every element in the population are more and more taken for granted as a result of the trend already described.

But planning, to be effective requires:

devices for controlling the development of science and technology;

devices for controlling the ways in which science and technology limit or refrain from limiting the free development of cultural and esthetic preoccupations;

devices for preventing the various catastrophes already described—namely war and despotism; and above all,

devices for conveying to the average citizen in the public schools and universities the urgency of the issues and a respect for those technically competent to work upon them. Common men and women need a readiness to assert their own self-interest with reference to such major issues as the standard of living; freedom of thought; freedom from disease; awareness of the role of research in finding answers if they are to enjoy the universe into which they have been dropped.

This is a very tall order. The attitude of helplessness; the belief that there is only one kind of scientific approach; the assumption that science must depersonalize and mechanize human nature—can stifle and destroy the potentialities for intelligent social choice which exist. But in the meantime they *do* exist, and the need for planning, howled down twenty-five years ago, is now widely assumed; indeed, it is more and more widely assumed that the planning is better when those for whom the plans are made are the planners.

But who could devise and expedite such plans? And in the society in which planning is done, who would have the power? Because of the great uncertainty that men with both knowledge and good will can find their way to the top control positions in a highly stratified society, we have to provide for the continuation and strengthening of complex democratic processes—processes by which at least the general assent by the common run of mankind must be obtained for those innovations upon which new social patterns may be based. This entails assent to the desirability of acquiring more knowledge and making it available for social application, a kind of belief in a "free enterprise" of investigation combined with a, so to speak, socialism of application, as is currently done in many aspects of medicine and industry.

There is, indeed, much of the old law of the jungle in the application of science; but there is a strong countermovement. Public opinion does not support "holding patents out of use"; and there is great pressure through economic, social, political, and moral forces toward the dissemination of new knowledge. Even "business secrets," enormously important for the competitive movement, soon leak out. It appears probable that a technically competent subleadership (that is, a circle of leaders just below the top political controls) can maintain itself in the task of gaining scientific informaton and making it known. Even while big businesses get bigger, economic evolution in recent years appears to have been characterized in the West by a rather high degree of group participation. (Ordinary farmers, small businessmen, and workers have usually been able to understand to a considerable degree and to use the scientific investigations which the elite have thrust upon them.) The story is not yet told, but, on the whole, the conception that the group can more or less understand and indirectly control some phases of economic and political evolution appears to be relatively justified. How much—and how well—can it control?

• Some Comparisons of Autocratic and Democratic Systems

After much musing on this question of whether democracy or authoritarianism or something else is psychologically the most feasible way to run a scientific-technological society, and after much uncertainty as to how much can actually be proved, I encountered some of the ideas of Norbert Wiener.[5] These, in collision with some others that were hiding in dark passages in my mind, produced some thinking which I shall try to describe. Wiener's central thought relates to "feedback," the process by which any event sets going processes which act back to influence the event, as a rising temperature in your living room acts on the thermostat to cut off the furnace.

Those who govern have always needed feedback from the governed, at least as regards their strength and endurance to perform and the possible dangers of revolt. As society becomes more complex, it is less and less feasible for an autocrat or a group of oligarchs to understand the control system itself and where it is tending. Those who operate at middle and lower levels are also facing more complex instruments with less and less certain outcomes. Just to go on governing becomes constantly more difficult unless better and better feedback is provided from all levels in the social machinery. Moreover, the nature of science and engineering stimulates curiosity rather than blind execution of routine tasks. Curiosity cannot be stifled without stopping the whole machine. Curiosity, however, involves more and more perception of alternatives. Unless those at the top get feedback from the constant exploratory behavior of middle and lower levels, they do not know where they are in the operation, and the impulse to revolt may be growing. Very complicated espionage and secret police becomes imperative. As

[5] *The Human Use of Human Beings: Cybernetics and Society,* Doubleday, 1951.

this develops, thought control must be standardized. Thought control, however, contradicts the exploratory attitudes themselves.

Here arise two further difficulties. The machinery itself must become dominant over those who guide it and those who operate it. There is no escape except by widespread re-educational processes which are built into the machine itself. We have a situation like that in which a machine is given an instruction —a "taping"—to transform itself constantly on the basis of new information. Such new information becomes available regarding the effectiveness of the machine at its various points only insofar as middle and lower elements have their own feedback techniques for finding out how well their activity is succeeding. Since this kind of feedback, at all levels, is essential for the master machine to operate, the feedback necessary to operate such a machine is feasible only under relatively democratic conditions. The question to be considered is whether the curiosity impulse at middle and lower levels might be so blunted and machine feedback so perfected that all essential controls should get into and remain in the hands of autocrats. This question resolves itself into one as to the sheer latent strength and latent potential for growth which the curiosity motives possess, and the degree to which these are nourished during the transitional period to the centralized world system toward which we are moving.

What is said here regarding curiosity would also appear to apply to fellow-feeling or the capacity for full feedback from the various members of the system to one another, their capacity to feel with and resonate to the wishes and hopes of others sharing their predicament. It must be admitted that over most of human history over most of the globe, it has been relatively easy to coerce or bribe middle-level leaders into the service of autocrats; armies and police have always known this. The present thesis about the prospects for democracy can be defended only on the assumption that the conditions of group living must and inevitably will continue to provide greater and greater reciprocity, both in act and in feeling, between members of the community (cf. Riesman's views, p. 98). All must be given a fairly high level of education if they are to operate or even to navigate among the engines and the social structures which express the technical society. With such education comes, to some degree, increasing understanding of others and a capacity to see through their eyes.

At this point, however, we must face the possibility that the economic, military, and political leadership cannot very well afford a period of general recession or loss, either in their own power or in the general strength and world dominance of the system which they have created, and that in any such period of recession or threat, the likelihood of tightened controls and rejection of participation by the center and bottom of the mass might well be upon us. Since there is no way of knowing whether this is likely to happen or not, the possibility of a scientific bettering of mankind in terms of its inner qualities and its control of its own interpersonal relationships must depend absolutely upon increasing knowledge, understanding, and capacity to use the findings and directives issued constantly from the leadership. If the intellectual leaders, upon whom scientific findings and their applications in the physical, biological, and social sciences depend, cannot make themselves heard and cannot bring society along with them, the game is up. Without a high level of community intelligence, at least sufficient to permit a general grasp of the leaders' plans, and wise selection among leaders, the system cannot work.

It may be thought that the danger of the loss of such control on the part of the elite and the loss of such communication between the elite and the common man is not a really serious risk. One of the largest risks, however, lies in a phenomenon seldom noted: the very limited number of persons involved in the basic work of discovery, in contrast to the very large numbers concerned with repetitive and self-indoctrinating techniques who look to short-range gains and who grow weary in the contemplation of the more complex issues that have to be faced at physical, biological, and cultural levels.

We can be grateful, of course, to the writers of science fiction, from H. G. Wells and Aldous Huxley right down to the dime-a-dozen space mariners of the paperbacks, for keeping alive a sort of readiness to speculate. The ruts in which such speculations run, however, are very narrow; and the turgid dreams of even the most imaginative and philosophically minded prophets cannot excuse a lack of disciplined knowledge of what is going on in all the sciences. Besides, it is not enough to know the physical sciences, not enough to know the biological sciences, not enough to know the cultural sciences unless one's thoughts can be shared in a process of group thinking capable of implementing the ideas into a system for action. Indeed, we may say that all such books as treat of "human destiny"—such as the present volume and those listed at the end of its text—can hope only to add a little bit to the thoughtfulness of those who are already thoughtful enough to realize the magnitude of the task: the task of creating a leadership wise and strong enough to make the big dent required of social institutions. This leadership will not only share in the development of the thought that is required; it will find how to get itself into a position where it may be listened to, both by those above it in the political system and by those below it in the center, upon whom some sort of effective democratic action would depend.

A species can die out if only a few dozen members exist at a given time. It takes a certain mass to weather the hardships and vicissitudes. The same is true of ideas and of those who bear them. The leadership needs not only to be well informed and oriented with reference to the democratic process; it needs to be strong enough to develop a morale based upon a sense of mutual responsibility and an overwhelming responsibility to the democratic mass which it serves.

The three kinds of social order described here are samples; and so far as I know they represent the major available forms of future societies among which choice must be made. It is the freedom, the sensitivity, the generosity of the educational system, and especially the capacity to whet and gratify scientific curiosity, that will be mainly responsible for making possible an effective choice. An educational system which prepares people simply for the ways of living which are regarded as traditionally desirable is not an education permitting intelligent choices. And an educational system preparing only for the fulfillment of a technical role is even less likely to permit humanity that view of the possibilities from which intelligent decisions can be derived. If it is to science that we appeal, to science we must go. It looks more and more as if the possibilities of weathering the succession of tempests to which humanity is heir will lie in the "third human nature"—the discovery-driven, science-driven human nature sketched above. Such a society, however, can operate only through the *planning* activities mentioned above (p. 173) and only under the relatively democratic political institutions described on page 213.

Tentative decisions regarding both the short-range and the long-range will soon have to be made, or go by default, which is another way of "deciding." But the task remains, in the chapters which follow, to consider some further problems of basic cultural and biologic change which belong not merely to this century but to all the foreseeable future.

Chapter 13:

Biological Changes in Man

At the beginning of the preceding chapter it was suggested that mankind faces not only a war threat and a threat to freedom of thought, but a threat to his own biological make-up.

Many people believe that man's biological structure and function have been crystallized for some hundreds of thousands of years, and that whatever evolutionary changes are to come will be cultural rather than biological. Indeed, as distinguished a scientist and convincing a writer as Julian Huxley[1] has sometimes said so. This question nevertheless seems to be still an open one worthy of analysis from at least three points of view.

Before we examine evolution, in the strict sense, it must be noted that rapid changes in physical type may occur through changed environmental circumstances, not presupposing any *genetic* changes—as, for example, the shortening of stature in Greenland over several centuries, even the shortening of stature in France within the last hundred years, and, most conspicuous of all, the increase in stature among the Japanese since World War II. Here we are evidently dealing with phenotypic rather than genotypic changes. But these changes are often profound. They include the changes due not only to climatic, dietetic, and disease factors but also to hosts of more subtle factors, such as the new regimen of urban as contrasted with rural living. Even without

[1] In L. Leary (ed.) *The Unity of Knowledge,* Doubleday, 1955, pp. 79-97.

alteration of the mating patterns, with resulting true changes in gene distribution, these factors may profoundly alter the capacity for life, the range of abilities, the sensitization to the environment, the interpersonal relations of all who are touched by them. It seems rather remarkable that those who say that biological change has ceased should overlook the fact that even in our own well-nourished population, marked increase in the stature of sons and daughters over their fathers and mothers has been occurring within this century, and it is entirely possible, as there is much indirect evidence to suggest, that the sons and daughters are likewise brighter than their parents. Surveys of school children in Scotland[2] show considerably higher intelligence-test levels today than a generation ago. This may be a reflection of "urbanization" of Scottish life in a broad sense—not merely the increasing size of the urban population but the urbanization and sophistication of the population as a whole. Any serious consideration of the future of humanity will have to take into account the question of the qualitative as well as the quantitative modification of the human organism through the control of nutrition, exercise, and standardization of ways of living, thinking, and feeling. Such change has already gone very much farther than would have been anticipated a hundred years or even a few decades ago.

A second, closely related factor altering the biological make-up of humankind is the decreasing prevalence of certain diseases and the increasing prevalence of others, a factor altering both phenotypes and genotypes. The general practitioner in advanced countries has at his command the means of preventing most of the deaths that one hundred and fifty years ago were regarded as acts of God; life expectancy in the United States has jumped from about thirty to seventy years within the last century. The direct and indirect consequences of disease upon anatomical and physiological attributes are now largely under control in the United States, as probably will be the case within another century for the whole human family. This can be viewed in a purely negative sense in terms of reduction of disease and its sequelae, or it can be viewed dynamically and positively in terms of changing

[2] L. S. Penrose, *Brit. J. Psychol.*, Vol. 40, 1950, pp. 128-136.

health patterns, and ultimately in terms of the remaking of the human body and its function.

It is intriguing to glance at the extraordinary remaking of livestock who have enjoyed the good offices of the veterinarians within the last hundred years. Quite aside from the effects of breeding, there has been almost complete control of most of the diseases and pests which ravaged them a few generations ago. A glance at the livestock of poor countries (such as Greece and India) which still lack such services makes one realize that the physical remaking of a stock through nutrition and disease-control is no fantasy but a simple and fully documented reality.

In some quarters the control of disease has already been making huge differences in the definition of "human nature," and systematic experimentation on diet, regimen, and disease control can rather rapidly achieve what has already been achieved by veterinary medicine in the case of domestic cattle. To talk of the consequences of food regimen and disease control in the case of human beings is often regarded as the work of a food faddist, a crank, or a crackpot, but those who have begun to embark on such thinking will not be much impressed by the unimaginative here more than elsewhere. In the two-thirds of the world where nourishment is a serious problem, attitude and character are directly related to malnutrition.

The human nature of poor and sick human beings who exist by the hundreds of millions, notably in Africa and Asia, will upset the applecart of "white civilization" fully as much as will their acquisition of technological skills. The story has only begun. Now that most diseases have been extirpated, or their ravages largely curtailed, in Western societies, the positive question of medical and pharmaceutical research elsewhere will be the improvement of the potentialities—physical, physiological, intellectual, emotional, creative—of those whom they serve; and even if no motive but the commercial is to be involved, we can be sure that the trend already under way to emphasize sheer comfort and enrichment of life rather than the attack upon disease alone will increase geometrically. Most of the doctors of a hundred years from now will be relatively little concerned with curing people of disease. They will have means at their disposal for enabling people to function better and enjoy life more, and they will be able to earn a good living in doing so, as in fact a minority of doctors already do.

Third, there is mounting evidence that, though the gene-pool (the collective hereditary potentialities) of the human family is not changing very rapidly, and relatively little is being added or subtracted by way of "good" and "bad"' genes within one generation, nevertheless profound changes are going on, resulting from the matings of particular strains, and that social changes may very well accelerate the creation of new types. As Sewall Wright has said: "Human evolution is still going on." If these observations are valid with reference to trends operative only over a few centuries, it is surely time for thoughtful men to ask what may be the directions in terms of a larger canvas.

• *Human Genetics*

Let us look now more closely at genetics, the basis of heredity. Remarkable indeed are the genes, the ultra-microscopic units within the rod-like chromosomes, the conjoining of which produces a new life. In the "reduction division," before the creation of a new life, 24 out of the 48 chromosomes in the father are randomly segregated from the rest, and the same in the mother, so that the new life contains 48 but in a combination different from that of either parent. The individual's inheritance depends upon a very large number of genes, the combination producing a new creature which never existed on the face of the earth. Its uniqueness begins with the uniqueness of its gene combination. Since there are thousands of genes and a small number of chromosomes, some of the genes are "linked" together. Thus, if one derives a given characteristic from the father, one derives from him also the characteristics linked on the same chromosome with it. The "mapping" of chromosomes to show where each gene is located is already possible with some animals.

Genes provide both *continuity*—the resemblance of each generation to that which went before—and *diversity*. In general, the process of natural selection by which each species has been developed depends upon wide variability in each generation, so that in a given environment some do better than others. Those that do better tend in the long run to survive, the others to fall by the wayside before the period of reproduction. Natural selection is the process by which a hereditary pattern adjusted more or less to a given environment has been selected through the survival of some, the elimination of others. If there is a tendency for those who bear certain genes to fail to reach the reproduction age, those particular genes appear less and less frequently in the stock. There is, in *short-range* terms, no way in which the human stock can be appreciably altered, except by a marked alteration in matings, the tendency of certain genes, so to speak, to be used more frequently—that is, more children may be born who have certain genes and gene combinations, whereas children with certain *other* genes and gene combinations appear less frequently, generation by generation.

Another factor operating against genetic change is homogamy, the principle that like mates with like, which in the long run strengthens characteristics present in both parents. There is, moreover, a tendency for certain traits to become "associated" with one another by certain matings: genes carried by one stock and genes carried by another stock tend to express themselves in the same offspring. There is no natural or necessary tendency, for example, for blue eyes to be related in any way to curly hair; if, however, there should be a tendency of the blue-eyed to choose the curly-haired, and vice versa, or if migration, occupational selection, and so on, should cause the families of the curly-haired and the blue-eyed to be more closely acquainted with one another, to form family contacts, to enter into marriages, and therefore to produce offspring which would contain the tendency both to blue eyes and to curly hair, blue-eyedness and curly-hairedness would appear more and more frequently in the population as a "natural" type of association. This is independent of the linkage based upon the fixed relation of genes to one another within the same chromosome, and hence may or may not continue to appear in later generations.

We have still to examine a fundamental, although only dimly understood, factor in the origin of species and in the constant proliferation of new characteristics in man. This is *mutation,* the sudden alteration within a gene—*i.e.,* the production of a *new* gene—which causes a new characteristic to appear. A mutation may occur through a variety of biochemical and bio-electric forces, of which cosmic rays, X-rays used in medical practice, and radiation from atomic bombs, and missiles are examples.

Mutations are usually damaging or lethal; that is, they produce inferior or defective genes or alter the gene for the worse or produce so profound a change that the organism cannot survive. Some relatively rare mutations produce salutary effects or, in the case of domestic animals, start new lines which man has selected and deliberately perpetuated through breeding. We hardly know how to plan for the human future in terms of the production of favorable mutations. We do know, however, some of the implications of those mutations which appear—*e.g.*, a genealogical chart in which all males are pathological "bleeders." If, when a mutation appears in a given individual, it is "dominant," the offspring may receive the characteristic, despite its absence in the mate.

A closer look at the behavior of these protein molecules called genes may be rewarding.

Sometimes the attributes of the growing individual arise through the capacity of the genes to accelerate, to regulate, or to limit specific biochemical processes of growth. In one curious type of mental defect,[3] the operation of a gene within certain families regularly causes a biochemical injury to the developing nervous system, with the result that all the individuals afflicted by this biochemical malady show mental defect. A single gene, specifically and virtually unerringly, marks certain individuals in certain families for this kind of doom, and this characteristic runs true through the various family strains analyzed.

Sometimes defective genes may express themselves more directly. The gene itself is defective, so that development defect appears in structures which are normally present in humankind. Illustrations are found in albinism (the lack of pigmentation of the eyes, hair, and skin) and in missing parts of many sorts, from those which we consider trivial to those to which, as "monstrosities," we turn an eye of fascinated alarm.

Sometimes genes, through operating in a specific way upon structures which would otherwise take on different form, help to give rise to specific anatomical forms. Every genetics text gives

[3] G. A. Jarvis, "The Genetics of Phenylpyruvic Oligophrenia," *J. Ment. Sci.*, Vol. 85, 1939, pp. 719-762.

us illustrations in animals and in men of the attributes of hair, blood, and bone, which run in family lines.

But in naming this third way in which the genes may give rise to the adult characteristic we have "let the cat out of the bag," for we have pointed out here that the gene does not, in itself, directly "cause" characteristics but is rather one of the conditions under which the growing organism, controlled from within and from without by myriad physical and chemical factors, serves to mold and shape a characteristic in one fashion in contrast to another which another gene in another individual would help to cause. Often two or many genes collaborate in such a molding process. The complex adult trait is usually traceable not to a single gene but to the combined effect of many. A given gene, moreover, exerts many different effects in various parts of the body and in various physiological functions, depending on other genes doing their work at the same time. The physiological system of the body expresses not a series of separate genes acting like a mosaic, but the intricate interdependence of many. The usual pattern is one of multiple-gene ("polygenic") causation— genes acting as a team directed toward a given total result—a result which is itself highly organized and patterned.

Does this mean that no gene can ever simply and directly produce a single trait in the adult man or woman? In a formal sense, yes. Sex determination itself is a matter of a single gene, but the intricate biochemical realities which make for maleness and femaleness are responsible for the development of primary and secondary sex characteristics, both physical and mental. And with these polygenic traits, so complex in themselves, massive environmental forces must often be given great emphasis. To say what maleness or femaleness means is to define the wide variability within the two sex groups. The more meaningful a trait is for social living, the further is it from simple determination through any single genetic factor.

Granting this, one must have much material, both on family tree and on circumstances of growth, to say anything very useful about the potentialities of any individual. In a gross way, one may say that the greater the number of genes pulling up, the higher the level of performance. In this gross sense, intelligence is additive. There is, however, as we know now from much modern investigation, a gradual differentiation in intelligence during the growth process into the many types of specific intellectual skills—verbal, numerical, spatial, etc.—the various "primary mental abilities" defined by L. L. Thurstone.[4] None of these many specific abilities is due to a single gene; rather, we are dealing here in the intellectual sphere with something like what we have in the physical sphere—namely, the pooling of many genic contributions. We encounter factors dealing with *general* muscular development and factors dealing with a *specific* development of specific muscle groups; or we encounter general speed of response and, superimposed upon this, specific speeds of various parts of the body. Personality is a complex architectural total with a wide base and a system of superposed additional skills, more and more specific as we ascend, but with the various levels interacting (p. 57).

From such a point of view there is no way to exempt temperamental, emotional, or feeling-tone factors from the general logic of development. We know from an abundance of data in nature and from a great number of experiments with animals that temperament is related to factors of nervous and biochemical make-up, just as are the various intellectual skills. Such data as we now have on human family trees suggest that these laws apply just as clearly to temperamental and emotional factors as to intellectual or special abilities. A man inherits not only his nervous system but his whole neurocirculatory and biochemical system; genes play a part in many of his special sensitivities (*cf.* p. 129), his high or low thresholds, his diversity of emotional response, his proneness to joy or glumness, his tendency to stable or unstable emotional discharge.[5] Individual physiology is dependent upon specific structures, and the specific structures are dependent upon the various types of interlocked genetic influences; and environment exerts its steady pressure in growth. The same is true for individual psychology.

It is from this point of view that any long-range view of human potentialities must attempt to answer the question whether there is anything new under the sun in the matter of human nature.

[4] "Primary Mental Abilities," *Psychometr. Monog.*, No. 1, University of Chicago Press, 1938.

[5] S. Diamond, *Personality and Temperament*, Harper, 1957.

Is it likely that some stocks, say within a given race, will tend to become more numerous, others less numerous, in such a way as to alter the predominant temperamental patterns found within a group? Is it likely that by gradual and cumulative shifts in various social patterns relating to mating there will be more and more sensitivity, or lower and lower thresholds for various sorts of rage- or fear-producing stimulation, or greater and greater equanimity and poise, or more and more volatility and unpredictability with respect to emotional discharge?

• *Control of Genetic Trends*

A few years ago we should have been unready for such questions as these. It would have been thought fanciful to suggest that humankind, by giving thought to the matter, could hope to control its biological destiny or could even understand the long-range genetic trends which will make the men and women of the future. There seems, however, to be a shift in sentiment, owing partly to recognition of the importance of constitutional factors in all the components of adequacy to meet the demands of life; partly to studies of the inheritance of specific psychological characteristics in man, as notably in the research of Kallman[6] on the inheritance of predisposition to mental disorder and neurotic tendency; partly to an increasing awareness of moral responsibility with regard to the utilization of such facts.

Quite dramatic, for example, was the declaration by the Pope in 1953 regarding positive eugenics. In sharp contrast to the frequent assumptions regarding the resistance of the Roman Catholic Church to the utilization of genetic information, the Pope has solidly declared not only the moral importance of research upon the reduction in the general proneness to various types of physical and mental weaknesses and illnesses by processes of elimination ordinarily called "negative eugenics," but quoted with sympathy the aims of "positive eugenics," as well; that is, as stated below, specific encouragement to individuals with special gifts to enrich the human stock by allying themselves with others likewise gifted:

[6] F. J. Kallman, *Heredity in Health and Mental Disorder*, Norton, 1942.

As far as possible, deficiencies already in evidence must be remedied and care must be taken that hereditary factors even of little value be not allowed to deteriorate still further by fusing them with a homozygote partner. On the other hand, it must be seen that positive characteristics at their full value join with those whose hereditary patrimony is similar.[7]

This does not mean that the Church itself takes sides on genetic questions, but "The fundamental tendency of genetics and eugenics is to influence the transmission of hereditary factors in order to promote what is good and eliminate what is injurious; this fundamental tendency is irreproachable from the moral viewpoint." The position of the Church remains, of course, clear in the matter of allowing each individual the right to contract a valid marriage in accordance with his own inclinations and abilities; there is nothing in the papal declaration which would apply pressure on any individual either to contract or to avoid a specific marriage because of consequences for the physical or mental characteristics of his potential descendants. Nevertheless, there is a moral recommendation contained within the Pope's strong approval of research which will make clear the social role of marriages which will be not merely free of negative consequences but endowed with positive potentials for the human family.

It must be added that through one large portion of the world, India, in which religious and ethical considerations have often been thought likely to interfere with man's taking into his own hand the general control of reproduction, the experience of the last few years has seen an objectivity and a willingness fully as great as in the West to study and to utilize biological phenomena. This does not, of course, mean that the religions prevalent in Southern Asia have the same strong position with respect to family limitation which is characteristic of the Roman Catholic Church. The case is offered merely as an indication that serious and objective consideration of facts and consequences, rather than sheer moral horror, is a growing response of

---

[7] Address to the *Primum Symposium Geneticae Medicae,* Sept. 7, 1953, excerpts from translation prepared by the Vatican Press office, *Eugenical News,* Vol. 38, 1953, pp. 146-149.

human beings with regard to the characteristics which their descendants are to receive.

• The Consequences of Mutations

All of the foregoing is independent of basic changes in human nature which may be expected in the form of new mutations; the assumptions made hitherto relate only to the relative increase in the prevalence of some groups of genes and the relative decrease of others. It must be remembered, however, that mutations are constantly going on (probably one mutation for about five new births), and that the concept of positive eugenics could well include the long-run arrangement by the human family that individuals with like favorable mutations might be encouraged on a purely voluntary basis to work at particular occupational tasks or to make use of certain facilities which are likely to draw them together. Any attempt to push any person into any group or place repellent to him would be alien both to religious and to democratic concepts; but since we are pushing people about by economic and political devices of all sorts, without regard for long-range consequences, it may be considered moral to enable them to move on the basis of their own choice to points where their more favorable characteristics might be likely ultimately to be of some benefit to the humanity of another period. Associations for scientific and artistic purposes are drawing people together today; as genetic knowledge increases in the coming decades it will make clearer the consequence of intermarriages of various kinds.

Another long-range line of thought which arises whenever the future of the stock is considered is the likelihood of true *emergence* (p. 252) of characteristics which do not exist at present, emergence based upon the fresh combinations of genes which may always occur. Fresh combinations of this kind occur, of course, in *every* new person: three boys in a family, each very much an individual, differ from one another, from either parent, and from everyone in the family tree. This kind of combination of attributes is of the very nature of the evolutionary process by which sexual reproduction augments the variability already found at simpler biological levels.

Unfortunately, many of the qualitative expressions of individuality which emerge are likely to be overlooked in the inevitably lopsided use of the methods of science. The problems of qualitative population investigation are nearly always related to intelligence or freedom from mental disease or some other broad, socially desirable characteristic. It cannot be asserted that any great attention has been given to the inheritance of those qualitative attributes which give rise to the unique attributes which we know and cherish in each person. It is unwise at this point to insist that science can *never* find a way to investigate individuality. Rather, we are here at the very threshold of a type of scientific investigation, a concern with the nature of individuality, which will be more and more central as the biological sciences mature, and more and more central to any mature psychology.

It is likely, however, that a problem of such delicacy and complexity as the development of a science of uniqueness will have to be worked out first through relatively simple forms—protozoa, flowers, and perhaps invertebrates—and that whole forests of difficulties will have to be traversed before we shall be in a position to define genuine laws relating to human individuality. Here and there we may be lucky in identifying a single gene, either an old familiar one or one arising from a mutation, which is unquestionably related to some uniquely appearing characteristic. Even this, in view of the complexity of the developmental process, will require a study of interactions of genes and environment and will scarcely enable us to bypass the problem of studying that virtually unexplored realm waiting for a new science: the nature of laws relating to the determination of qualitatively new phenomena.

In the meantime, the process of directly utilizing the everyday qualitative uniqueness of individuals in the same family as a way of understanding basic potentials for human development will be slow. The trouble is that just as an enormous number of genes took part in the unique process which gave rise to one particular individual who never before appeared and whose like will never appear again, so we are unable to define, even in the case of very intimate knowledge of two marriage partners, what the likely qualitative combinations to be found among their various children might be.

From a quantitative point of view, we can very considerably reduce errors of estimate for a population from which these two are drawn; we can say, for example, that the taller they are, the greater the improbability of a child who does not exceed a certain height. In a statistical sense, we may greatly reduce our errors. In the case of the patterns of genes working cumulatively together, the likelihood of an individual's being poorly equipped with respect to a trait, despite excellent endowment both on the mother's and on the father's side, is very small. But, except for these quantitative generalizations, we are in no position to speak of the idiosyncracies which new individuals may possess. We can keep in mind Darwin's principle that the greater the variability of the stock, the greater the likelihood of individuals of any special type appearing; but confidence is sobered by the reflection that when a high degree of endowment exists in both paternal and maternal stocks, our hope of desirable characteristics depends precisely upon the limited variability which the great similarity of the two parents here entails. Considering the human family as a whole, our greatest hope, under present condition, lies in the enormous variability of human hereditary strains, so that there is a very great deal which can and will appear from which some sort of selection can be made; and our resultant hope is that a selection will be made with some degree of wisdom.

Incidentally, if we are interested in persons with especially valuable gifts, there is a gain to be realized in sheer numbers, however little the point may be recognized. Individuals with superior endowment, although especially likely to come from parents with outstanding endowment, come in larger *total number* from parents in the middle of the distribution, for the simple reason that the middle is so heavily endowed with sheer numbers. When children can be properly reared, the number of individuals will be a major consideration in determining the likelihood of finding, in any given epoch, a certain number of individuals with some especially precious attribute. A qualitative argument based upon the restriction of numbers and restriction alone would be contrary to the evidence as to the inevitable tendency of great numbers to produce, now and then, individuals surpassing any given point on a distribution curve. This principle and the principle of encouragement of reproduction among the specially gifted are not opposed. On the contrary. The principle of having a large amount of good material from which to choose and the principle of *special* encouragement of those especially likely to have something useful to give to the future are coequal aspects of a unified philosophy for the encouragement of human potentialities.

• *Positive and Negative Eugenics*

We have preferred to emphasize positive rather than negative eugenics: the long-range encouragement, direct and indirect, of favoring the stocks freest of defective genes. But the negative approach is also important.

Defective genes are of enormous importance in human evolution, and the progress of applied genetics will depend in large measure upon knowing how to identify stocks which are relatively free of defective genes. For the immediate present an important task is the discovery of devices by which the increase in the numbers of those with many defective genes may be prevented, relative to those who have few such defective genes; or, stated more positively, the encouragement of matings by those who have more to give to health, stamina, intelligence, creativeness, and the various other attributes upon which any kind of a civilization, no matter what its character, will have to depend in some measure.

It must indeed be emphasized, as Julian Huxley[8] has pointed out, that complex civilizations could function better with a very wide range of variability from very competent to very incompetent and with appropriate matings according to "social class." His brother, Aldous Huxley, drove this in an extravagant direction in *Brave New World*. But the commonplace genetic principle that extreme homogamy along sharply defined class lines would produce a biologically structured class society has to be admitted. The degree of homogamy is extraordinarily sensitive to a number of social factors: (1) vertical mobility, the tendency of those lower in the scale to move up; (2) horizontal mobility, the tendency of those at a given level to move into other

[8] *Man in the Modern World,* Universal, 1947.

positions at the same general social level; and (3) sheer change of habitat (apparently about one American family in five moves from one city to another each year). An old New England town such as Newburyport, Mass., the "Yankee City" of W. Lloyd Warner and his associates,[9] shows a high degree of inbreeding, class with class. A "boom-town" of the Middle West, where "whirl is king," shakes off this tendency to a considerable degree.

Homogamy is important in another respect. It might seem more or less axiomatic that if there is some hereditary factor in the production of differentials in intelligence, *and* if there is some tendency of the natively more intelligent to become more successful, *and* if there is a lower birth rate among the most successful (all three propositions seem to be rather probable in the light of present knowledge), we might conclude that the general intellectual level of the public is slowly declining. It has been shown mathematically, however, that this conclusion actually depends upon the degree of homogamy, and no conclusion can as yet be drawn. It remains true that the great mass continues to produce offspring who are by definition not very far above or below the mass average; but some offspring at any given time draw "better" and others "worse" genes than their parents with respect to any attribute. It will follow necessarily that from time to time there will be highly able individuals from the middle or even the just-below-middle strata, and history very strongly supports such a conclusion. (The likelihood of moving from the *very lowest* to the *very highest* level reduces statistically to almost zero.) Relatively, then, the likelihood of a highly successful child would be somewhat greater among the favored groups quite aside from the special environmental opportunities which could be offered. But the sheer numbers of those in the great middle mass would be so great that they would tend to produce more such high-level achievers.

All this would appear to be true whether one is dealing with "general intelligence" or with special gifts which are important for special adaptations in the society in which the individual is born. This same general logic will apply, in fact, to such groups as composers and mathematicians. The son of a composer is

[9] L. W. Warner and P. S. Lunt, *The Social Life of a Modern Community* (Yankee City Series, Vol. 1), Yale University Press, 1941.

more likely to be a successful composer than is the son of a mathematician or a bricklayer, but considered historically in terms of sheer numbers, more composers are the sons of artisans than of composers. A reduction in reproduction rate among the gifted in any field would not necessarily mean that there would be a loss of this elite group in the future, because so many of the gifted are the children of ordinary people. But it *would* tend to deprive humanity of very valuable persons, partly because the gifted are a fertile source of the genes upon which creativeness depends and partly because the home environmental opportunities involving identification of children with the parents, closeness to them, and exposure to their ways of thought can best be guaranteed in this fashion.

But where does sober sense about human heredity pass into the extravaganza of science fiction? It is not very difficult for the writer of science fiction to imagine a new humanity derived through a stockbreeder's skill in the selection of favorable characteristics and the mating of those who possess these traits in marked degree. Add a little about the cult of science as a way of managing the breeding process, and you have Aldous Huxley's *Brave New World.*

It remained for a very sober scientist, himself the author of a long series of competent experimental studies, Henry J. Muller, to show the realistic possibilities for a new human nature based upon the application of the principles of genetics. His volume, *Out of the Night,*[10] which appeared more than twenty years ago, is easier to accept today than it was then. Freed of ignorance and superstition, future man, he believes, will plan for the wisdom, the creativeness, the stable temperament, the joy in living which will become the precious inheritance of his descendants. One reason why this is more credible today is that there is more knowledge of mutations than there was then.

There is also a deeper understanding of the fact that two stocks may each become stronger through mating, without losing anything in the hybridization process. On this point the recent studies by W. R. Thompson[11] are instructive. Thompson points out that if the father is especially gifted in one field, the mother in

[10] *Out of the Night: A Biologist's View of the Future,* Vanguard, 1935.
[11] "Traits, Factors and Genes," *Eugenics Quarterly,* Vol. 4, 1957, pp. 8-16.

another, the children may well, by the operation of ordinary genetic principles, be gifted in both without necessarily any reversion to mediocrity with respect to other characteristics. It is also probable that regions of extreme "racial" hybridization, as in parts of Southeast Asia, may teach us much about the children of parents of differing abilities and temperaments.

The kinds of characteristics we are considering are not, of course, the expression of *single genes,* such as produce pathological bleeding. Since it is increasingly evident that many important attributes of head and heart are polygenic, it is therefore only the experimental genetics of specific attributes that can make clear what the results of various combinations may be; and since experimentation at the human level is impossible, the only feasible procedure is a systematic integrative study utilizing genetics, physical anthropology, and psychology, to ascertain the outcome of those matings which occur in the cultural conditions of our own and other contemporary societies. This is a mammoth enterprise requiring huge long-range support; but it is only when such support is available for long-range studies that the factual material can be amassed to ascertain whether the stock is gaining or losing with respect to any particular group of characteristics.

It has long been known that the prevention of procreation by those with simple Mendelian defects or those with gross polygenic defects, such as ordinary mental deficiency, can have no great effect for many generations. If, however, marriage customs alter with respect to age of marriage, marriage across social class lines, marriage across ethnic lines, and so on, some effects can be observed within relatively few generations. Here we are dealing no longer with Utopian possibilities, with strange and adventuresome brave new worlds, or with the ultimate selective breeding which might occur under a dictatorship which happened to be minded to create a new humanity and have the power to do it. Rather, we are dealing with an immediate present factor, a factor already at work, already capable of being studied, already known to have marked consequences, and likely within a few generations to be a factor of weight with reference to such practical issues as the percentage of our population capable of going through college, of achieving certain levels of scientific work in the laboratory, and so on. Those reaching any given "cut-off point" which we may wish to establish will increase or decrease in numbers as the requisite changes in attitude toward marriage restrictions occur.

The term *restrictions* should be stressed, for it is the removal of restrictions, not the predetermining of a mate, that is involved. The issue is usually falsely represented. The question is not the advice of any individual to marry another individual; the question is always whether certain barriers now operative—for example, those of religion, race, economic class, and immediate neighborhood or residence—are to be maintained with the rigidity which at present obtains. As long as such criteria have greater force than intellectual or temperamental attributes, so long will they mold the development of those special concentrations of intellect, creativeness, sensitivity, and so on, to which we have earlier given so much attention. Indeed, the first principle is always the matter of sheer acquaintance of young men and women. If, because of social gulfs and barriers, they cannot get acquainted, they cannot marry. No question of social control or even social advice is of any great importance here. The primary issue is ease of getting acquainted, which is a question of social distance; equality, not only before the law but in terms of status; readiness to move in another's world, to see through his eyes, quicken to the pulse of his values. It is under such conditions of reciprocity of response that the most natural intensification of outstanding social attributes is to be achieved.

There are, of course, many important subsidiary principles, to which Frederick Osborn[12] has pointed—principles having to do with the restriction in birth rates operative in modern society at various periods, especially limiting the reproduction rate of the most gifted of the youth of the United States and of Western Europe. This trend has been reduced since World War II, but long-range outcomes will depend upon age of marriage, spacing of children, and many other unpredictables. An urgent step is to consider the conditions under which socially favored groups *surpass in fertility* those in the unfavored categories. The analysis appears to indicate that all major forces at work in modern

[12] *Preface to Eugenics,* rev. ed., Harper, 1951.

society toward equalitarian improvement of educational and other social facilities and services should quasi-automatically reduce the relative differential which has existed in the reproduction rates of unfavored as compared with favored elements of the population.

Ordinarily the debates between environmentalists and hereditarians become more and more tortuous and more and more emotional as the issue becomes narrowed down to the question whether the socially successful tend to be brighter than others, and whether the large families of the unsuccessful represent the deterioration of intelligence. For the reasons suggested above, this is not an answerable question. Intelligence is a composite of many things, the separate aspects of which have not been followed through from one generation to another. We can hardly even talk intelligently about whether the sum total—aside from environmental effects—is increasing or decreasing.

Secondly, as just noted, we do not know the degree of homogamy and what effect this may be having upon the hypothetical average of any intellectual score we wish to set up. It is tragic, however, that the issue has become focused on this rather unreal problem. The question is not whether in the span of two or three generations we are sinking a little in some composite score. The question is whether we are moving toward realizing our potentials. Many human geneticists are now pointing to the apparent rapid increase of defective genes of many sorts. If, moreover, there is no decline in "general intelligence," that composite of all the abilities, there may also be no increase. It would appear of major moment to the human family in an age of science and technology not merely to be holding its own but to be making some appreciable gains; and even more, to be focusing on research which would clarify the genetic dynamics of such gains.

With regard to other attributes, such as self-control, emotional stability, capacity for cheerfulness rather than moroseness, and so on, which are probably of as great importance as intellect, and with regard to persistence, esthetic sensitivity, creativeness, sound judgment, and so on, we again need much more knowledge. As elsewhere throughout this book, the aim is to show the implications of existing knowledge and the need for more rather than to offer a proposal for immediate action. As knowledge comes in, we can plan at least to do what we can to encourage those with the greater talent, the greater creativeness, etc., to maintain or perhaps increase their numbers. It is hardly enough to argue that we are not going downhill biologically in an era in which we shall need our potentials in all these attributes to do the best we can against the enormous odds which the threats and hurdles of today present to us.

There is another reason for regret regarding the argument whether the stock can be improved: the fact that the substance of modern proposals for betterment of the human stock and for betterment of the human environment turn out to be practically identical; instead of being antithetical, they strongly support one another. As Frederick Osborn[13] has shown in the most thorough analysis yet available, factors favoring higher reproduction rates among the most gifted and competent are regularly factors recognized by environmentalists as likewise salutary. The improvement of living conditions among the mass of mankind will tend to make the *primary* factor in reproduction rate the interest in and love of children rather than the blind processes generally operative, the unfavored elements producing large numbers of unfavored descendants. A vigorous euthenics movement, such as has recently been put into action in many parts of the world, may result in a fairly clear classification (aside from socioeconomic class) of families into those that want children and those that do not, and an accentuation of advantages for the former in the matter of birth rate.

There is another practical reason for emphasizing, for the present, the environmental factors that are good in their own right and perhaps also capable of a beneficial effect on marriage patterns; and waiting for a little more information before pleading for a massive program of positive eugenics based on present genetic knowledge. One of the many reasons why we do not as yet know just what genes might well be thinned out is that genes which are beneficial in one society, *e.g.*, genes related to capacity to bear extreme pain, are not necessarily beneficial in another. Maybe sensitivity, not ruggedness, may be useful in a future society. It has become clear that we must distinguish between those

[13] Osborn, *op. cit.*

genes which produce bad results in *any* society and those which do so in one society but not in another. Indeed, many genetic contributions which would have destroyed their possessors a few generations ago can now be conserved and integrated into new orchestrations.

We have for some decades been told that we are preserving the unfit. There is truth in this. But the issue is complex. Often we must ask: Unfit for what? Most of us are unfit for the arboreal struggle for existence of the first human societies that made their fire by the caves beneath the trees. In fact, we have for a very long time been bred in unfitness for that kind of existence and in fitness for a different kind. What military selection through the ages may have done we do not know, because it selected the tough and eliminated large numbers of them before the reproductive cycle was over. Certainly we are in many ways less tough than those only a few generations behind us, but the success of the toughening process, as we know from experience with preparing men for work with submarines and in Arctic maneuvers, may demonstrate that our softness is not a true genetic deterioration but merely a phenotypic modification under the less stressful physical setting of industrial living; today's softness may be superficial, permitting great hardening when it is needed. The discussion of all these issues as to whether man is "degenerating" has distracted us while a vastly more important issue has crept upon us. This is the fact that genes which would have been eliminated throughout organic evolution until very recently are now being preserved; and sometimes they are linked or associated with many which may well become constructive in terms of social contributions. It is important to learn as much and as rapidly as we can regarding such matters. Osborn has shown that for the first time in history the elimination through deaths has ceased to be a major factor in human evolution. No one knows how rapidly this will produce a yield of mounting defect (of the type which will be defects in *every* society); nor, on the other hand, does any one know what the interaction of the genes which are being preserved will do under constantly changing marriage patterns and environmental stimulation. It would be nonsensical, however, to argue that such a colossal new factor as the sudden end of "elimination through death" could leave the human stock unaffected.

• *The Effects of Radiation*

A profound impression was created in 1956 by the publication of carefully prepared material to indicate the degeneration of the human gene-pool as a result of radiation.[14] A certain amount of this radiation has, of course, gone on for countless eons through the action of cosmic rays and through the action of light and heat in certain special instances, but medical and dental use of X-rays has very greatly increased the radiologic dose which human beings in civilized countries receive during their lifetimes, and it has become clear that there is no really "safe" dose. All radiation may produce undesirable mutations. Indeed, it is probable that even the effects of atomic bombing in Japan, though cumulative for a long time, are less serious than effects cumulatively produced in civilized countries by medical and dental radiation. It is simply impossible to shield the patient and, indeed, the technician, from *all* radiation. Effects received are accumulated within the germ cells—generation after generation—until ultimately eliminated in the course of the struggle of the race for adaptation.

A rather macabre thought necessarily imposes itself sooner or later: Since mankind cannot plan systematically the long-range reproductive trends of its own kind, it can systematically plan, as one of the aspects of that positive research program upon which a better human stock may ultimately be based, a study of the *consequences* of deleterious or lethal radiation. The issue of trying to be objective about that which is very terrible is not very different from the standard practice of waiting for the body of an automobile-accident victim by whom, through an immediate graft while the tissue is still warm, a patient's eye or a major blood vessel may be saved. It is conceivable that by planning in advance one may utilize the information which radiation damage

[14] See the summaries in B. Glass, "The Hazards of Atomic Radiations to Man—British and American Report," *Bull. Atomic Scientist,* Vol. 12, 1956, pp. 312-317.

will convey. One will do this exactly as an astronomer will plan many years in advance the few minutes of observational and photographic work that can be carried out during a total eclipse of the sun. The minutes are soon past, but years of research then go into the study of the data. We need not wait for another super-Hiroshima for such planning. The world's present medical and dental dosage, spasmodically increased from time to time by weapons tests or war, already provides the basis for such calculations and such research.

So far, nothing has been said about the possibility of direct experimental modification of genes. Sir George Thomson[15] offers us two comments on opposite sides of the issue. On the one hand, to try to produce favorable mutations by present methods, such as X-ray, is "like trying to improve a statue by spraying it at long range with bullets from a machine-gun." On the other hand, if an electron beam "is directed at a particular chomosome, or even a particular part of a chromosome . . . it seems possible that this could be controlled and that only one or two genes would be affected." This is followed by cautious speculation about plant and animal improvement, with huge implications for the human food supply; but with reticence regarding man himself.

● *Overpopulation and Natural Resources*

A few words must be said here to explain an otherwise extraordinary omission. Many highly competent students of the world's resources—such as fuels, food, water, and many of the things essential for industrial productivity—are convinced that we are using up these resources at an appalling rate and cannot long maintain present standards of living, even with a stable population.[16] Moreover many of the same experts have given us reasonably detailed information about world population trends and have indicated that the rapid growth to be expected in the next century or two will crush any hopes that we might entertain regarding a decent standard of living for our descendants.

[15] *The Foreseeable Future,* Cambridge University Press, 1955, pp. 120, 121.

[16] Harrison Brown, *The Challenge of Man's Future,* Viking, 1954.

There is no wisdom in belittling assertions such as these, coming as they do from wise, thoughtful, and earnest men. One reason, however, for avoiding this issue here is the feeling that many whole volumes are needed—and are indeed available—to spell out this very evident and important cause for alarm. A second reason, however, lies in a certain reluctance (which many will regard as sheer timidity) to embark on grim speculations regarding trends which are less knowable than most of those with which the present effort is concerned. Believing that mankind cannot exist at all except with some reasonably democratic system of control applying both to national and to international effort and believing that the combination of science and self-control will produce startling changes in humankind even within a century, I cannot believe that blind reproduction trends, as such, are really among our most serious enemies. They are serious, but there is as good reason for faith in the human capacity to deal with them as there is in the competence of humanity to deal with the issues related to war and dictatorship. If mankind achieves enough democracy, science, and self-control to weather this century, it is hard to believe that it will destroy itself through population pressure two or five or twenty centuries hence.

As regards the exhaustion of the supplies upon which human life depends, it seems likely that if humankind can settle its population problem, it can likewise settle long-range problems regarding foods, fibers, fuels, and water, and without mortgaging interplanetary possibilities far in advance, either. The immediate threat of chaos or war from overpopulation and the ignorance and disease often caught in a circular relation with the fact of overpopulation constitute obvious and immediate threats. But long-range thinking is different from short-range thinking. As a Japanese friend of mine says: "Some people are already born." Short-range issues relating to the threat of world disaster I have tried to sketch briefly in Chapter 12, and the long-range issues are, so far as I can see, related essentially to changes in the human stuff and the nature of human culture rather than to problems of resources and problems of population as such.

What is missed in the ordinary view of the population problem and of a slowly changing human nature through the permutations and combinations of human attributes is the *vastness of the range of unused hereditary potentialities for individual development and expression.* Cultural changes, we have seen, are already producing a wide variety of important *biological* changes, not only in our own bodies but, through our genes, in our descendants. Changes in marriage patterns will change the trends of "human evolution" and, even without benefit of favorable mutation, will re-enforce some of the urgently needed qualities important for many kinds of leadership and give them a more prominent place.

Chapter 14

The Fulfillment of the Three Human Natures

The first human nature—the human nature of our organic make-up, our capacities, our cravings, our need to use the equipment with which life supplies us—might be satisfied in a wide variety of physical environments and even of social environments. From this first human nature, as we noted in Chapter 3, developed a second human nature full of "acquired tastes," cultural needs, insatiable new demands upon the environment. These demands are not only in potential or actual conflict with one another; they are often in conflict with the demands of the first human nature. Wordsworth put it well: "A few strong instincts and a few plain rules." Can a social order serve both the first and the second human nature?

Superposed, in turn, upon the second human nature stands the third human nature, the insatiable craving to understand, hoping to be realized in a world of science and arts; and no longer limited to an elite few, but demanded by common men and women everywhere. This third human nature is often embattled with the second, because the second often prefers that which is familiar to that which challenges understanding. But where shall we look to find a social order, a kind of humanness, that can fulfill the potentialities of *all three* human natures?

The most useful first steps can be found in a principle originally developed in physics, then in biology, then in psychology. I shall take liberties with all the modern formulations of this principle, but will begin by paying a grateful tribute to its effective use by Kurt Lewin, about whom more will be said in Chapter 17. The first statement of the principle sounds self-evident; as it is developed the thesis sounds stranger and stranger until, when it is half developed, it contradicts our most cherished assumptions and "puzzles the will" whether to go on or turn back to question the rightness of the path we chose.

- ### The Impotence of Heredity and the Impotence of Environment

Out of the infinite complexity of the biochemical interactions within the germ cell, and between the cell and the maternal environment, would you guess that the capacity to see or to hear, the capacity to walk or to talk, is latent? There is no connection for the untrained eye—and not much, either, for the trained eye—between the delicate and intricate system so well shielded from chemical and thermal irregularities and the finished product. From the unfinishedness of a tiny human embryo or even from the little fishlike creature with its gill-slit and its piggish nose which follow, one could not at first easily believe that it takes but a few more months to make ready the birth of a boy or a girl. We take it all for granted. After birth we take for granted the slow but steady maturation of inner forces coaxed along and given direction by parents and the cultural whole, so that in a few years there is somehow a recapitulation of the family type and the cultural type, with idiosyncracies profound enough but ordinarily not too great for the tether which the biology and the social life of the group impose.

It is, however, astonishing, when you look at the basic simian stuff, to see it turning not just to the art of stone-polishing but the art of painting supernally vivid mammoths, reindeer, and bison on the walls of Spanish and French caves. One might go to sleep a minute and wake up to see the intricate pottery and jewelry of the civilization of Sumer and Akkad; sleep again and see the paintings of the Sung dynasty co-eval with the Gothic magnificence of Western Europe. Who, having studied all this utterly unpredictable potential of the human animal, would have guessed that at his next awakening he would see the material order of nature reduced to mathematical abstraction and even to the laws of evolutionary growth and of atomic structure? The changes are often so abrupt and so incapable of extrapolation from anything previously known that we are forced to think of human potentials as hammering out, over and over again, a reality which contains almost nothing to remind us of the raw material. Fragments, for example, of the scientific method as known to the Greeks and fragments of the capacity to dabble in clay and ochre survived in the fifteenth century. But the transition from the fifteen century to Newton and Rembrandt in the seventeenth is as breath-taking as the transition from the one form of life to another more complex. There is a sense of the utterly unpredictable at each new venture in human nature.

Some will say: "Not so fast; there is the potential within each stage to create the next." Indeed there is. But he who has already struggled to point a clear way historically from one stage to the next will be the most cautious in predicting what will follow after an age of scientific and technological supremacy, or in saying what, in such an age, is to be the role of the arts, of philosophy, of religion, and of the amenities. Let us indeed make the most of whatever skill in extrapolation we may possess. But let us maintain a humble tentativeness with respect to the kinds of creatures which the human beings just around the corner, a few centuries away, may be. The kinds of things which human beings do today, a few seconds in the geological time-piece after they emerged from the last ice age suggest—if we recognize the principle of accelerating development—that the humanity of our great-great-great-grandchildren may already be so utterly different from anything we can conceive that we shall be like Longfellow's "skeleton in armor" or the mummies of the Pharaohs.

They will still be human, but humanness is a matter of definition. The social elaboration of human nature now going on at so extraordinary a pace makes us wonder what it is to be human. It does not lie in the *evident* human nature of today, any more than an eye or an ear is evident in a protein molecule which we call a gene. Human realities at every point are *inter-*

actions between potentialities in genes and potentialities in environment; nothing is foreseeable from heredity or from environment alone.

• *"Adaptive Radiation"*

From this point of view, what will happen when there is a new kind of habitat for all three of the human natures? We can get some insight from the biologist's conception of how life manages to find a *new place* for itself, and thereby to become a *new life:* the principle of "adaptive radiation." As developed, for example, by Simpson,[1] this refers to the way in which a species adapted to a given habitat may grope its way into many other habitats, as if exploring and experimenting, like the boll-weevil "looking for a home." A few may survive in each of the new habitats, being especially well equipped to meet its demands or capable of exploiting its opportunities. Through natural selection the species may then undergo differentiation into forms well adapted to each of the various niches which nature has unwittingly provided. Add to this the principle of segregation of species by barriers to interspecies hybridization, and we have a possibility of stable and continuous occupancy of these special niches for very long spans of time.

It is generally believed by students of evolution that the environments do not in themselves *elicit* the mutations which prove appropriate for these environments—*i.e.,* there is no "macro-evolution" or cosmic trend to which individual biological variation and development are a sympathetic response. However that may be, we need only assume at this time that there is sufficient activity in the form of mutation and sufficient fertility to provide the various stocks from which individuals and their descendants are appropriately selected and maintained in each habitat.

Now, if the principle of adaptive radiation is biologically sound, one must ask whether the principle is not likewise sound at levels both *below* and *above* that of biological evolution. It seems probable that the structure of atoms depends likewise upon adaptive radiation, insofar as different temperatures make viable

[1] G. G. Simpson, *The Meaning of Evolution,* Yale Univ. Press, 1950.

various kinds of atoms. In the electric furnace of today, for example, one may create environments in which certain kinds of atoms can "live," and in the unimaginable ferocity of the temperatures of many of the stars, it appears likely from spectroscopic analysis that certain kinds of atoms are "at home," whereas others, which we think of as the "normal" form of the atom, cannot "live." It would look as if a kind of experimentation were going on in the electrical constitution of matter with variations which may appear spontaneous but are ultimately traceable apparently to that combination of internal and external circumstances, that "field relationship," upon which all interaction must depend. Given the right circumstances and the right internal structure, degrees of instability are converted into new opportunities; and since stability is never absolute, forms are never fixed.

At the cultural level, simple human societies which have adapted themselves to island or mountain regions have gradually undergone an ecological adaptation which involves changes both in physique and in customs and skills. The Eskimo with his very simple but very adequate equipment made of skins, bones, teeth, wood, and blocks of snow and ice, and a ritual and cycle of life which permits the group to exist despite incredible physical difficulties, is more than an example of the adaptation of physique to the conditions of the Arctic; he is an adaptation at the cultural level, as well. His life is a product of a new biocultural interaction.

There is, moreover, an interdependence among the various folkways, arts, and skills, making possible an integration of life ways. It is not a question of throwing together one method of making a harpoon, another method of paddling a kayak. There must be a system of interconnecting strands. The meeting of two independent systems of folkways often makes for nonviable cultural progeny, just as the mating of different species makes for noninterfertile progeny. This appears to be the simplest answer that can be given to the question whether the potentials of culture are finite or infinite. Human potentialities do not consist of mathematical permutations of the possible; they consist rather of finite families of coherent patterns. The number of elements is not infinite. Just as there appears to be a limit to the number of ways in which protons and electrons can be organized, so human societies consist of a rather small number of patterns in which basic adjustment processes can be organized.

But the principle of adaptive radiation holds whenever a human society is cast loose from its traditional isolation and faces a number of potential habitats. There are ways in which the social structure may respond to the challenge. The number of habitats available to a moving tribe, for example, is finite; and the tribe may, as it stops off at various places on its sojourn, develop compact and viable institutional modes of life as numerous as are the habitats to which adjustment must be made. The implications for industrial societies are obvious. As man creates complex new industrial societies, he brings into being new worlds into which fresh waves of adaptive radiation can move; new biological trends are set going which fulfill themselves insofar as the social environments permit. He may, by taking thought, further the biological trends, making the human stock fit for a new world; but some biological change will occur even if he remains blind to what he is doing.

In terms of the principle of adaptive radiation—with men changing in response to new environments—the possibilities for humanity may at first sight seem infinite. But the more we study nature, the more we are reminded of the principle of the "emptiness" of nature, the fact that nature itself can do nothing at all unless the conditions are exactly right. Most of space—whether between stars or between atoms—is unoccupied. So, too, most of the creatures that we can imagine would not be capable of life on this planet; there are gaps, so to speak, not filled in; "impossible" animals. Theoretically, we should imagine that there might always be room for more, not only at the edges of our imagination where we must touch realities but all through the middle. Actually, nature is a honeycomb structure, full of gaps, though revealing its own regularity.

It is not unlimited capacity for adaptation to new environments that is implied. Whatever is to exist must come to terms with whatever exists already, both in the living and in the nonliving environment. There is such a perfect balance among the forms of life that if any species is to increase in numbers, others must decrease. The balance of nature is being constantly disturbed by a frost or a drought, and the relative gains and losses of the various species immediately reflect the altered situation. Every now and then, a new form appears. The geological record shows many alterations in the balance of nature. There have always been gaps which could be filled and which at a later time *were* filled. The fullness which Darwin describes is relative to a situation, not to the entire dimensions of the life potential.

• *New Dimensions and New Fields*

Does this mean that there is always room to squeeze in more and more components in human life or human society? Does it mean, for example, that you could squeeze more and more elements into a human life without crushing it? Probably not. But the real point is not the squeezing of more elements into a given dimension but the discovery of a *new dimension,* as was suggested on page 151. In the case of the table of the elements, one discovers the dimension of temperature: raise the temperature to that of the electric furnace and one finds that many sorts of new elements appear. This principle runs through the whole realm of science, invention, and the arts. What is happening is not that more material has been squeezed into one dimension of reality but that man imagined a new way of thinking—has, so to speak, gone off *at right angles;* has conceived a new way of structuring the situation. It is like the problem of arranging six matches in such a way as to produce four triangles. As long as one works in two dimensions one cannot solve the problem; but let the third dimension be added and the trick is easy. The very nature of discovery lies not so much in the more and more thorough exploitation of the material given by a given dimension, a process of infinite subdivision, but rather in the process of conceiving new dimensions.

One comes to the same conclusion with respect to the cultural limits which have been reached by any period of great creativeness (*cf.* p. 154). What happened to Italian renaissance painting when the Florentines had done their utmost? The only thing that seemed to remain was the development of texture, particularly textures of skin, clothing, and clouds which the Venetians so radiantly perfected. One thing did remain to be developed, however, in the painting of the seventeenth century: the study of human personality, carried through with rapidity by the Dutch and Flemish painters and realized at the highest level by Rembrandt. One might then recapitulate the point that in each instance the period of great creativeness starts at right angles from a previous period of creativeness.

But what determines the fact that in some instances no further turn can be made, no further dimension seems discernible: what is the explanation of the fact that in the representation of the human body no one could carry on beyond Michelangelo? Indeed, even within his own lifetime something seemed to say: you can go no further; and the *Last Judgment* is a muscle-bound negation of the earlier grace. Perhaps the assumption that power must become ever greater was a self-defeating one. In the same way, in the great Romantic period in British poetry from Burns through Coleridge, Keats, Shelley, and Wordsworth, something happened which put an end to great Romantic poetry. Perhaps it was an *assumption* engendered by the new "Satanic mills" of the Industrial Revolution; an assumption that romance is "sentimental." Most limitations of individual and cultural inventiveness lie in *assumptions;* if you challenge the assumptions, there is a new dimension.

Challenge the assumption that a refractory human nature must be pounded willy-nilly into a shape demanded by society, and you have a whole new conception of education; challenge the assumption that the individual must be at war with himself, and you open the door to modern conceptions of healing, especially of psychotherapy.

Through much of history, and in many societies, there is a deep distrust of human motives, and it is assumed to be necessary to teach the reasoning faculties to dominate, to coerce, or to crush the life of emotion and impulse. Restating the issue today in terms of the integration of all the basic components in our nature, the essence of the modern view might be phrased in terms of a challenge to the assumption that one part of man must thus coerce the other: In *The Prophet,* Kahlil Gibran[2] writes:

> . . . consider your judgment and your appetite even as you would two loved guests in your house.

[2] Knopf, 1923, p. 51.

> Surely you would not honour one guest above the other. . . .
> since you are a breath in God's sphere, and a leaf in God's forest,
> you too should rest in reason and move in passion.

There are a few clear cases in history where the removal of an assumption has liberated a geyserlike jet of new ideas. Such was the removal of the Greek assumption that to putter about with sheer *things* is the work of a slave. The men of Alexandria believed otherwise. It was only in the Alexandrian world, after the decline of the Greek city-state, that science as a worldly labor demanding toil commensurate with the toil of the arts became worthy of the recognition of free men; only in Alexandria and in Syracuse that the beginnings of optics and mechanics could be defined. Even Euclid, center and core of later Greek and medieval mathematics, appeared on the scene long after the practical geometers of Egypt and Greece had taught how to measure fields. Today, with a more fluid social order, the invention of tools and instruments may indefinitely increase the range and subtlety of our powers of observation. Such new devices as electron microscopes and X-ray analysis of chemical structure suggest to us that the chief blinders we have are those which deny that there is something new to see.

Sir William Dampier points out that the modern view of man stems from the liquidation of the assumption that man himself is inaccessible to scientific study. Today it does not even sound very rebellious to say that, by discovering the nature of the processes of perceiving and thinking, we can develop our powers of understanding and analysis. And a major effort of psychiatry and experimental psychology is devoted to an objective investigation of the process of self-deception and of ways of getting rid of it.

The very nature of the scientific enterprise has itself been far more explicitly studied in the last few decades than ever before. Passing beyond the study of the inductive sciences and the canons of logic offered by John Stuart Mill, one encounters more inquiry as to the nature of science—a sustained effort to discover what is really knowable and by what steps it can be made known. In such an atmosphere one can rightly ask whether a strategy for the organization of knowledge can be achieved in the twentieth century which will bear the same relation to the nature of twentieth-century science that Bacon's *Novum Organum* bore to seventeenth-century science. One can ask at the same time whether the knowledge of human nature can in like fashion be approached through such a strategy—a strategy, perhaps, which will bring out the ultimate oneness of human nature and of cosmic nature, showing not only, part for part, how man's potential knowledge and creativeness corresponds to each potential of the world but how the structural organization of human personality is related to the *structural organization* of the various types and forms of things of which the world is made. Perhaps we shall find that the structure of the world and the structure of our minds are essentially the same (*cf.* p. 300). Perhaps we can develop human minds to be more ready to grasp cosmic patterns that are waiting to be grasped. Perhaps the third human nature will find itself, as its flexibility increases, glimpsing the cosmic pattern that will release its own inner pattern.

• *Extrapolation versus Emergence*

Let us look more closely at the steps that need to be taken. The study of adaptive radiation has suggested that new inventions, new customs, new values in human living must fit into the structure that already exists (winning some of the battles against existing ways, losing other battles, making many compromises). Often a new step in evolution occurs when everything is ripe for it; not simply because *one* aspect of the world (such as temperature) is becoming more favorable but because a *combination* of circumstances permits something to come into being which never could occur before. It is perhaps a new form of life. Indeed, this could be true of the origin of life itself. Perhaps it was not the decreasing temperature, or the reduction of clouds, or the salinity of the sea, etc., but a peculiar combination of many circumstances that made life possible. Schrödinger's[3] doctrine of the "step-function" suggests that the step from nonlife to life was not a question of a slow transition (as it were, up an inclined plane) but a leap; similarly, change from one form of life to another by way of a leap. *Perhaps the three human natures, still in conflict with one another, can integrate in a new emergent whole.* A life

[3] E. Schrödinger, *What is Life? The Physical Aspect of the Living Cell,* Cambridge, Cambridge University Press and New York, Macmillan, 1945.

driven by the need to *understand* may achieve both a biological and a cultural fulfilling, and such lives might in time become the common human nature of the future.

The principle of emergence means that new conceptual tools are required at each level of integration—or that the data inherently and in their own right, require new methods of conceptualization. In discussing the nature of life, C. D. Broad[4] distinguishes between "substantive vitalism," which looks for new substances as realities become more complex, and "emergent vitalism," which looks not for new substances but only for new *modes of organization*. The latter view is clearly prevailing today. Emergence requires the use of new concepts to deal with the new forms which appear at different levels of progressive integration —and, likewise, new concepts to deal with the integration of the three human natures.

Thus far the concept of levels involves essentially an architectural building process. Components are built into ever more complex totalities, but the totalities give a special function to those individual parts which are caught within the functioning unit of the whole. Even the individual card in a card house depends for its function—say, for example, its sidewise slipping—upon other cards above, beside, and beneath it, and the processes become progressively more complex as the number of interacting components increases as we go up the physical and biological scales.

In each expression of emergence, the higher levels react upon the lower. Every individual in our society expresses in a sense the character of that society. The degree of dependence upon the group, the degree of coercion, or the degree of autonomy enjoyed expresses the kind of social organization which prevails. My own personality could scarcely exist in a society like that of ancient Attica or contemporary Pakistan. The part is dependent upon the whole or, in the language of Gestalt psychology, each event has "membership character" in the whole. The same is true with reference to each cell in my body. Each cell is bathed in fluids influenced by the general acid-base balance, the metabolic idiosyncrasies, the toxic remnants which reflect my own path through life as a living system. The phenomena at the lower level

[4] *The Mind and Its Place in Nature*, London, Kegan Paul, and New York, Harcourt, 1925.

express in some degree those of the upper level in the same way. By the same token, each of the three human natures will be profoundly influenced by its place in the new integration with the other; it will be a new thing because it has entered a new emergent. Every motive, every attitude will be transformed. Just as the very quality of the sex motive is different when tender and romantic components in culture have done their work upon it, so the attitude toward the partner in love is altered by the sense of discovery as one moves toward deeper understanding, as a sense of discovery brings a dynamic view of personality to replace a static one. Attitude toward one's own individuality, already profoundly marked by cultural emphases, becomes enriched by excitement in discovery, as in all new experience in education, in therapy, in group membership; and deeper interest in discovery of the values of other human groups can directly alter one's primitive feelings for them as well as one's culturally ingrained stereotyped attitudes about them. It is likely that *new emotions* come into existence as emergent integrations are formed.

• The Unity of the Sciences

A most challenging derivative of "emergence" is the problem of the "unity of the sciences." Is it possible that emergence involves not merely a progressive identification of new levels but the recurrence at each level of certain universal principles which must therefore be viewed as *master principles which are essentially the same at all levels?* It is possible, for example, that there are certain formal principles having to do with organization in time and space, the dependence of parts upon wholes, and the like, which are the same at an anatomical level and at a sociocultural level. It is possible that there are laws of nature which are not the laws of physics, or the laws of biology, or the laws of sociology, but simply laws relating to the intrinsic organization of the real. Herbert Spencer was the prophet of such a view and attempted in his *First Principles* to lay down certain laws regarding differentiation and integration which are today sought among even the most complex and evanescent phenomena as guides to the unity of nature. Today, with a hundred years of scientific material, concepts, and methods not available to Herbert Spencer, there is an effort to define the modes of organization which constitute these natural keys to the unfolding unity of nature.

Such conceptions simplify our task; for if there is to be such a thing as the development of *human* potentials and their release in a changing physical and social setting, there will be laws which relate to *all* unfolding and to *all* fulfillment of potentialities, as well as those laws which relate to biological evolution, psychological development, or sociocultural unfolding as such. There will be laws of the highest, most general sort. Such laws, as they make their appearance in physics or in biology, are of the liveliest concern to those who ponder what human beings may become. Thus, in Lancelot White's *Aspects of Form,* we can see reappearing at all the levels, from that of the crystal to that of culture, the basic problems of the relation between time-space form on the one hand, and the world of function, self-realization, and purpose on the other. As one attempts to skim the huge array of materials developed by mathematics, crystalography, botany, zoology, psychology, and the social sciences, one encounters at every level the traditional issues which Aristotle defined in his controversy with those who followed Democritus—issues regarding the priority in reality of material events as contrasted with the priority of formal or functional processes which gave the definition and place of each physical event.

Now what does it mean to say that the *same* principles appear at different levels? Does it mean that principles can be arrived at deductively, as if they were matters of mathematics or formal logic and that they are, on that account, sublimely indifferent to all problems of content? Does it mean that the laws appropriate at the basic level, that is, the level of the physical sciences, are of necessity basic to the biological, and these to the psychological and social, etc., so that the most general laws, those obtaining at the base, are, of necessity, capable of generalizing to the whole system of reality? Does it mean, on the other hand, simply that the ways of nature are uniform; permitting us, for example, to conclude that the laws of cultural change, psychological development, and enzyme function exemplify *general* principles? There is truth in all of these propositions; any plan for the realization of human potentialities must be based on utilization of the principles of *all* the sciences at every level, and the principles which exemplify not specific sciences but generalized cosmic principles.

• *The Logic of Predictions*

In the light of such an analysis, what are the possibilities of predicting the human future? If we make no limiting assumptions—such as the assumption that "as things have been, they remain"—the problem is to find the kinds of *new* potentialities that exist for the fulfillment of the three human natures. What are the guidelines to the form of the interrelated biological and social changes which we believe to be coming? This question involves our readiness to consider the possibility not only of gradual change but of abrupt transition to new levels. Both kinds of social changes are well known. Let us see how far we can go in social analysis by supposing that changes of the types already going on will continue to appear; this is the method of extrapolation; the analogy from past and present to future. Let us compare this with the contrary supposition, which we considered when looking for "new dimensions"—namely, the thesis that changes must appear which *cannot* be predicted from extrapolation but only by positing a new level, a level of emergence, a level of qualitatively different events.

Let us first try the method of extrapolation as applied to the *biological endowment* of mankind. It will be recalled (p. 238) that at an earlier period in prehuman and in human history, biological change based upon *selection by death* (and utterly blind as far as human awareness of its direction was concerned) offered the chief basis for changes in the inherent intellectual and emotional attributes of the race, the potentialities for the development of language and of the arts, and in time defined within very broad lin.its the kinds of civilization which a given physical structure could produce. This is no longer the case. Today, the biological changes, although continuing many trends inherent in germinal material (the material of the human "gene-pool"), are more and more dependent upon differential birth rates, the circumstances of mating, and, above all, the relative encouragement and discouragement of the various types of genic potentialities. Whereas formerly the "biological" called the tune to which the "cultural" had to dance, today the cultural calls the tune and biology dances or hobbles as best it may.

At first sight, this may mean that biological extrapolation is even more difficult than cultural, but this does not really follow. For biological change (except insofar as it may be produced by radiations, the effects of which are mainly lethal or disease-producing) must in general follow various lines laid down fairly explicitly by cultural change. J. L. Fuller and W. R. Thompson, among others, have pointed out that, quite rapidly within a few generations, the changes in attitudes as to who would be a good wife or a good husband can have powerful effects upon the frequency with which various phenotypic attributes appear and upon the intercorrelations between attributes. If, as in the example used (p. 233), there should be a tendency among boys bright in mathematics and physics to marry girls who are bright in literature and the arts, correlations between these attributes can begin to appear rapidly, although at the genic level there is no reason to believe them to have any necessary biological connection. A large number of associations of this sort between attributes are appearing and are literally producing new types. It is, of course, quite true that if social changes were initiated in which these spouse preferences no longer obtained, the trends might reverse; but we are thinking now of cumulative trends or cumulative social changes, and it is quite possible that, on a very wide front, biological changes based upon such associations of genes are arising from the cultural trends of today. Thus, social tendencies such as changes in the prevalence of certain values could in a few generations find expression in new biotypes, particularly emergent attributes, new kinds of thinking and feeling tone which have never been present in the human stock before.

In terms of the accelerating rate of cultural change, it is therefore possible that biological extrapolation would give us within a few hundred years (say, twenty generations) amazing combinations of intellectual, temperamental, impulsive, and impulse-controlling tendencies, of esthetic and imaginative potentials, which could occur only furtively and on a small scale during the entire historical period when the human gene-pool was subject to relatively slow-moving cultural transitions. Indeed, new types might be created, insofar as the consistent trends in socioeconomic circumstances relating to marriage can be maintained. We must even ask whether the trends of biological change which might occur within a few hundred or a few thousand years, along with cultural evolution, might not well be so profound as to make the concept of "human nature," as we now use it, less and less precise.

The method of extrapolation has a value which depends on the kinds of factual materials available. Although the extrapolation of steps to physical invention is impossible, the extrapolation of human modes of dealing with such inventions is feasible. Such extrapolations depend upon what little is known about the general potentials of the human gene pool and the biological principles which relate to its modification and elaboration, and similar knowledge regarding the range of human *institutional* variation and the types of further elaboration that can be expected. It follows paradoxically that these types of extrapolation, being based actually upon factual material *about humankind,* are in many respects much more feasible than are the short-run extrapolations which relate to atomic fuels and ways of coping with them.

Of course, the basic limitation of extrapolation of any sort is the fact that continuity can be assumed only if the underlying causal factors responsible for the existing trend can be assumed to continue. In biological matters, this is a fairly reasonable way of proceeding when working with a compact and stable form of life, such as an amoeba, concerned with uniform life tasks of feeding, locomotion, and defense within a stable environment. The evolutionary process rapidly gives rise to mutations, new selective processes in the form of death on the one hand, acceleration or reduction of reproductive rates on the other hand, and that which has been stable for an eon can rapidly become unstable or indeed become extinct. Extrapolation is a question of mathematically simplifying the course of a path into the future when something reasonable can be said about the interacting factors that are involved in the continuation of a series of observations.

Extrapolation, as we saw, may be contrasted with "emergence." Emergence defines the process by which co-working factors result in a *new form of organization.* It is the appearance of a new total arising from a series of interdependent changes, *no one of which has any specific predictive power for a new system of functions.* New functions appear in the evolutionary series which are not foreordained by a genetic drift or series of mutations, or series of selective processes operating with respect to any one organ, but rather in consequence of interdependent or structured patterns. The synchronization, however it occurs, and however long one waits for it, gives the new emergent reality.

In the realm of social emergence, likewise, one may note many instances in which a new invention could in itself produce but little. Think of the amazing steam engine of Hero of Alexandria, which in an era of slave labor had nothing very important to contribute and was used only to amuse the crowd. Think of the invention of gunpowder in ancient China, which, in the absence of powerful martial classes concerned with the invention of weapons, simply suggested no new power opportunities to any of the long-moustached generals, who contemplated such holiday delights as fireworks and Roman candles. What cannot be extrapolated in general is the sequence of events to which the term *emergence* may be applied. Emergence depends upon a system of relationships not directly derivable from a knowledge of the changes and separate functions considered.

Perhaps, however, the gap between extrapolation and emergence is not so enormous. If the principle is offered as a fatal obstacle to the prediction of new events occurring at higher levels of organization, there is a "catch" somewhere. There are certainly many instances in which it is possible to predict biological events—*e.g.,* fatal illnesses—on the basis of simple physical chemical knowledge. Medical men can often prevent dangerous possibilities when foods, drugs, bacteria, and accident-causing objects in the environment are involved. They often take a lowly form. "The trouble was not just the cold that he caught, but on top of that he was all run down, and on top of that he had been neglecting food and sleep for weeks." In these cases we ordinarily assume that certain interactions, essentially of an emergent sort, are beneficial or dangerous.

What the advocate of the theory of pure emergence means is that it is only by experience with the actual interaction that one can tell what a similar interaction in the future will bring. But even this is not strictly true. The chemist knows what is likely to happen if certain classes of objects are put together, and he knows this, whether the particular action, such as an explosion, has already occurred with similar substances or not, because he knows something about atomic structure, about acids and bases, and consequently, about the forces that govern the potential interactions of the substances. As a matter of fact, special skill or information in almost any field involves a good deal more than the capacity to carry over by analogy predictions from one type of action to another; it involves some conceptual formulation of potentials that lie within the structure of two or more interacting ingredients, whether they be chemical, biological, or social. If you know something about human sensitivity to wounds of self-esteem, and something about the need for show-off or swagger on the part of certain components in the population, and something about the sanctioned uses of weapons of various sorts, you are not much surprised to learn that when these three things interacted in Sicily in 1781, or in Denmark in 1246, they produced a duel. Injured pride leads to violent explosions. If you understand certain tendencies or predispositions, you are by definition able to take most of the mystery out of emergence.

The reason why the mystery of predicting an emergence ordinarily remains is that we do not know enough about the underlying structure of events. From this it would follow only that the emergence is baffling, not that it is inaccessible to scientific prediction. It is baffling just because the specific subject matters have not been mastered. It is not an instance of a truly unknowable, a true shift to another plane about which no conclusions can be made at an earlier stage or at a lower level. It is possible to predict the emergent expressions of human potentialities, whether at the biological or the cultural level, insofar as one knows enough concretely about the changes going on at either level, and how the various biological changes are likely to interact, and how the various social changes are likely to interact, in new emergent forms at specific periods of development.

• *Historical Emergents and Their*
  Relevance to Today

Certain tentative predictions *can,* therefore, be attempted whenever it is felt that sufficient information about the component parts and the necessary forms of interaction among such parts can be gleaned. An attempt is made in what follows to offer a historical example of emergence which can be used without too much fantasy or irresponsibility, together with some implications for the three human natures.

The purpose is to illustrate the principle that a basic change in society, lifting it from one mode of organization to another, depends upon the interrelations between many components, all of which must be ready and capable of interacting with the rest at a given time. The example is offered by the materials gathered by historians with respect to the Industrial Revolution.

The establishment of a market based upon rather free communication over large distances, independent of political restraints, with capital and banking facilities on the one hand, competitive bidding or a buying public on the other, had already brought into existence the Commercial Revolution, which flourished from the later medieval period to the early eighteenth century. The "men of the market" had, by then, had their way. Men of many classes were finding and using capital, and there was communication by new transport routes by land and sea, with men specializing in the transportation process, the skills of competitive buying and selling, and the acquisition of the capital and the skills required in large-scale banking.

This situation, however, could not possibly by itself engender *industrialism*, nor could any one component lead, by exaggeration, into industrialism. On the contrary, at least the following five *additional* components had to be present, at the right time, and interacting with one another.

1. There had to be a rapid acceleration of productivity, so that the same capital investment in productive equipment could yield a much larger volume of goods to meet an available demand. In other words, there had to be inventions. These appeared first on a large scale in such devices as the "flying shuttle," making possible the greatly increased productivity of weaving.

2. There had to be concentrated utilization of power to supplement the power of human muscle; and to this end some of the new inventions, notably the steam engine, rapidly paved the way, enormously accelerating the effectiveness of the productive machinery.

3. Those who were to operate the inventions, whether in the form of machinery or in the form of power, had to be brought together in convenient places for the exploitation of these new roads to wealth; and this meant a factory system.

4. To keep pace with all this, there had to be rapidly improving transportation, which indeed was accelerated by the very existence of the preceding three factors, notably the use of steam as expressed in the steam locomotive and the steamship, and secondarily in the development of roads.

5. Complicating the whole, there had to be an increase in mass purchasing power so that the new goods could be bought and used, and more and more demand made available for more of the same goods; and in particular for the *diversified* goods which the inventive process and the available power and capital brought to hand. It is hard to see how the large quantities of capital obtained through the Commercial Revolution could have done this alone, even after the conquest of India and the huge metal and jewelry supplies could be converted into material wealth on the part of the entrepreneurs. It is hard to see how large-scale labor-saving devices could have done the job effectively without the supplementation of human power by great quantities of nonhuman power. Moreover, once commenced, it is hard to see how the process could have gone far without the elevation in living standards and the population increase which derived in part from the foregoing steps, which were acting not separately but in combination. It is all very much like Schrödinger's "step function" principle already quoted: the circumstances must be such as to lift a structure to a new structural level, a new mode of organization.

Much of the same problem of combined social forces involved at a new level can be witnessed in contemporary India. The advent of modern science and technology on a large scale is paralleled by the development of political democracy and some socialist principles, limiting, controlling and often decisively transforming capitalist enterprise as it has existed in the West, with the standards of living for most social classes jacked up at an extraordinary rate despite the increase of population. Indeed, some have suggested that it is only by the very rapid combination of a number of factors which raise productivity and living standards that the Indian village population can achieve that general outlook and alteration of social organization in which a decline in the birth rate can occur. If the changes on any front are *slow,* the result will be larger families (through lower infant mortality and general increase in population because of the reduction of disease through better nutrition and sanitation). The integral action of *several* vigorous forces in modern Indian life, say some observers, might thrust India over the line into the type of industrial society which we know in the West, rather than simply pouring all the gains from the new technology into an increasing population.

It might be added, at a speculative level, that the "decline and fall" of many great societies such as the Roman society of the third and fourth centuries of the Christian era, and the Indian society of about A.D. 800 to 1000, may well have been due to failure at one critical point, in the sense that a complex structure could not be maintained unless all essential components remained well articulated. Of course it does not do very much good to say that Rome fell because of soil exhaustion, or India fell through the supremacy of the Brahman priests as they struggled against the impact of Buddhism; for the structural way of thinking requires one to ask *why* these factors were determinative in a strong and complex society, which we might perhaps expect to find a means of rectifying its own faults.

It is nevertheless likely that just as a building or a dam may collapse through a structural defect and a man die through the failure of a single component (*e.g.,* the inability to maintain body temperature against severe cold), so a society may fail through a single Achilles' heel. It is also likely, however, if our analysis be correct, that viability may fail through a subtle *interaction* of components; and that viable new societies will depend on an *interaction* of components which are not altogether unpredictable.

• *Emergent Interaction in the Institutions of Today*

We found ourselves (Chapter 12) forced to assume that there will soon be a world scientific-technical-political system in which the question of the independence of sovereign states is less important than it seems today. Such a system—if it is to survive—

will have to be characterized by three higher components, in emergent interaction with one another:

1. Curiosity about man and his environment, and eagerness to apply the findings of investigation, with the resulting standardization of ever better physicochemical devices and of social-relationship devices in the service industries and in community organizations. The scientists, arranged in their own hierarchical system through vertical mobility within their own ranks, will become more and more a special "class" of human beings, aware that they may soon hold destiny in their hands. Curiosity will also be invested in the discovery of new economic and political institutions, and, in less systematized fashion, in new arts, crafts, and hobbies.

2. The development of a fluid "power elite" capable of handling the physical inventions and social interactions which result. Such men, the superexecutives of today, are already very different from the Vanderbilts, the Harrimans, the Carnegies of yesterday; they are not primarily money-making tycoons but artists in the manipulation of top-level organizational problems. They arise from the armed forces (Strauss, Marshall, Eisenhower), or from engineering (Morgan, Hoover, Quarles), or from industry (Stettinius, Wilson), and their essential roles seem to be the same regardless of how they may be shifted about. We have long assumed that a Secretary of the Navy can be a newspaperman, or that a Secretary of State can be a utilities financier. We decided during World War II that the production of synthetic rubber should be intrusted not to a chemist but to a railroad man. We have apparently found that executives of high ability are almost interchangeable parts in the system; it is not knowledge of the task, but interpersonal skill—and toughness, shrewdness, persuasion, tact, knowing when to use the tweezers, when the sledge hammer—that produces results. These men will share power with the scientists, and when there is conflict, they will win in short-run battle but be worn down by the long-range inexorable movement of science and technology. In another generation the discoveries of social science will begin to make a big practical difference to these management-artists, and scientific methods will infiltrate the management craft.

3. Good vertical communication—communication up and down the ladder. Riesman suggests that "other-directedness" is an aspect of a general modern trend of the highly placed to keep their ears to the ground. If for no other reason than the commercial, the advertiser needs feed-back from the "hundred million guinea pigs." Actually, with the vertical mobility required to keep science vital, and the need to sustain mass purchasing power (through education, earning power, and alertness to new appeals), the system cannot work without a good deal of response back from the *led* to the *leader* (p. 213). Everybody is watching his neighbor or looking back over his own shoulder. Stores must be "friendly." Companionship must be exploited, even at times organized to death. But the "masses" may more and more be liquidated in favor of citizens who can be pushed around less and less. Insofar as the social skills, derived from social-science research can be made intelligible to the common man, they will be used to challenge, as well as to make accepting contact with, the power group at the top.

Some of the implications for the "three human natures" are clear.

The biological remaking of man, through disease-control, nutritional gains, etc., is under study by medicine and by the World Health Organization and the many agencies having to do with improvement of the lot of men and women in the underdeveloped areas. The scientific-technical approach of today is clearly asking how the economic gains can be channeled into a more endurable and a culturally richer life rather than into sheer increase of population. Very great gains in health (especially infant and childhood health) and longevity are already evident. As we suggested above, the scientific approach to human life must be combined with a scientific approach to conservation of world resources if sure gains are to be effected. And the scientific-technical advance over the face of the globe, we are belatedly discovering, can effect cultural gains without gross damage to existing cultures only if social-science skills and concern for the life of plain, ordinary people of other cultures are maintained.

The genetic consequences of all these biological trends will be great. Of especial importance is the creation of new biotypes by hybridization, a factor of huge importance in all human history, and of course more important today in our shrinking world, which has even less place than ever before for "pure strains." The first step is to study the trends. It is likely that many years will pass before negative eugenics will be generally accepted, and many more before a democratically oriented society will effectively move toward the elimination of those social barriers which play so large a part in controlling the selection of marriage partners. Here the role of research will far outweigh the role of action, whereas in the earlier-mentioned biological application the converse is true.

But the gains in the more impersonal kinds of curiosity (science-technology) and in the more personal kinds (arts, hobbies) will prove so fulfilling to the second human nature, the human nature embodying culture, that it will flourish or even undergo hypertrophy with respect to the first human nature. Just as the baseball lover's virtuosity with respect to the strategy of the game surpasses his own physical capacity to throw or run, so the *cultural* form of virtually every human activity, notably under the influence of mechanization, takes precedence over the *biological* form. You don't show off your chest; you show off your car. It is less and less feasible to knock your opponent down; more and more important to barb—or polish—your words.

In the matter of rigidity, it must be granted that the technical product (the machine, the labor-saving device, the hi-fi set, the supermarket standard wares) subtly standardize the man and woman who use them, providing some ripples of equality and democracy along with a tidal wave in the direction of mechanization—and resulting loss of any hope of escape. But as we have already seen (p. 172), the counterthrust of individual creativity in the spaces between great standard blocks of uniformity, together with vigorous creativeness in science, offer the only evident respite, the only encouragement of that continued freshness on which the flexibility of culture must depend.

And all this seems to mean that the devices favoring cultural inventiveness, expressive of the third human nature, must be zealously guarded if the interaction of the trends favorable to all three human natures as spelled out here is to be enhanced.

But this is just scratching the surface of the problem of discovering how to identify and to use the emergent conditions leading into a new society. The scratching will go deeper in the next chapter.

Chapter 15

Moral Issues

This chapter deals with two fundamental moral problems: first, the moral issue which arises from the control of society by forces set free by science; second, the broader question as to whether present-day mankind has any moral right to choose among the possible futures towards which posterity may move.

• *Science and the Temper of Civilization*

Science may give strength to those already strong and arrogance to those who first become aware of their power. If the civilizations of the past may be classified in terms of their mode of production, the civilizations of the future may be classified in terms of their control over the development of science and its application, the liberation of the yen to discovery, and the applications to which creative curiosity is turned. We who applaud science may find ourselves applauding whole societies with whose structures—and the human consequences of such structures—we may be reluctant to come to terms.

We have already wrestled (Chap. 12) with the question *who is to control science* and have argued that decentralization, or democracy, or at least a high degree of dispersion of controls, has some enormous psychological advantages. Surely the question of the ownership and control of the means of production will partly determine whether production will be mainly for use or mainly for profit—and thus answer the question of relative equalitarianism or relatively sharp gradients in the consumption, prestige, and power levels within society.

But more important than the question of gradients in consumption is the question of the ideological atmosphere which must accompany a scientific-technological society. The scientists, and those close to them who glimpse the possibilities of practical applications, must in every future society stand close to the commanders, the makers, and the distributors and may be subject to control by them. The heart of the question is the *direction in which scientific investigation is to be pushed;* the atmosphere affecting the choice of problems to be studied. Science can be pushed in the direction of gaining greater understanding of the physical world—through astronomy, for example. Or it may move toward a greater understanding of man—through social psychology, for example. Or it may aim at a greater understanding of the immediate physical environment—through organic chemistry, for example. If all three can grow and keep in balance, we can gain in wisdom as well as technology.

The obvious moral danger is that we allow the third of these, the immediate practical goal, to overwhelm the first and second, as might occur either through the quest of power, prestige, and material gain, or through a mass concern with comfort and gadgetry, without awareness of the role of understanding.

On the whole, the reduction of science to the production of practical inventions is just one more case of a goose to be killed for its golden eggs. A democracy without intellectual curiosity, without love of science as science, will produce an unfulfilled humanity just as surely as could any fascism. If science aims at a flexibility commensurate with humanity's need to understand itself and its environment, the pressure of a humanity which needs leaders who understand science can help it.

One of the most dangerous modern temptations is to think of science as a single, indivisible expression of human capacity and human effort. The profound reality contained in the phrase "the unity of the sciences" must not blind us to the fact that, as science develops, it expresses itself in radically different ways. The basic thirst for understanding and for ordering the world in terms of intelligibility is an utterly different thing from the practical investment in specific scientific laboratories and personnel who carry out investigations which will make life immediately more comfortable and which will yield good returns on the investment. There is everything in favor of better television and color photography—more broadly, for all the comforts and amenities of modern living—and the alert intelligence which meets consumer demands is an important element of modern cultural evolution. This must not, however, be confused with science in the sense of digging deeper into the tissue of reality.

There have been several dramatic studies of American expenditures for basic scientific discovery as contrasted with those involved in industrial and military expenditures to meet immediate practical problems, and we are certainly on the safe side in saying that the former does not amount to one percent of the latter. In the flurry of excitement and fear related to Sputnik and its younger siblings which will soon populate the skies, there has been an increasing recognition that unlimited government and private expenditure on weapons, even in the broadest sense, is not likely to meet the real challenge. Indeed, even when gauged in terms of the adequacy of guided missiles, the short-range or emergency definition of science is inappropriate. At a much deeper level, survival is defined not only in a race with another power but in a race with all the threats which face humanity. There is no substitute for basic understanding, for the cultivation of all those cultural inventions, such as schools, universities, books, magazines and newspapers, and radio and television programs, which will strengthen humanity's *desire to grasp where it is going*.

Indeed, from this point of view, the distinctions among the physical sciences, the biological sciences, and the social sciences with respect to subject matter shrink daily into smaller and smaller compass, and the need for an understanding of the very structure of science itself, as it turns to all these various forms of inquiry, becomes ever more precious and ever more indispensable to life in the era into which we are moving. Instead of the weak and often trivial studies carried on today, for example, with reference to the process of education, there will need to be deeper understanding of the transformation of human nature in the educational process, and likewise a deeper understanding of the nature of the interpersonal relations into which we are educating boys and girls, young men and women, so that they themselves may grasp the sense of participation in a changing social order, and look forward to their own opportunity to take part in the creative reconstruction of society. Even in terms of the reduction of maladjustment in mental disease through a more enlightened use of educational forces, this would repay a thousandfold the investment which men will have to put into it, which, in turn, is a tiny fragment of what will undoubtedly continue to be put into short-run industrial and military necessities.

A deeper probing kind of science will act back upon those who take part in it. As in Newton's third law, "To every force there is an equal and opposite reaction," so the process of discovery acts back upon and changes those who take part in it. There are minor changes in people who take part in research in new plastics, greater changes in those who take part in research in the prevention of disease, and still greater changes in those who begin to ask what science and all its ways, the discovery yen in all its forms, could mean to those who trust the impulse and follow it.

If, moreover, it should be inferred that there is just one scientific view of the universe, and that all men must be forced to accept it, many of the purposes of science will be curtailed, and the basic intellectual hungers, as well as the hungers for the things that science produces, will be less and less adequately satisfied. An essential issue is whether free groping into what challenges understanding is to continue. For science, as it takes new forms, generation by generation, will give new forms to other institutions.

Is there an infinite number of such science-dominated societies to be imagined? The answer seems to be that there is only a small number of viable modes of organization of science and that, after a period of "natural selection" among scientific developments, one or perhaps a few will find their way through "adaptive radiation" into the physical and human ecology which this planet affords. The first is that of the "institutional mind" already briefly sketched (p. 161), with which there is relatively little place left for the maverick investigator, and the honor goes to him who finds his way up through the rich branching of the trees of specialization. The second is the anarchic or ultra-individualist method which would thrive through the encouragement of all sorts of odd innovations, even among those (like the perpetual-motion inventors) who, from the viewpoint of established science, are crackpots. The third is a system of rewards for creativeness, the leader choosing his problem. All three methods are to be seen today in nascent form in our own industrial age. If all can be kept going, there may perhaps be a natural selection from among the three systems, as well as among specific ideas. In consequence of what science can do to the face of the earth and, indeed, of the planets, it will be interesting to see what "natural selection" among scientific ideas might do. As science is fitted to nature, and nature fitted to science, through their mutual interaction, a kind of dynamic science might be developed which would represent a flexible adjustment of scientific activity to man in a given era.

But the great problem is to prevent "scientific standards" from becoming ossified. For it is certainly idle to assume that the structure of knowledge is now rigidly set and that all that remains is to fill in more facts; it is idle to assume that the very nature of the scientific enterprise is at last known. For the nature of science and of logic, the nature of the process of understanding, are themselves being investigated far more thoroughly than ever before, and what is not known becomes, as in all other fields, far more vast than what is known. Bridgman talks of a time scale in the universe within which the scientific laws themselves, as we now know them, may be outgrown; there may be a process of drift in the basic laws themselves. Similarly it is entirely possible that if man gives himself time enough upon this planet—or even other planets—he may find himself faced not only with a new structural core of the universe, or one structural core after another but with a new structural core of his own personal and social nature. He may discover that there can be no destruction of the new entities which the "sorcerer's apprentice" calls into being; that there is no end to the realm of knowledge and resultant action forced upon him when once the Pandora's box has been opened.

As soon as the lightheadedness resulting from such sudden exposure to infinite possibilities has passed off and one finds himself facing the reality of a world very much too big to cope with, one may settle down to the problem of control—a bigger one than humanity encountered after the discovery of the New World. Since the dawn of history the Mediterranean world had known the pillars of Hercules as the Western outpost of the land. There was no more beyond; *ne plus ultra.* When Columbus, "Admiral of the Ocean Sea," had shown that there was in fact more beyond, the word *ne* had to be stricken off; and the mood of the age appeared on new coins: "There is more beyond." So, too, knowledge whirls forward, not only with respect to content but with respect to the extension of new modes of knowing.

Some years ago, Nathan Israeli developed the magnificent conception of a "museum of the future": a systematic and orderly display of the various potentialities which the future may indeed bring. Just as we may use a museum to see what Egypt once produced or a museum of science and industry to show the interrelations among the sciences and engineering and invention today, so a study by all the methods of analysis and extrapolation might reveal to us the *possible future directions* of cosmic and human development. In such a museum, we should have to go far beyond the classification of scientific enterprises already attempted in terms of observation, analysis, abstraction, generalization, the principle of levels, and the discovery of new forms of emergence. The task here would be to find ways (like those of the encyclopedists of the eighteenth century) of defining systematically what is known, so that one can fill in the gaps and at the same time extrapolate in directions suggested by existing trends—for upon this possibility intelligent planning depends.

The more serious social science predictions, the Utopias, the science fiction of today would all occupy alcoves in such a museum, with alcoves being constantly made ready for new possibilities which begin to take shape, and with constant reconstruction of the exhibits to give them greater reality. Here would appear, for example, the various educational systems which may be glimpsed as possibilities emerging from the conservative and the progressive trends of today, and the children and young men and women who will emerge from them. Here would appear lovers of the arts in whom greater freedom of expression has colored the whole process of personality growth; likewise those to whom the arts are perfectly ritualized and mechanized; and those caught in the confusion and conflict set up by these different conceptions. Here would appear the supertechnologists who, having mastered the details of their limited fields, will believe that they represent the spirit of science; likewise those who are mainly concerned to understand a field of knowledge as a whole, and those who would like to understand the nature of the scientific impulse itself. To do justice to Israeli's idea, even to sketch its possibilities, would take another book. The great moral problem will be the self-control necessary to get these possibilities arranged in visible form in this museum, so that thoughtful men and women can study them, taste their possibilities, and make choices which, being well-informed choices, are *free* choices.

• *Who Has the Right to Plan for Whom?*

But what right have we to choose, or to plan—which is much the same thing—for men and women unborn? J. R. Oppenheimer has told us that scientists have discovered *sin:* they are now aware that their work is morally significant; they are like Adam and Eve *after* they ate the apple and knew good and evil. Planners, too, are discovering sin. They are sensitive to the public question "For whom do we plan, and by what right?" They have not quite forgiven the old reactionary skeptic William Graham Sumner for writing: "A and B put their heads together to decide what C must be made to do for D." The dig is fair. It must be felt as pain and as sin; and then considered thoroughly.

With regard to the ethics of any plan for the realization of man's potentials, one is always asked how one can judge one mode of development to be *better* than another. How, without an absolute ethics, can one say that mankind "should" move in one way, "should" realize one possibility more than another? Is it not an act of impudence or insolence to define the human potentials in such a way as to suggest that one is in fact "better" than another?

In a sense the point is well taken, and there is a certain insolence in any dream of Utopia whatever, even though one may believe that people will be happier in one condition than another, and even though one's aim is simply to make issues more clear as to where decisions by thoughtful people are possible. In a deeper sense, however, the question leads to the following reply: Suppose it should turn out that when the issues as to human potentialities are really *clear,* virtually all human beings would make essentially the same kind of choice regarding the main issues. Suppose it should turn out that the stubborn or even violent conflicts as to the desirable directions of human development arise from insufficient information on relatively simple points. Suppose it should turn out that evidence is already in hand, or can soon be marshalled, to indicate the nature of those societies in which human beings can function relatively well and happily, with evidence that marked deviation from such a mode of fulfillment will continue to cause suffering until the situation is rectified. These suppositions are worth close study.

It does not follow that humanity will choose a conflict-free mode of existence. A certain amount of intrapsychic conflict and a certain amount of interpersonal conflict may, indeed, at times make for a healthier society. But our direct study of persons through psychiatry and psychology, and of societies through anthropology, sociology, and history indicate that this desirable modicum of conflict is frequently exceeded. There is often much too much conflict—enough to interfere with effective individual and group living, and growth. Our first thesis, then, would be that that society is *good* in which intrapsychic and interpersonal conflict are below such a level. Such conflict usually reveals rather rapidly where and how it is helpful, and it need not be perpetuated beyond the period of its helpfulness. This ordinarily means, in the case of the adult human being and in the case of the stable society, that most conflict must in general carry the "burden of proof" that it is a useful means toward the happiness and growth of individual or group.

If this is the case, our primary task would seem to be to find tendencies within the individual person which give intrinsic satisfaction and cause no excessive conflict, falling foul of other tendencies. And if it should turn out that those same tendencies are causes of serenity and effectiveness to individuals and likewise to the group life of which the individual is a part, there would seem to be a strong case to give them their way.

Can we find any such tendencies in human beings? There are

at least two kinds of tendencies that meet these specifications. First, it is apparent that before the specific maternal and sexual forms of love have developed into well-crystallized form, there is a large area of general affection, outgoing warmth, social feeling, generosity, sympathy.[1] These impulses are common in small children and through reciprocity with others they grow stronger yet. A great deal of this basic good will persists, as a context within which more specific affections arise. There is no conflict between this broad matrix of good will and the development of specific maternal interests directed toward an individual child, or erotic or other affectional response directed toward an adult. Erotic love may produce competitive or disruptive consequences, but this does not indicate that the basic reservoir of warmth is in itself disruptive. On the contrary, it often serves as a solvent to the more violent forms of the feeling, such as the possessive and demanding types of love.

It seems clear likewise that this fund of affection can predispose to (and work well with) an interest in the esthetic and creative satisfactions which have played so large a part in the thesis developed in this book. As a matter of fact, without going into the Freudian doctrine of sublimation, we can see that this diffuse love pours into love of the form or content of a work of art, or the process of creating, or the fellowship of those working in creating a beautiful thing together.

Must the thesis be maintained that the *only* solvent of the obstacles in the way of the unfolding of human potentials is this matrix of general human warmth? On the contrary, the case has already been made that there is likewise a variety of cognitive-affective tendencies of a broad sort which one might call *curiosity* or *interest* in the world as a challenge both to understanding and to esthetic ordering. There is a world of discovery, a world of joy, in understanding, creating, and mastering, which is the basis of science and the arts, which in itself is a basically "good" world of activity. This world, as a matter of fact, is often more real (particularly to young males) than is the world of love just defined; and there is no reason why the young scientist or mechanic "should" feel inadequate because he is more devoted to

[1] L. B. Murphy, *Social Behavior and Child Personality: an Exploratory Study of Some Roots of Sympathy,* Columbia, 1937.

his specimens or his electronic equipment than to humanity at large. But if he is devoted to them, one may well wonder whether *interest* and *love* are so utterly distinct from one another. They seem to overlap. Sometimes they fuse.

It seems clear that liberation of the human impulses in these two vast areas—curiosity and love in the broadest sense—is a major component in what makes a good society; and that they prove not to be in conflict with one another at all but rather to give one another mutual support. It seems that only a studied blindness could make us unaware that it is good for the soul of man to be curious, to be inquiring, to seek answers, just as it is joyful to love persons and to be loved by them.

To plan for future men and women to have and enjoy them does not seem arrogant.

• *Freedom of Choice*

Another answer to the question about planning: Are planners such as ourselves trying to take away the free decision of future generations? My feeling is that man today is very far from free and that it will take him a very long time to become free. Man is unfree not only because of his imperfect biological nature and the conflict between impulses and judgment but even more because of his cultural nature and, above all, by virtue of the blind assumptions he makes about his own limitations, especially his assumption that he can find no freedom essentially greater than that which he envies in the man nearby who has a little more freedom than he.

The world has become so sensitized to freedom that the words and symbols of freedom strike deep resonances everywhere. To be free is first of all to live a life unburdened by toil coerced by others. But equally precious is autonomy in decision. To be free is to be able to move in space and, even more important, to be able to move in the world of thought and expression. One might be tempted to say at first that those at the apex of social structure are always free; but closer study—as, for example in Japan, in India, in the Middle East, in ancient Greece and Rome—has indicated that those at the apex are also coerced by structure below. Freedom, in the sense of autonomy from social control, the sense that one's life is one's own, without any impairment of the power of individual decision (provided only that no damage is done to others) is an idea which has been with us only a few centuries, and with us more as an ideal than as a consummated reality.

The fact that freedom has this intense meaning as a result of its origin in escape from tyranny may make difficult a rational inquiry into the basis of the human potential for freedom. Let us begin with the assumption that there is everywhere a demand for freedom. This is supported by the fact that those societies which openly deny freedom must resort to elaborate and often cruel rationalizations to justify delay or restriction in the extension of such freedom. The implication is likewise clear that we may be buying such freedom as we have in a market in which we are bargain-conscious, making the most of those precious freedoms which are genuinely ours, and inclined to belittle or deny the vast and coercive restrictions on freedom of act and of thought which still prevail.

Viewing the matter in this way, we cannot but agree with Erich Fromm,[2] who has shown that during the medieval and early modern period there was an objective—and, for the most part, successful—struggle against the restrictions of a rigid social order, a social order in which men had been bound to the land and to a "station in life," as well as a habitat from which they could only slowly and with many tears free themselves. The history of the covenanters of the *Mayflower* who faced the grim wilderness—half of them to die in the first winter of their settlement—is a story not of delightful, pioneerlike expansion into the ever-promising future but of escape from almost unbearable coercion and tribulation in a society wrenched by cataclysmic change. Most of the modern urge for freedom was an escape. It was not so much a movement toward self-realization as a catapulted or explosive tearing loose from fetters which bound men to a painfully immediate present.

The roots of the desire for freedom were, however, many; and two other roots must be described. One was the freedom from irrationality, the freedom which came from a reason above im-

[2] *Escape from Freedom,* Farrar, 1941.

pulse, from grasping the nature of things rather than impulsively responding to momentarily presented aspects. This kind of freedom had been stressed in many phases of Greek philosophy, especially Stoicism. From this point of view, only the wise man was free. The poor man, even the slave, Epictetus, could be free in spirit. As a later German version had it, "Thoughts are free." The other idea, ultimately fusing with the idea of freedom as rationality, was the thought of *freedom to choose the good* as a form of escape from the *bondage* of sin and the wages of sin, which are death.

The Greeks, of course, never went far in the development of the idea of sin, or of choice between the noble and the base. They knew what a noble man was and what a base man was. Thersites, who tried to persuade the Achaean soldiers to abandon the siege of Troy, was portrayed by Homer as intrinsically and basically so foul in body, mind, and spirit that what he did was a blot on human nature. Thersites, however, could not do anything else but what arose from his own nature. It is impossible to imagine Thersites as *choosing* the good. In the same way action was conceived to flow from the nature of a man and therefore not to involve any special conception of "free will," such as later characterized Christian thought.

As a matter of fact the Hebrew thinkers, at least until the later prophets, had an idea somewhat like that of the Greeks. The idea of sin as free choice of the bad invaded the Western world from Persia through the system of Zoroaster, in whom good and evil are not only ultimate realities but aspects of nature in both of which man shares. In the later Hebrew tradition and in the Hellenistic world, in which Hebrew and Greek thought are interfused, there begins to be more and more emphasis upon sin as the expression of *arbitrary choice*. In these terms the Garden of Eden story takes on enormously foreboding meaning. From this point of view sin itself was *not actually in the nature of Adam and Eve,* whom God had made; on the contrary, their nature permitted *freedom* to obey and to disobey, and they *chose* to disobey. It was sheer perversity, sheer sin, a deliberate and free choice on the part of Adam and Eve which resulted in the invasion of the world by evil. The conception of sin as the arbitrary expression of willfulness—the conception of a free will as something not flowing necessarily from the nature of the individual but representing a momentarily creative act for better or for worse—was slowly developed in the early Christian period. It was, of course, greatly enriched and magnificently formulated by St. Paul, and later by Augustine, from whom it became central in the Roman Catholic tradition. From the Augustinian point of view, man has genuine freedom within the limits determined by his understanding and his situation. He can choose to do God's will or he can choose the opposite.

So well-defined a thesis could only be attacked, so to speak, in bulk, not by erosion; and this is why Calvinism, slightly more than a millennium later than Augustine, defines the abject *unfreedom* of man as a sort of fulfillment of that helplessness of man to which Luther was pointing. Soon science was defining an ordered, lawfully determined universe, of which man was just a part.

There is something of a paradox perhaps in the fact that modern Protestantism, struggling with these issues, has seen fit to assign enormous importance, as does Roman Catholicism, to free choice. The free act is defined not at all as that act which follows naturally from the full nature of the person at the time. For, according to the Protestant belief, two or more kinds of action can at a given moment equally well flow from his nature, a good act and a bad act; the act of will is itself outside of the causal series.

The question of freedom to choose is fundamental in all our thinking about the future. How can we speak of choices among future possibilities unless we define the kinds and degrees of freedom the individual or the race possesses? Although we shall disclaim any attempt to say anything new on this issue of freedom, a few obscurities need to be ironed out and a few possibilities explored.

William James distinguished well between "hard determinism" (or fatalism), which puts the control of mankind utterly outside of himself, and "soft determinism," choice springing from character.[3] Hard determinism is "necessity." Heracles, returning from abroad, is overpowered by a demon and slays his wife and children. The force is external to himself. It is indeed

[3] "The Dilemma of Determinism," in *The Will to Believe and other Essays in Popular Philosophy*, Longmans, 1903, p. 149.

a *deus ex machina*. It would not be the *nature* of the true Heracles to do this. Man is conceived to act in accord with his nature
except when invaded by a demon. The demon expresses Fate.

"Soft determinism" consists, on the other hand, of the conception that the man acts from the whole of his nature. He sees,
feels, and acts in accord with what he basically is. He may, indeed, be "inconsistent" if his inner nature is "inconsistent." He
may negate, regret, repent, re-do, remake. He may start in new
ways; he may attempt to undo the past; he may turn away. All of
these actions are real, and they are expressions of the diversity,
the turmoil, uncertainty, and conflict within him. Insofar as he
achieves a unity of goal and of value and pursues it knowingly, he
is acting out his nature. This is self-determinism.

It must be admitted that an utterly base man concerned only
with the torture or destruction of his fellows might likewise act
out the wholeness of his being. The concept of wholeness must
not be taken to imply goodness. It can, however, be noted that in
general we can agree with Socrates that most men in general
often mean much better than they do, or with Paul, who said,
"The evil that I would not, that I do." There is much love in
mankind but there is also much fatigue, much conflict, much uncertainty, much rage, and much terror. Not pretending to
have the ultimate truth about the unknown and unrealized potentials of mankind (for if we had any such knowledge, even the
thought of such volumes as this would be a waste of time), we
can nevertheless note the basic truth that those men are free
who are not tripped up by internal contradictions, by unconscious impulses which drive them to goals which broader considerations would not actually justify. Self-determinism, then, is utterly and absolutely distinct from hard determinism. It looks for
the unity, the continuity in life, deep in the structure of the individual person.

This is, of course, determinism in a philosophical sense. It has
no place for what William James called "arbitrary spontaneity";
sheer absence of causality. Indeed, *"arbitrary spontaneity" would
be an interference with such freedom.* It would entail a source of
actions essentially *external to the character of the person* and
would therefore be actually closer to hard determinism than to
the everyday naive conception of free will.

Freedom to choose means the operation within the person of impulses to gather information relevant to his decision and to see the issues clearly. If these impulses and this information are not present, it is difficult to see what freedom would mean; and it is difficult to see how this kind of freedom could *precede* the impulses seeking freedom. This kind of freedom arises from a human context, and to some degree we can help to find freedom for ourselves and others by providing rich contexts. But none of this is done causelessly. There must likewise be the personal hardihood and capacity to act upon the understanding of the issues. If these things are available, there is freedom.

Let us imagine a person of generous impulses and wide vision who dissents from all this. In the midnight bull session, many a sophomore desires to demonstrate the reality of what he thinks to be free will. From his own inner nature as it exists at a given time there is a recognition of ways of accomplishing a generous act for the benefit of those whom he loves. But the only way in which he could possibly "demonstrate" the popular, man-in-the-street type of free will would be to do something base in order to prove that he was not controlled by utterly deterministic forces! Actually, if he did this, he would only reveal, in a sorry fashion, that he had become confused as to the nature of freedom, and that he was allowing a bizarre impulse to become dominant in an otherwise well-structured personality.

Indeed, the contradiction inherent in many attempts to prove the reality of free will is evident in the indoctrination in children of a group of impulses which are held to guarantee right conduct. If one succeeds, success occurs by virtue of a system of thought which is rooted in the most fundamental of deterministic assumptions. The person could not then from this point of view be free if his nature, shaped by such training, chose the right; he could be free only if he chose the wrong! When, however, different teachers are compared with regard to their love of the child and their skill in enabling him to find a right way of living, the relatively larger number of misdeeds on the part of those taught by certain of the teachers will lead to an unfavorable comparison: look how much better another teacher did! In other words, it is basically presupposed that there are interpersonal devices to enable individuals to see things from a right point of view and

make appropriate selections. The very disciplinarian who insists
upon vigorous control and the formation of stern habits thinks in
an utterly deterministic fashion until his pupil has done the opposite of that which is expected; then suddenly the pupil is said
to have arbitrarily exercised free will and the negation of that
which was right! In short, freedom is being taken away by the insistence upon causelessness or arbitrariness of action.

A popular objection has, in every generation of philosophy,
been reiterated in some such form as this: "But if it's all predestined, all arranged in deterministic fashion, why do you write
such a book?" This is of course a reversion to *hard* determinism,
and a failure to note that it is about 180° removed from the self-
fulfillment or soft-determinism principle which is here being
advocated. It is *because* the tissue of the world is believed to be
structured and orderly that any individual may hope beyond all
arbitrariness to influence his own future conduct, and that of
his fellows. It is because of structure and order that he can
hope, indeed, to play some part, to take some place in the forward movement of those on this planet who likewise share such
aspirations. He can thus count on causal and lawful human forces
(guided by such cosmic forces as science cannot at present comprehend or claim to know how to investigate) to the end that
predictions can to some degree be better and better fulfilled
through further knowledge and more steadfast action. Insofar as
one believed in arbitrary spontaneity or causeless action, or action springing from something other than the character of individual human beings, to that degree would he negate the kind of
thinking and the kind of long-range concern with the possibilities of a better human society, which it is the task of thoughtful
science and its application to serve.

PART V

Man and World

Chapter **16:**

The Boundaries Between the
Person and the World*

At this point in our journey we face the largest of the philo-sophical issues with which evolution confronts us—the question whether man's development on the face of the globe is a unique, essentially accidental event, having no deep affinity to anything which the universe as a whole is doing, or whether, in some sense it *represents* ways of the universe, the stuff, the trend, the meaning of the universe, or one of the meanings of the universe. Our intent here is not theological; it is not concerned with divine purpose as such; it is based on studies of the universe as known to science. And since not much is yet known to science, it is highly speculative.

The issue, I think, was fairly stated in T. H. Huxley's memorable essay "Evolution and Ethics," in which we are told that ethics is simply a human invention, out of tune with the essentially non-ethical principles realized in the development of life. A half century later, Bertrand Russell, in "The Free Man's Worship," returned to the challenge, arguing that there is nothing in the universe outside of man to which he can respond with a sense of oneness. Man and World are two, not one; man can find a corner in the world for his own little life, but the universe as a whole has no interest in him.

* Most of this chapter was presented to the 14th International Congress of Psychology at Montreal in 1954 and was published in the *British Journal of Psychology,* Vol. 47, 1956, pp. 88-94.

These ideas made history because they were already *in* the intellectual history of the era. But I think they were immature, exaggerated responses to man's feeling of alienation after the earth on which he stood had lost its place as center of the universe and after his own life had come to be seen as one of thousands of expressions of a struggle for existence.

I think the sense of alienation blinded man to the deep affinities he has with his cosmos. I think it will be worth our while to give a whole chapter to the problem of man's distinctive or unique position, his supposed separation from the cosmos which engendered him, the possibility of his defining, so to speak, a path to his own potentialities which is independent of the paths which honeycomb the cosmic structure.

A central aspect to be treated here is the question of boundaries—spatial, temporal, functional, and conceptual—which mark off the realities and events called personal from those called extra-personal. To suggest the range of possible ways in which we may conceptualize the relation of the person to the world may perhaps help to make clear what we do not at present understand about the nature of persons and may help to focus experimental, clinical, comparative, and other research procedures toward the attainment of a clearer and more workable formulation of the possibilities.

The boundaries between person and world may be viewed in terms of the physical, the biological, the psychological, and the social.

• *Physical and Biological Boundaries*

From Democritus to Schrödinger[1] the physical view suggests that what is inside man is essentially like what is outside; he is a bit of the cosmos, duplicating it in substance, frequently also in structure.

The world as envisaged, for example, by Democritus, consists of particles, some of which are bunched in the form of organic beings, and some of the particles within such sentient beings make up the "mind" of the person. From this conception, through Lu-

[1] E. Schrödinger, *What is Life? The Physical Aspect of the Living Cell*, Macmillan, 1945.

cretius, La Mettrie, and the monistic systems of today, an essential identity of thought can be observed. From this point of view, there is a clear and obvious boundary between person and non-person, namely, the capsule, the envelope, the spatial boundary, essentially the skin of the living individual. At times, the monist espousing such a view glimpses a larger and more complex relationship, as when La Mettrie, for example, compares man to fire, the process of respiration involving a subtle and fluid interaction between person and world. Though the cosmos permits momentary isolation of small portions of itself, biochemistry has made clear that in vital processes such as respiration it is meaningless to define a sharp boundary. Thus, in L. J. Henderson's "nomogram" of the blood,[2] the living system within the skin is not sharply separable from the non-living system in which it is bathed; oxygen in the red-blood cells can be regarded either as part of us or as part of our environment, indifferently. The gradient between man and world is a gentle one indeed.

Biological research nevertheless forces our attention to an apparent paradox: the fact that the organism is ultimately inseparable from its environment means that its very existence depends upon its obedience to principles quite different from those which generally obtain outside it. In an "open system," for example, specific processes, such as the maintenance of homeostatic balance, prevent the irruption of the outer form of order into the protected inner realm within which a fundamentally different kind of order prevails. As C. D. Broad[3] (p. 253) puts it, we find, in contrast to the principle of substantive vitalism, the operation of "emergent vitalism," a conception according to which the same material particles which are found in the universe at large are found under conditions of such organization and at a level of such emergence as makes vital phenomena essentially different from those occurring in the outer world. We may thus, if we choose, avoid dualism of substance, yet provide dualism of functions.

Thus, despite this conception of homogeneity attempts are still made to develop some plausible basis for the fundamental strug-

[2] *The Order of Nature: an Essay,* Harvard University Press, 1917.

[3] *The Mind and Its Place in Nature,* London, Kegan Paul, and New York, Harcourt, 1925.

gle of the individual against the world. The conception of home-ostatic balance enables us to envisage ways in which particles essentially like those of the cosmos at large may, nevertheless, as it were, fight against the disintegrating forces of the cosmos, maintaining for a while their own tightly structured internal coherence. Lifting this conception to the cultural and ideal sphere, we have the views propounded by Huxley and Russell already referred to, in which the value system of human beings negates, opposes, and stands in stark opposition to the valuelessness and impersonality of the world.

But it will surely not suffice for science to declare only that we are both one with the environment and also embattled against it. The empirical issue is to ascertain just when and how far Henderson's conception of the *gentle gradient* holds good, when and how far the *sharp gradient* of homeostatic isolation prevails, and just when and how our relative independence of the environment is to be defined. The term *gradient* is used here for no single physical continuum. The most important continuum lies in *degrees of interdependence.*

• *Psychological Boundaries*

Turning now to the viewpoint of psychology, we find the gradient between person and world ordinarily treated as very steep. We speak of individual and environment as two utterly distinct things, with a sharply defined boundary. Our diagrams show no region of transition; everything is either inside or outside the organism. Yet despite all this, contemporary psychology offers at least three other possible approaches.

First, the Gestalt conception of *inner structure,* such as the structure of thought or the structure of personality, in contrast with a lower degree of order in the environment, reveals a parallel with the sharp gradient of homeostatic balance.

The concept of isomorphism is an effort to give the individual a structure and an autonomy, while providing resonance of inner to outer reality. The term *isomorphism* has been used in two senses: first, to denote the correspondence of mental structure with the structure of neural response; and secondly, to denote the correspondence of inner structure with environmental structure. It is to the latter that I refer. Isomorphism, indeed, is a special case in which inner structure mirrors outer structure, not through capitulation of the inner to the outer but through their capacity for attunement. For Arnheim,[4] isomorphism is that structural correspondence between the physical environment and the psycho-physical processes in the person which makes adequate reaction to the world possible. In relation to music Arnheim writes of "the structural kinship between expressive effects and specific patterns of rhythm, pitch, harmony, timbre, or volume."

A second concept characteristic of modern psychology presupposes formal independence of person from world, combined with absolute dependence through the ceaseless give-and-take tennis game of acts and signals, the world of cybernetics and of information theory, of navigation through a sea of uncertainties, of complex contacts with heterogeneous reality—a world where *reality is reciprocity,* not the world of events-within-the-individual-person which our self-reliant grandparents knew.

It is not ordinarily noted that in many such cases the interdependence of part of organism No. 1, say its vocal cords, and a part of organism No. 2, say its ears, is very much closer than the interdependence of many parts of organism No. 1, such as toes and ears. Functional interdependence is what we are now studying, and the lines of functional interdependence do not neatly run in closed circuits inside one individual.

The third psychological conception goes even further. By all means the most original and radical of the modern efforts to transcend these traditional dichotomies is the field theory of Kurt Lewin.[5] Incomplete and in some ways self-contradictory at the time of his death, this was, nevertheless, a brilliant adaptation of the general scientific conception of the field as developed first in physics and then in biology, transported into psychology to indicate the relative inseparability of person and world. As a matter of fact, it is only in Lewin that one refuses to accept the ancient question: Are we one with the world or isolated from it? Neither, says Lewin, and proceeds to show how those aspects of a response which are properly called personal and those aspects which are

[4] R. Arnheim, "Agenda for the Psychology of Art," *J. Aesthetics Art Criticism,* Vol. 10, 1951, pp. 310-314.

[5] K. Lewin, *A Dynamic Theory of Personality,* McGraw-Hill, 1935.

properly anchored in the environment come to meet one another in one organized field dynamic. In the "life-space" of Lewin there need be no fixed division into outer and inner.

In some types of field theory a unified world of person and environment yields at some points a gradient as gentle as that of Henderson. In many empirical problems, such as the preparation of a life history, the field conception, with its fusion of outer and inner, notably improves our powers of explanation and prediction. Although all concepts of the nature of the individual encounter deep-seated resistance, the notion that we tend to melt into our environment encounters a resistance which is perhaps proportional to our culturally engrained conviction that there *must* be something which is utterly our own.

• *Selfhood*

Up to this point the terms *person, organism,* and *individual* are used more or less interchangeably. This is because we have been considering ways of attempting to view objectively the relations of organism and environment. There is, however, another issue— namely, the problem of the way in which the barrier is viewed by the experiencing individual. This is the problem of our awareness of our own individuality, commonly called the consciousness of self. Classically, throughout both Indian and Western traditions, the thing known as the self, the observed me, develops like an object of experience, comparable in all fundamental respects to the development of other percepts. The newborn have no clear awareness of self; but gradually through the observation of body surfaces, muscular contractions, the sound of the voice, cathexis upon these physical entities and constant comparison of them with other entities observed in other persons, an "empirical self" is woven and given abiding structure. This self may undergo transformations and elaborations, but it represents a relative continuity from the cradle to the grave, is given a name, is given a social position and sense of responsibility, and around it in time cluster the goals, values, norms and ideals which give meaningful purposive continuity to life. It is fundamental to most such theories that the self becomes a loved object.

Freud's "narcissism" is the clearest of the Western formulations of such self-love.

There is, however, constant reciprocity between the image of the self and the image of others; and this means, from the point of view of an empirical psychology, that the contours of the self are often blurred, and the distinction between the self and non-self made indistinct. The question arises, whether the self ever does become sharply separated from the perceived selves of other individuals and consequently whether a sharp delineation of the self is ever achieved. One might set up a splitting or "dissociation" so profound that selfhood is separated by a deep gulf from all else in the world. This is hard to imagine in view of the endless social commerce of selves which have to be perceived as phases of a process of social interaction in a context of wholeness. Yet in certain types of mental illness, this extreme separation can be observed, while at the other extreme other types of illness involve an incapacity to separate the regions definable as self. Empirically, then, there are *degrees* of independence of self from non-self.

There exist, however, in human societies a great many phenomena of awareness in which self is not distinctly marked off or in which it has properties quite different from the self as we know it. There even appear to be some completely selfless experiences existing momentarily, and experiences of complete immolation or identification in group or cosmic processes. Some of these experiences have been studied in early childhood, through the clinical methods of modern psychiatry, through the methods of ethnology, and occasionally through the methods of experimental psychology, especially in the case of depersonalized hypnotic states. Such investigation shows that the sharp isolation of the individual is merely one special case of consciousness, like Euclidian geometry among non-Euclidian systems. There is, moreover, some experimental material on the conditions which lead to such impersonal states and which throw light on their broader significance. There is, of course, an abundant opportunity here for self-deception, and it would be ridiculous to maintain that the person's experience of boundaries between self and nonself is a safe guide to the real situation. He may be a psychotic whose illness consists in large part of his inability to accept the real boundaries. But if the fusion of selves is experienced by some persons as a reality, this constitutes a psychological problem which may merit study, along with the problem of the nature of the objective boundaries.

This soon leads over a bridge which to many will appear to be perilous indeed. For selfhood is seen from all these vantage points to be capable of only a relative definition. It represents a reality which is only partially detachable from a flux of experience not sharply organized around the self. This re-opens some issues raised in ancient Greece and in ancient India regarding the real separation of one person from another, and reminds one of John Donne's words: "No man is an island." Such a conception, developed by mystics in both the Eastern and Western traditions, has pointed to a type of psychological reality which is not anchored in any single self. It has insisted that there is not only the reciprocity of self and social environment but at times a true and intimate fusion of selves, of personal identities. This view has usually been conceived in religious terms through identification with a deity, or as in the Greek mystery religions, as identity of the fellow worshippers in their identification with the deity. There is, however, more here than a system of religious and philosophical possibilities. There are challenging psychological problems which have been posed by studies of sleep, trance, hypnosis, ecstasy, the phenomena of 'possession' described in the ethnologists' and historians' records. The empirical problem of the degree to which selfhood can disappear leads on into the problem of the interaction between two or more selves in which the isolating sense of individuality tends to be lost in a sense of communion.

I do not mean to suggest that the individual's sheer belief that he is dependent on others, or independent of others, should be taken as anything more than just a belief. He may, of course, actually be more dependent on others and on the environment than he thinks he is, or he may be less dependent. My point, rather, is that the problem of dividing the world into experienced self and nonself is a problem that needs to be pursued conjointly with the problem of the nature of the objective biological gradient.

It might be thought that an appeal for a study of conditions of selfhood with very fluid and indistinct boundaries is essentially an appeal for a study of queer, bizarre or abnormal states. On the contrary, it seems very inappropriate to use terms of evaluation and derogation when dealing with states of consciousness about which we know so little, and which in the nature of the case appear alien to our more customary ways of thinking. Rather than trying to finish in all completeness the study of one kind of awareness, it may be better to strive for an openness towards the possibility of areas of experience as yet unexplored.

The reluctance to investigate these phenomena is perhaps related to the vigorous individualism of Western history, and likewise with the feeling that our long cherished emancipation from philosophy and religion will somehow exempt us from coping with problems of this order of complexity. As a matter of fact, the same motives and the fear of losing caste among positivist scientists has interfered on a huge scale, even with the investigation of relatively simple and objective laboratory phenomena. Such laboratory phenomena, for example, are now available in the field of parapsychology, meeting the challenge for strict experimental control. A huge range of empirical materials is now at hand, interconnected by a very considerable body of coherent systematic conceptualization. Most of this conceptualization is unknown to psychologists; indeed, even the empirical material is largely unknown. One often hears the remark that one might begin to believe in the authenticity of the many experiments in telepathy to which no objection has been pointed out if there were some sort of coherent theory regarding it. Yet several coherent theories have already been developed in intimate relation with the experimental facts, and progress in development of repeatability of experiments goes hand and hand with clarification of the conceptual systems.[6] Science can seldom afford to be afraid of investigation, and in this instance, as in so many others in the history of science, fear can actually cripple the types of investigation which would give true unity and resolution to what have proved otherwise to be insoluble problems.

[6] W. Carington, *Thought Transference*, Creative Age, 1946.

In the experiments of Soal and his collaborators,[7] it has been possible over a span of several years to observe meaningful variation in telepathic scoring level between subjects working in different rooms, with independent observers in both rooms, with randomized stimulus materials and careful and cautious statistical treatment. The phenomena were not only in conformity with reasonable psychological hypotheses regarding the dynamics of the process, but exemplified the specific point here suggested, namely, the interpersonal nature of the telepathic phenomena. In some experimental series, two separate individuals working independently each possessed some information about the stimulus material, but neither one knew its whole character. A third person, C, the sensitive subject, was able to piece together the material, so that this mind C actually represented, at the time, an integration of the contents of three minds—A's, B's, and his own. I ask only that this be taken as a challenge to read or to think. It is perhaps of interest that many of the phenomena suggested by unconventional ways of looking at the person raise essentially the same kind of question, namely, the question where one person begins and another ends.

• Social Boundaries

Finally, in the social-science approach we have been pushed by more and more evidence in recent years to admit the profound interdependence of members of society, the full membership character of individuals in their group, and the reality of processes which are fully interpersonal, not simply the accretion of the behavior of distinct individuals. Again societies differ in the degree of autonomy allowed to the individual, with autonomy varying from great to little, but never suggesting the reality of any wholly self-sufficient person, any more than psychology, biology or physics could allow such absolute self-sufficiency.

How did we manage to forget so much of this in erecting a pedestal upon which the individual was to stand—poor Simeon Stylites, alone in his elevation above the group? We forgot, per-

[7] S. G. Soal, and K. M. Goldney, "Experiments in Precognitive Telepathy," *Proc. Soc. Psychical Research,* Vol. 47, 1943, pp. 21-150; S. G. Soal and F. Bateman, *Modern Experiments in Telepathy,* Yale University Press, 1954.

haps, because we are parts of the Western conception of individuality, made razor-sharp by the Commercial and Industrial Revolutions. We grow today in actuality more and more dependent upon one another, but the rugged individualism of a tradition is still spread all over our psychology. Is it really necessary to give the Western conception of individuality not only the right of way, but actually the sole berth in the establishment of psychological science? Is there a possibility that by greater openness, we could recognize that in Western psychology we have only one of an infinite variety of possible relations of self to world?

• *The Need for Research*

Not, of course, that we are fully consistent. Perhaps we might conclude that some aspects of persons are relatively sharply bounded, others the reverse. Paradoxically, we give heroic stature both to the Whitman-like "individualist" and to him, like Gandhi, who is "selfless" in devotion to a social goal. In an era in which humanity can hardly expect to survive without fuller knowledge of the biosocial value of individualistic and social impulses, research is needed into the sources both of man's need to isolate himself and of his need to soften his individuality in the presences of his fellow men and of the sea and the stars; we need to understand how his culturally molded selfhood sometimes leads him to make the gradient seem much *less steep,* sometimes much *steeper,* than it is.

From such speculations as these one would conclude that mankind will need to study very closely both the question of the autonomy of each man from his fellow and the autonomy of the species *homo sapiens* from the deepest structural laws that represent the ways of the cosmos. It would seem at best rather rash and wild to mark man off as in Bertrand Russell's essay, from the rest of the universe; actually he is a "brother to the insensible rock." There is indeed a gradient: there is much in men that fights and must fight for its own life. But the trouble is that we do not know when this involves fighting for liberation and when it involves fighting against man's nature. A familiar example: man's long struggle in many cultures against sexuality, in the name of purity or spirituality, has often created an artificial division in his na-

ture, and ultimately produced a self-deception and self-hate
which has poisoned the soul.

By learning to accept his place in the world man can better realize his nature. To prejudge what this place is, to prejudge how
his potentialities are related to the inscrutable laws and meaning
of the universe, is as fatal a mistake as to assume in advance
either a classical dualism (the doctrine that mind and matter are
utterly different) or a classical monism (the doctrine that mind
is simply an expression of matter). Both of these doctrines are
probably false. A serious philosophy of man's ways of fulfilling
his nature must be as skeptical and as deep-probing in its quest
to understand the structure of the universe as in its quest to understand man's own nature.

Some will say at this point that we have come to a wall of un-
knowables, the scaling of which is nothing but a prophet's folly.
But we shall get further in the long run by stating our program
in tentative but positive terms: that man, being of the stuff of
which the universe is made, whatever that stuff may ultimately
prove to be, may have deep affinities with it, deep resonance to it,
deep isomorphism with it; inevitably a tendency to become, as
microcosm, what it is as macrocosm, at least in many fundamental
respects, and so realize his nature more and more as he discovers
the nature of cosmic structure and cosmic movement. If, of course,
the cosmos is nothing but a matter of movements of masses according to gravitational and other pulls, the view of human nature could hardly become more than the view of the ancients
that man might, as it were, learn to hear the "harmony of the
spheres" or might make some trivial use of the mechanical attributes of this world about him. If, however, our concern is with
the biology, the physics and the chemistry of man's frame and
function, and with that psychophysiological function which we
call his mind, self, or personality, the attempt could be made to
find the nature of his being *in* this unknown stuff which microscope, test tube, and the instruments of the future will reveal.

In terms of the thesis developed here, this would be far indeed
from deriving man from a "physical" or "materialistic" law.
Rather, the meaning of the physical and of the material (if these
terms are preserved) would be compared with the meaning
which we discover in our own life of values and purposes, and the

attempt would be made to see what the ultimate dependence of each reality may be upon other types of reality. If, as we have pleaded, there are basic trends in nature which have worked themselves out in the evolutionary process, these trends have utilized such stuff as was at hand. The basic laws of physics, chemistry, biology, and so on have, so to speak, simply exploited the stuff and the processes which were available for the completion of their own dynamic. In John Masefield's words: ". . . something that the things not understood make for their uses out of flesh and blood." To say that man's material structure has caused him to have such and such specific psychological attributes is very much like saying that a man must be five feet, nine inches tall because these are the clothes which he has to wear. Actually, the suit, the stuff embodying the basic laws of nature, is at hand to respond to the basic forces.

Take, for example, the principle of adaptive radiation mentioned above. This principle presumably applies regardless of the specific forms of life involved. Indeed, as we tried to show above, it holds even for inorganic realities of various sorts. From such a viewpoint the general dynamic of development on the face of the earth logically *precedes* rather than follows the specific biochemical and physiological events; the biochemical and physiological events are *expressions* of a broad dynamic which includes both cosmic trends and human trends, both being ultimately the expressions of the same requirements. To understand man more fully is, therefore, to understand more of the nature of the cosmos and vice versa. It is likely (as Edith Cobb so brilliantly shows in her forthcoming studies) that the tiny child, long before he can verbalize, resonates to cosmic patterns with a deep sense that this is basically he himself; long before there is a socially defined self he senses a rhythm, a dynamic pattern in the world which he also senses in an isomorphic form within himself. To the rhythms and cadences of sound about him, he makes a re-echoing response through his own limbs and his own vocalizations, not through an instinct of imitation, but because he is of the same stuff as the world. The *Aspects of Form* in the world, described in the volume by L. L. Whyte, are the aspects both of galaxies of crystals, of impulses, and of perceptual responses. There is an empathic response not only to the human but to the subhuman realities about him, catching and maintaining those rhythms and patterns, large or small, which make up the visible texture of the universe.

This visible texture we are only beginning to understand. The world of the electron microscope is beginning to reveal the vast complexities which underlie the structure of the world. Man can realize his potentialities through catching and making the most of the potentialities which cosmic structure permits. He can, however, at the same time, within his own limitations, alter cosmic structure insofar as his own nature may be able to make minor variations in the nature of the rhythms or processes which he sees fit to call natural law.

He can fulfill himself, of course, by the principle of emergence —by complicating nature far more than it has ever been complicated before. Just as the brain of man, for example, is an elaboration of biochemical and neurophysiological realities to a degree very much more intricate than is known to exist anywhere else in the universe, so it is entirely possible that man's psychological and social nature may represent refinements and elaborations, cosmic potentialities, cosmic trends as yet unparalleled elsewhere in the knowable universe.

This does not, however, preclude the possibility that the very discovery of these complexities may throw light back into the mirror of life in such a way as to suggest a dynamic, a rhythm and a law in a natural process which was not earlier glimpsed. After all, this is the kind of universe that made man. Whatever lies beyond that universe or within the latticework of its own textures, unknowable to science as it now exists, may well prove to be intelligible to a far greater degree as man becomes aware to a far greater degree of the subtleties and complexities within his own nature. There is no longer any place for the "nothing but" kind of explanation of man. In no branch of science has the "nothing but" method proved successful in recent decades; it is a poor method in the biological sciences and poorest of all, indeed, in the case of man.

In summary, although we cannot set limits upon human potentialities or tell what can and cannot come into existence, it seems a fairly reasonable principle to say that what will come into existence will mirror, because it basically represents, the inherent moving predispositions within cosmic structure. This, of course, will not tell us which of the particular kind of cosmic movements will next occur or will supervene in any given era. This is, however, somewhat different from the rather vague conception that man might become almost anything. And far from believing, with the Aristotelian school of thought, that it is simply the business of man to realize his own nature, our thesis would be that there are many possible natures within him from which he must *freely* choose; there is no law of self-sufficient entelechy or self-fulfillment which could act in the manner of "hard determinism." Rather, the potential self-fulfillments lie scattered there beyond the horizon; and man, with all the wisdom which he can marshal, must strive to define them—and then to choose among them.

Chapter 17:

The Human Natures of the Future*

In the preceding two chapters an attempt was made to show that the realization of human potentialities involves a much deeper understanding than we now possess of the relation between man and his environment. If we ask regarding anything that any man or any historical epoch ever saw, felt, or did, or anything that any man or any epoch ever will see, feel, or do, the answer is always, "Yes. *All* this is human; man is *all* that; but he is *infinitely more.*"

I am now going to attempt a freer sketch of the potentialities of man, borrowing again from the thoughts of Kurt Lewin. For it was the genius of Kurt Lewin that gave us the most appropriate tools for analyzing this problem of the diversity of human natures and the correlative problem of the flexibility, the range, the potentialities of human natures, both as they may take shape in the world of today and as future human societies may know them. Rather than inviting approval by emphasis upon the solid facts which today are at our command, I will endeavor by a sort of stretch-out method, a sort of "testing the limits," to see how far we can move in the direction of charting the unchartable domain of the potentialities latent within human society and within the individual personality.

* Most of the material of this chapter first appeared in the Kurt Lewin Memorial Address, presented to the Society for the Psychological Study of Social Issues in 1953 and published in the *Journal of Social Issues*, No. 7, 1953.

Let us begin with the fact, already noted, that nothing is in-herited, nothing acquired; everything is the realization through the environment of a specific potentiality permitted by the genes; or, if you prefer, the realization by the genes of a potentiality permitted by the environment.

Let us go on from this to the self-evident, yet shocking fact that in my experience nothing springs from *me*, and nothing from my environment, but everything from the interaction, the "life space" in which I, as a person, navigate.

We can visualize this state of affairs by imagining a large cir-cle *S* to represent the situation acting upon a man at a given time and a large circle *O* to represent himself, the living organism.

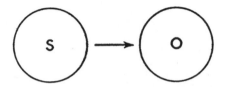

Instead of saying now that the situation acts upon the organism, it will appear more correct to say that certain aspects of the situa-tion act upon certain aspects of the organism. And, indeed, the specific aspects of *S* that are to be involved depend on what *O* is present; and the specific aspects of *O* that are to be involved depends on what *S* is present. There are, then, certain aspects of *S* and *O* which mutually select one another, which, so to speak, pull upon one another and create a field, create a new region, which we can visualize as a large shaded ellipse. We shall say now that the psychological reality is not the *organism*, for part of it is not active at the time, nor is it even the organism in relation to the situation, for neither all the organism nor all of the situation is involved. Our interest is in the area which encircles the inter-action of *S* and *O*.

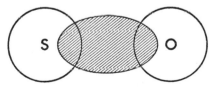

In any type of personal or social analysis, it is always reciproc-ity, mutual selection, the creation of a new unity that is involved. This does not mean that the life history of the individual is a chameleon-like response to situational changes. In all such analysis, the life-continuity of O is presupposed, and it is only O himself, not somebody else. The changes in O, based on O's life history, interact in this case with the succession of situational possibilities. One might, if one liked, write a history of the situations which have surrounded the person: a sort of reverse of the ordinary obverse which we undertake in writing a biography. Indeed, we might learn much from doing this. Better, however, in trying to develop the skill to tell the story of a man, would be the study of the mutuality of person and situation, a biography which is as full, as intimate, as human with reference to the forces that work on the person as with reference to the inner world which constitutes himself as person.

Such a point of view is of intense practical importance if we are to try to do what Julian Huxley did in his incisive *Man in the Modern World*—namely, to foresee what various environments will be appropriate for the biologically changing human family and what kind of biological responses will be made to these successive environments. We cannot plan, Huxley says, for man as he now exists as a biological entity, because in the planning of events at some distance in time he will be different. And indeed it is the social changes that we envision that will be largely responsible for the biological changes which appear through different matings, different nutrition, etc., at a later period. We have to do the two jobs at once—the social planning, the biological planning—each being relative to the other.

Actually, I have attempted above to go further than Huxley, since I disagree with his principle that the "main" evolutionary future of mankind is social. I see no reason to deny the continuous and even accelerated biological evolution of man, both as result of the social forces at work in the world today and as result of increasing understanding and application of genetic knowledge. The field principles which I have sketched above would apply in point of fact to the engineering of social changes even without reference to biological changes. That is to say, a field principle is involved in trying to define genuine satisfactions and opportunities for the release of potentials for men as they will be in another era. And instead of extrapolating man—as he now exists—to be acted upon by new cultural forces, we shall have to imagine a continuous succession of forces acting upon new men. Our imaginations, in other words, will be stretched to the uttermost even without reference to the principle of biological changes running concurrently with the social changes.

Fortunately, we are not without parallels for the task. The five-year planners, the long-range city planners, the agricultural and engineering planners must often ask themselves how they are to effect changes in something which will not come into existence for a long time ahead, and to try to see, like a captain on a pitching and rolling ship, where a projectile fired at this moment and subject to action of the wind will land in relation to invisible and distant enemy ships moving in a zigzag line more or less oblique to that of the motion of his own vessel. All these types of thinking have become a matter of course in pure and applied science, economics, business, politics, and even to some degree ordinary family budget planning; they are the core of modern "programming."

The issues presented here, however, are of a different order, not only in terms of greater complexity but in terms of a certain fuzziness in the raw material itself which is supposed to be undergoing the transformations. The situation is not altogether unlike Alice's croquet game, in which the mallets are flamingos, the balls hedgehogs, the wickets bent-over soldiers, any of them likely at any moment to change their minds and desert their roles. Indeed, the common snide remark, "You can't change human nature," would, if we could half believe it, become a great comfort in the croquet game of the sort with which we are now concerned.

The short-range planners generally make the mistake of holding too many things constant. They say "other things being equal," but of course they are not. The long-range planners, on the other hand, make the mistake of assuming for the most part that human nature itself is a constant. Here I refer both to long-range social planning such as that of the Soviet Union, and to the writings of almost all science fictioneers, who make humanity a constant through eons of time, though the physical habitat in which they dwell is utterly transformed. Those that will let their imaginations run away with them in regard both to fantastic inventions and to fantastic changes in human nature are far wiser. They may be completely wrong as predictors; this is not the point. If a few little efforts are made, here and there, to begin thinking about the range of *possibilities*, there will be raw material to sketch out, as in a great chess game, some preliminary questions, so that better players than ourselves can ultimately develop a strategy.

• *The Lewinian Life-space*

We are now ready to cast these rather abstract forms of thought back into the reality of daily living and to use the mode of thinking associated with Kurt Lewin. Much of what has been said in this book will here be recapitulated with a new accent.

The first fundamental conception is that of the *life-space,* the experienced totality of the individual, comprising a fluid yet indissoluble unity between the experiencing self and the experienced world without, and comprising not only the clearly conscious but likewise the half-conscious and unconscious dispositions and attitudes which color and give meaning to all that is experienced. This conception has proved to be a remarkably flexible, subtle, and productive tool in research thinking, and if I develop it in a somewhat unorthodox fashion, I shall make my plea that this is the very virtue of flexibility and remember with affection and gratitude the way in which Kurt Lewin sat and laughed when speakers challenged his findings or rejected his theoretical constructs.

Much of what follows is very familiar, but here it will appear in a perspective rather different from what is current in psychology. Ordinarily we begin our accounts of human nature very much as Aristotle or Thorndike did—by assuming an "original nature" which is intrinsic, implicit, needing only to be guided into one form or another by processes of growth and learning. Growth and learning can lure into being whatever is potential in the inner stuff of humanity, but nothing more. Most of the environmentalists shift the accent to an educational process and show how man may become what the social environment dictates, for the social environment is usually conceived as acting upon an essentially formless human nature. Here and there, as in the writings of James Harvey Robinson and Gordon Allport, there has been a glimpse of man's endless becoming. It is my own prejudice, however, to believe that this last conception is still somewhat handicapped by a Platonic idea of intrinsic human nature as something guiding human destiny and that it needs the benefit of field theory to achieve coherence and credibility in an era in which both man and his environment need to be seen not as two realities but as two phases of *one reality*. The result would be literally the discovery of a new human nature.

The world which we might first examine is the world of music. Katydids, frogs, birds, and men exploit devices by which parts of their bodies vibrate, giving off sweet sounds, perhaps attracting females, showing off, or at least beguiling a swampy or sultry evening. Where does this music come from? Often from the throat. Apes find, however, that drums may augment the body, and preliterate man may accompany the vocal cords with pipes or strings. Some voices, and some strings, sound better than others and, by common consent, the singer and the instrumentalist appear on the scene. So our first conclusion might be that man, to supplement his glottis, has invented vibrating strings; from these in time come harps, pianos, violins.

But while inventing vibrating strings, he has also been inventing the art of playing upon the strings; he invents the process of plucking or rubbing, and of combining the strings with one another and with the voice. He invents partly to please himself, but partly also because other men enjoy it too; Saul wants to hear David play, and today we gladly pay to watch and listen while a hundred men, to the rhythm of a stick waved in the air, scrape horsehair fibers upon catgut strings or swell their cheeks to push air through brass tubes while deft fingers lengthen or shorten the appropriate air column.

Do our textbook accounts of the so-called "basic drives" seem able to carry the weight of explaining these experiences? Are these experiences merely derivatives, by sublimation or the like, of simple visceral drives or instrumental acts which derive their inherent quality of fulfillment from the fact that they lead into other activities which in themselves bring satisfaction? To Schubert, and to many of us, too, music is not only a preparation for other good things but a good thing in itself.

Where, in the course of evolution, did music arise? From the survival value of response to tone? From the elaboration of techniques that fulfill the visceral drives? Or perhaps from the elaboration of human experience itself into a new dimension? I think the last of these statements, though excessively vague as it stands, may be a move in the right direction. Let us try, then, to discover something more definite regarding such new dimensions of human experience.

The usual analysis stops before it even makes contact with the problem, for the usual way of thinking anchors the music of the violin at some point in the body—the fingers or the ears or the viscera—whereas the fact seems to be that we make music as much with our brains and our muscles or even, if it be great music, with our scalps, our spines, and our skins. Or it anchors the music in the instrument. Of course the violinist's tone was good, we say, for he played a Stradivarius. But I can make no sounds on a Stradivarius that you would willingly hear. Then, we may say, it is not just the instrument but the virtuoso in relation to the instrument. But this will not serve either, for the instrument and the virtuoso alike represent a phase of human culture in which complicated operations carried out on a hollow wooden instrument with resonating strings have taken on certain rich meanings located neither in the instrument nor in the individual, nor in the relations of the two, but in a complex interpersonal invention known as violin music.

Now my thesis is very simple—and to a reasonable psychologist, very shocking. If it is katydid nature to scrape, frog nature to croak, warbler nature to warble, it is human nature to play the *Air for G String* on a Stradivarius. To reply that the last named of these is a learned activity whereas the others are innate is not relevant, because the whole question is what sorts of things does any species *tend to learn;* what are the lines of development which it follows when it does what it wants to do? To talk about the infinite variety of human cultures is also irrelevant. Even if we assume that culture is infinitely flexible, we still have to face the question of the range of human potentialities. We must locate the individual human being, with all his complex organs, tissues, and learning readinesses, in the picture, not outside of it. The real problem is the range of conceivable possibilities

for human nature in which we allow for all possible transactions between persons and conceivable environments, neither
the persons nor the environments being the absolute arbiters of
what may happen but rather the modes of reciprocal interdependence that might develop between them.

This conception is what is missing from most of the Utopias.
They devise an ideal society which would satisfy the known demands of the humanity that we now know to exist in terms of
existing or recent cultural arrangements. But even if the trick
could be done, there would be no way to stop that evolution of
the interrelations of man and culture that goes on because human beings are human and won't stay put; a Utopia which would
fit the men of today would be insipid or become a strait jacket
to the men of tomorrow. The problem is to try to envision not
the society that would satisfy the men of today but the forms
of potential interrelations that might exist between potential
men and potential environments. It is not that the one must be
made, Procrustes-like, to fit the other but that among the organic
potentialities and the cultural potentialities those that might fit
must, through reflection and social experimentation, be selected.

It is easy at this point to say in despair that we might ultimately
develop a science of persons and, perhaps long after that, a science
of environments, but that it is unthinkable that there ever could
be a science permitting prediction and control, relating to interactions of persons and environments. But this despair may, as
we shall see, derive from insufficient attention to the development of several sciences which attempt a similar task, and in
particular, from inattention to some phases of psychology which
are already oriented in this fashion.

• *Human Potentialities in Terms of Fields*

In the specification of a field science of human potentialities,
the first step, I suggest, is quantitative, the second qualitative;
the third relates to the addition of new elements, and the fourth
is configurational.

The *quantitative* changes are changes in alertness, range of
information, skill, sensitivity—indeed, all the measurable attributes of personality. If the young men and women of today are,

as is very probable (p. 219), taller than their parents, they may likewise be brighter; perhaps it is a nutritional matter, perhaps a matter of exploiting more thoroughly the abilities latent in the tissues. In any event, we should be prepared to think of the humanity of a few generations hence as considerably altered from that which we know today. Whether one thinks of genetic factors or cumulative cultural changes or both, there is every reason to believe that now that we have discovered the art of measuring one another, we shall find that the measurements change with time.

In the matter of *qualititative changes,* we might draw examples from the arts and from science and technology. From Cimabue and Giotto to Leonardo and Michelangelo, the time span was about five generations—not much time in terms of cultural evolution. It was enough time, however, to transform Byzantine flatness into Masaccio's three-dimensional and tactual qualities, to transform dull, hard colors into molded tints and shades that tell of enchanted landscape, women of unearthly beauty, and the divine majesty of a world conceived beyond the clouds; time enough to turn stolid, sober faces to faces that challenge you and threaten you, escape from you, plead with you, and show mercy to you. No one man did this. What happened was essentially like a conflagration kindled by a spark. In every city where the transformation went on—Florence, Siena, Perugia, Milan, Venice—the feeling for richer experience guided the accumulation of skill, and as the skills were mastered, new enthusiasms, new realities to be grasped and represented, were defined. You read at the foot of a painting not the name Sandro Botticelli but the careful collector's scrupulously reserved annotation: "From the School of Botticelli." They learned to mix and spread paints as the master did just as they learned to see as the master did. It has been regarded by many as a scandal that some of the immortal Rembrandts were painted by his pupils. Why so? The flame caught in the ready fuel, as it had in Italy. Rembrandt did more than add range; he added depth of perception.

In music the same social development of a unique new human experience is very evident, as, for example, in the Vienna of the period from Haydn to Schubert and Beethoven. In philosophic efforts one may similarly scan the era from Thales to

Aristotle, or in literature the Romantic period, or in science the period from the whetted curiosity of Faraday and Maxwell to the passionate devotion of the Curies. In all these experiences, I would suggest there is much more than the logical fulfillment of a trend once set going by a genius; there is the development of a transmissible quality of new experience, which then is further enriched as it is further transmitted. There is no single quality that gives fulfillment to the trend; rather, as one watches the development of painting in each of the North Italian cities of the Renaissance, or of biology from the school of Cuvier to the pupils of T. H. Morgan, there are as many qualities coming into existence as there are groups of human beings who have caught the excitement of seeing in a new way.

The point is that there is no meaning in the conception of fulfilling human potentialities by rounding out a man and making him perfect, for he becomes qualitatively a new man as he grows; and there is no such thing as a society which will offer fulfillment to human nature, for human nature and society are evolving together not only along a line indicating quantitative increase in this or that but into ever new qualities.

Perhaps some of the steps of qualitative transformation that are evident in the history of music and science may appear also in the growing individual. In our fascination with a purely quantitative approach to the process of learning, we have given singularly little attention to the need to observe, describe, and understand the qualitative changes of the person into something rich and strange. But we can open wide this area of research if we wish.

The *third* aspect of new experience relates to the discovery of new elements of experience, never known to human beings before. Industrial chemistry, for example, gives us a wealth of new color experiences yielded by no sunset, no geological formation, and new qualities of olfactory and tactual experiences; new musical instruments and new devices for altering the familiar instruments reach the sensitive ear and brain with a volley of unfamiliar tone. New drugs, new foods and drinks are also vehicles of new experience. Most of the new products, of course, are not viable, as is true also of most biological mutations. Man is not absolutely but only relatively free. But in the same sense in which Nature is creative, the mind of man is creative—namely, in the discovery of the qualitatively new.

In his *Politics* Aristotle remarked that "most things are known"; and that what is needed is not further knowledge but the application of existing knowledge. If one meditates for a moment on what was *really known* to the men of Aristotle's time— if one compares, for example, Aristotelian physics and Hippocratic medicine with the physics and medicine of today—one can match this self-assurance only with that of the mid-twentieth century, which believes that we have now at last discovered all the real essentials within human nature. Having watched the tides of sentiment that have moved so massively against many of the findings of psychoanalysis, of cultural anthropology, and of parapsychology, we may wonder whether the primary affect involved might not be the simple fear that we might find out something new about man. But defensive barriers of this type can be safely left to their encounter with the creative insistence of new evidence.

Our *fourth* principle is the configurational; it relates to the combination or reorganization of the familiar into new forms. The simplest verse or drawing represents the principle. Anthropologists tell us that even the major emotions are ordered in different fashion in different societies. Jules Henry finds that the usual inventory of emotions which we use to describe the affective life is insufficient to describe the experience of the Pilaga of the Gran Chaco. They have, for example, a type of experience which is neither fear nor rage but, as he names it, fear-rage. In similar vein, the muted rage which Karen Horney describes as characteristic of the child who dares not express or even *experience* hostility has its peculiar affective quality which, although related both to rage and to fear, is experienced as neither the one nor the other.

If this thinking regarding the reorganization of affect is in the right direction, we direct our affects at different cultural objects from those known to the men of the Mediterranean world, or even our great-grandparents of a pre-industrial order; and our affective life contains much which they never knew. I believe that as one reads of the attitudes toward children entertained in the Calvinist era in New England one may find oneself tempted to call these attitudes inhuman; in quite literally the same sense, our great-great-grandchildren, experiencing much of which we today know nothing, may quite as rightly refer back to us as inhuman—that is, not human in the sense of sharing the experience which they regard as human.

There are more complex examples of that class of new experience which I have called the configurational. Science, if we may borrow from Conant's absorbing essay on scientific history,[1] seldom consists of noting a fact not noted before; it consists of a process of relating, or the construction of a configuration. Now the relating is not just a matter of putting two external events together. The observer puts himself into the equation, simply because, as Einstein so well put it, there are no "privileged positions" from which observations can be made. As the philosophy of science and the sociology of knowledge make clear, the science which emerges is just as much a matter of the man as of the external event. Eddington reminds us of the sculptor who wagered that a figure of Galatea sat hidden in the marble block; and when he chipped away the outer husk that hid her, he showed her sitting there. The scientist has to have the chisel and the block of marble; he also has to have his own intellectual and emotional predispositions, or he will see nothing. So science, as it comes into being in any society, is more than a technique for chopping off a chunk of reality; it is an expression of a new man-nature interaction.

The same process which goes on in the arts and sciences goes on also in the quality of relationships which men establish with one another. Affection and trust, belief in the unrealized potentialities of other human beings, call into existence not only what is waiting to bud but what never could otherwise be; and others, responding in their turn, lift those who reach out to them to a level which they themselves could never have defined.

Shall we conclude, now, that these four classes of experience created and maintained by society are dependent upon the environment in such fashion that the individual reared within such a society must be daily reminded, reinforced, transfused with the

[1] J. B. Conant, *On Understanding Science: an Historical Approach,* Yale, 1947.

spirit of his environment, like a man in an iron lung, so to speak, depending for his existence on external arrangements? In a sense yes, in a sense no. Yes, insofar as the man shining with a light whose source is gone shines with less and less conviction, like the great Venetian painters after the bright light of the Renaissance had begun to fade; but no, insofar as any great experience from the past, whether in philosophy or in the arts or in science or in the relationship of men to one another or to the unseen may reach across a thousand years and requicken the men of a later era. Essentially, however, the answers both show plainly that the new experiences depend on a complex field of interpersonal realities and that men in the group achieve experience-qualities which lie not within the skin of the individual as potentialities waiting to be tapped, in the way in which a firecracker has the potentiality of going off when ignited, but rather within a relationship between what is inside the skin and what is outside it; in other words, in the *life-space.*

Even within the lives of those present there may emerge new and significant types of human experience which are functions of newly discovered ways of organizing our group life. In the physical sciences this creation of the new is taken as a matter of course. Mendeléev proved once and for all that there could be only ninety-two elements in a perfect "periodic table." He was right—that is, under the conditions which he knew. But in the electric furnace, there are more, and in these days of isotopes, one comment might be: "What do you mean 'elements'?" Much which cannot exist can exist when the circumstances of its existence are altered.

The quality of interpersonal relations is again much more than a compounding of the qualities of persons in relation to milieu. No list of the biological components in human nature or even of the components arising in the mold of culture is adequate for the purposes of prediction. The conception of personality represented by field theory envisages the appearance of attitudes, outlooks, feeling tones which were never released before and which go on proliferating into amazing new forms. Social inventions of all sorts, arising from a combination of curiosity, the gain motive, persistence, the ability to scrape up capital, can turn the social order upside down, introducing qualities of life which are nothing like the ingredients that went into the recipe.[2]

• *Using What We Are*

Human potentialities are given by the *action* of that which sleeps within us upon the unformed potentialities of the world. As David Levy has shown, interference with activity is as dire a blow to health as interference with nutrition. Bela Mittelmann has pointed out that the activity needs are indeed as fundamental as is the nutritive need. We are provided with a complex set of organic equipment, and if it is not allowed to function, something

[2] In the Kurt Lewin address in 1953 I included the following paragraph which has an odd ring today. Some of the predictions are already painfully fulfilled; others sound already like the nightmare of another era.

I received in the mail an ad of a device known as "choosit" which makes it possible to pull into my television set any one of hundreds of recorded operas, plays, prizefights, skating races. Note the following from the *American Psychologist* for July 1957:

"Some readers may be interested to learn the history of the present craze for psychodiagnostic novels. Beginning in April, 1955, Archibald Ribber of Pocatello, Idaho, began to stay at home evenings to hear the operas over his Choosit set. Each member of the family wanted to see a different thing. So Archie squelched Junior who wanted to see Hopalong Cassidy when the set was tuned for Traviata; Junior in turn squelched his baby sister, who, not being content with squelching the cat, developed psychosomatic allergies. Her mother took her to a clinical psychologist at the university, who gave both mother and daughter the Rorschach. When Archie heard this, he went to work to develop a method of administering the Rorschach over TV which could be scored and interpreted for you for free by the Scrubbo hour if you can correctly rearrange the three words: suds Scrubbo makes. This new way of getting oneself diagnosed over TV resulted in such a degree of public sophistication regarding psychology that the new type of literature which is known as mass psychodiagnosis has been rapidly displacing the whodunit literature at the drugstores. In the meanwhile the interest in this literature in Japan, Norway, Northern Rhodesia, and Burma has produced a marked increase in interest in American culture, and the overseas libraries have been forced for security reasons to allow only those psychodiagnostic novels which have been written by authors who have been analyzed by analysts who have been cleared by the FBI."

happens to us, just as in using it we find joy. If we have tissues within us which through learning and thinking develop and enrich us, we shall in the same way find joy both in the new and in the old activities and in the process of learning and thinking. If thinking becomes a group-supported activity, we may, like the Athenians, foregather just to think, as the Icelanders foregather to play chess, or the Germans to make music. In the long run, the use of the brain, if not pre-empted entirely by the sheer process of keeping alive or keeping up with the Joneses, leads, over the centuries, to more and more exquisite cultural products. Those, according to my thesis, which supervene after ten generations of cumulative thought are just as directly and fundamentally an expression of human nature as breathing or eating. Because man has this rich potentiality for sensory, motor, intellectual experience, and has to combine all this in fresh acts of cultural creativeness, he is doing nothing more than realizing these potentialities when he writes Macbeth or flies a plane at Kitty Hawk. And it is not only human to invent oneself out of one world into another; it is also human to keep moving toward a destination which is not set within man's present nature but keeps changing as the nature of his environment changes. The biocultural reality keeps rolling up on itself.

Now if we once make up our minds that there is a vast and challenging area of human potentialities, we may view the issue either passively or actively. The passive attitude would involve delight and bemusement, expressed by ordinary mortals in terms of *ohs* and *ahs,* and by the poet, as for example by Shelley in *Prometheus Unbound,* in terms of a ravishing ecstasy of joyous anticipation of man's future. The active attitude would be embodied in a quest for definite principles governing the discovery and release of these potentialities. Not being a poet, and being somewhat constrained by the responsibility of emphasizing a thinking rather than a feeling approach, I will now attempt to sketch out a few principles which I believe may help to point the way and may be tested, experimented with, and replaced by better ones.

I would begin this task by asking what good teachers, parents, group leaders, clinicians actually do to release the potentialities of those whose development they cherish. First of all, good teachers seem to me to be concerned with more than helping to fit a child into a socially specified pattern; they seem to be on the watch for the reaching out, the sense of exploration, the insatiable curiosity, the urge to new experience, the delight in manipulation and mastery of new media. Those who conceive of education in terms of systematic mastery of all that one's culture has achieved, as for example in the incorporation within oneself of the one hundred great books or the great central ideas of western civilization, seem to be missing something very fundamental; indeed, I fear that the very heart is missing. For the heart, as I see it, is the demand of the person for life, the nourishment and the enrichment of what he already is.

The great teachers whom I have known are forever alert to the fact that the individual, whether two or twenty years old, can tell us more about his unrealized potentials than can any norm prepared in any office. There will, indeed, develop in him in time a need to share experience with his fellows and with the men and women of other regions and other periods; but these likewise will be richly and rapidly released if the teacher watches for their beginnings and feeds the flame with good tinder rather than attempting in advance to determine the directions to be taken. It takes a good deal of faith in the raw human stuff to do this; but those who have watched good teaching will agree that it can be done. In the same way the parent will let the child tell him where his tastes, his loves, his demands upon life lie. The parent will supply restraints and disciplines primarily when the child is defeating his own ends, especially when the child is clearly showing, as most children do sooner or later, that he actually wants goals, order, and a sense of direction rather than chaos. But it will be his first concern that the child live in the child's own idiom before he be asked to understand the idiom of others.

The same holds true for college education and for graduate schools. It may seem that the older a person is, the less able he is to tell us where the creative spark in him lies. Fill him up with the standard psychology that is good for him, we say; make him choose a dissertation problem that will teach him the nature of science. In the course of some thirty years of watching this process, I have seen the creative impulse of many students muted, and

I cannot think of anyone who was made into a creative scientist by such pressures. The discipline of sound method, scientific caution, respect for solid facts will come if there is a little seed which in time can be nourished into such a flower. But if we deny our students the right to explore and to speculate, they will in time play by the rules in their own specialty and dogmatize all over the lot in every other area of life. If we do not respect what the language of the organism tells us, we can learn only the hard way—namely, in sterile science and in the soured personalities whom we have created. Those of us who have watched the so-called "raising of standards" pursued in an impersonal spirit, and the cut-throat competition imposed upon students for grades (*e.g.,* in the attempt to make out of graduate students of psychology something that they have no desire to become), will hardly be surprised when you encounter a man who has been so thwarted and misdirected that he cannot even be civil with a frightened patient, or free himself from moralistic clichés when he finds a child unable to face its own aggressions or insecurities.

• *The Discovery of Individual Potentialities*

The first of the principles of permitting the discovery of human potentialities, then, is to take them where you find them. But a more systematic theoretical answer involves five principles, the first two negative, the other three positive.

First, note that in the equipment of man there are some needs so simple that they cannot to any considerable degree be culturally complicated into progressively richer satisfactions. The maintenance of body temperature is one, the maintenance of oxygen tension another. You can get delight from warmth when you are cool and from coolness when you are warm, but it is difficult to build symphonies out of such experiences. The idea of fulfilling human potentialities by simply *giving the individual all he needs* runs afoul of the fact that many of the needs just disappear when gratified, and nothing more can be done.

The second negative principle is to avoid overemphasizing the competitive. Competition is not always bad, but it frustrates and benumbs most of those who fail and, for those who succeed, it can at best give only the ever iterated satisfaction of winning again.

This may destroy the ability to risk failures for the sake of attempting new and more interesting goals. In the direction of competition lies, of course, a convenient way of maintaining a status-minded society; but I am speaking of something quite different—namely, the release of human potentialities.

Now for my three positive principles. First, study within the equipment of mankind the satisfactions that are capable of *progressive development*. Look at the sensory equipment, which the history of the arts shows to be capable of practically limitless variety, and which, in combination with the affective experiences linked with sensory qualities and their combinations, can evoke creativity in many lives. It is sometimes asked, "After all, what proportion of the general public can become seriously concerned with the arts?" Many Indian villages channel the creative energies of a large proportion of their boys and girls into the making of beautiful things; whole communities in Germany and Austria have grown up with a craving for and skills in music. Sandlot baseball, sidewalk hopscotch, and radio mysteries can all give something to the growth of boy and girl; but it is not clear that they necessarily give more to the fulfillment of human nature than many other satisfactions which cover the face of the earth and which have, as a matter of fact, grown like mushrooms when once encouraged, until blocked by the competitive spirit as incarnated in power struggles, militarism, an overlong working day, status anxiety, or some other circumstance alien to the need we are now considering—namely, the need for rich and progressively richer experience.

The second of my positive principles grows out of the first; it is that new potentialities are realized not so much by passive exposure to culture as by *active effort at self-fulfillment*. The venture into the new, and the return to the old with fresh understanding, are among the satisfactions everywhere known to common people in the form of proverbs, adages, plays upon words, and plays upon life. At a higher level comes the mastery of principles or laws—for example, the laws governing a radio set or an internal-combustion engine, which most boys love to master, and the manipulative skills of the artisan or the engineer. So, too, from the primitive satisfactions in early companionship and understanding one may pass to the satisfying worlds of the nurse, the teacher, the clinician, who delight both in the people with whom they work and in the self-enhancement that comes from a job well done. There is an unlimited range of human potentialities that can be released when one recognizes the danger signs set up by the two negative principles mentioned above, and notes both the sensory factors and the activity factors that can be exploited if once we let the growing organism tell us the directions in which it is seeking understanding and mastery.

But there is a final principle that calls for emphasis. In addition to the sensory messages to the brain, the fusion of sensory with affective qualities, the delights of smooth-running activity, there is the huge resonance chamber which we call the vital organs or viscera. In addition to the specific functions in the service of life, and their intimate relation to the obvious drives which every textbook defines and emphasizes, they serve to give a rich and continuous accompaniment to the themes that attract our greater attention. We feel well or ill, friendly or hostile, confident or cautious, grateful or resentful, reflective or active, partly by virtue of the endless circuits from higher centers to visceral patterns; indeed, the effects of everything, from drugs to music, are being studied in terms of the physiological rhythms that bespeak the ebb and flow of our feeling tone. But we are finding, as in the case of the world of sight and sound, that there is no limit to the range and complexity of new experience that may come in this way. We are, in fact, less and less sure that there is any basic difference between these interoceptive experiences initiated within the body and the experiences initiated outside the body (through our seeing and hearing) to which psychology has given so much attention. There is a limitless area for the psychologist in the exploration of these interoceptive processes, and for humanity at large as they are systematically described and used. In the Western world, at least, our practice has been to wait for some odd chance to yield a new experience, toying with drugs, for example, or trying to rig up a technique through hypnosis or yoga. Our whole attitude toward our own insides has hardly been serious. When the artist or musician gives us new experience, our attention is upon the art form, the medium of communication, not upon the realms of inner self-realization that are thrown open. But if the men in Rembrandt's school actually felt a sense of unity with other men by learning to look through the master's eyes, they became organized as new men, not simply as new painters.

In the interconnectedness of all that we are, the Aeolian harp upon which the world of beauty, of love, and of challenge perpetually plays yields blends in which no component can be sharply separated out; and if there is sexuality in the response to music—as there often is—there is likewise a powerful contribution from sensory beauties in the full measure of the erotic. No single drive could ever pre-empt the orchestration of the total without leading us back to a simple catalogue of independent drives, waiting each by itself to be fulfilled, which we earlier rejected as an unworkable picture of human nature.

If we think, therefore, of love and sublimation in these expanded terms, which are indeed not essentially different from those suggested by Socrates in Plato's *Symposium,* you will perhaps come to the conclusion that the enrichment of the qualities of love is a good goal for those who believe that human potentialities can be expanded and deepened. This conception of love, however, to be broad enough to include the love of looking down a microscope to see a Brownian movement, or the love of discovering a rare record in a rummage sale, or the love of discovery of order, rhythm, and meaning in the world, is something rather close to Spinoza's intellectual love of God.

But to be consistent should we include all satisfactions—say, for example, the satisfaction of a good cigar, or of proving your case in an argument, or of not getting found out when putting on a big bluff? My criterion, from the viewpoint of the present study of human potentialities, would be simply this: do these latter satisfactions make one more sensitive to new experience? Do they enrich one's capacities? Do they lead on in turn to more and more, deeper and deeper satisfactions? If they do, I have nothing whatever against them. I have known, for example, a man who smoked his cigar in exactly this spirit of adventure. In general, however, most such satisfactions are dead ends, and although this is nothing against them, it means that in the long run they give us a great deal less than those that open areas of experience which, once open, keep opening out ever more *broadly.*

The heart of the human potential lies in that sensitive, flexible, creative, self-fulfilling deployment of perception, feeling, and impulse in which no single drive controls the architectural pattern; in which no single task of selection, discrimination, or action rivets the mind to any self-sufficient goal; but in which each activity, satisfying in itself, is an aspect of a larger activity—a phase of a plan, a phase of a life, a phase of the nexus of the lives of many. It is distinctively human to use what one has as a person, and this involves using the forms of understanding, remembering, imagining as well as the forms derived from the outer situation and the forms derived from inner impulse. The impulse life is not simply the life of instinct, however sublimated, however complicated, however enmeshed in other impulses. It is just as much a part of human nature to make discoveries and creative integrations as it is to crave cold water on a torrid day. And the life of knowing is not simply the life of perception or of memory, however much the individual perceptual response or active memory may entice the person at the moment. The need to find concepts, to understand the whole, leads to its own intense gratifications and fulfillments. To begin to realize human potentials is to utilize the whole sensitized system of the molded perceptual and intellectual habits.

The scientist as scientist, for example, however much the perception of a specific precipitate or wing-vein or spectroscopic shift may be involved, is freely deploying the cognitive apparatus as a whole and reveals his potentialities as a human being just insofar as he ceases to be stimulus-bound and becomes concerned with the broadest implications of what he does. In the same manner, the artist is most completely human when he transcends the utilization of line, surface, movement, or symbol and undertakes to render the fullness of the world as he sees it. The philosophical, religious, political, and other value-fulfilling phases of human life express the humanness of movement in the directon of integration—fluid, sensitive, ever changing integration as a step toward further integration.

There is not the slightest objection here to those types of reductionism which undertake to find the primitive components still subsisting in the more complex structure; only to those types of reductionism which deny the reality of the emergent

processes, the organic creativeness, and above all the free movement of mind as a whole as contrasted with part minds, part
impulses, and part acts.

Gratefully here we may use Aristotle's "movement toward fulfillment" or entelechy, the efforts of Gestalt psychology, of Kurt
Goldstein, of Gordon Allport, to find fulfillment in the wholeness of the living individual. Yet there is such a thing as showing
the self-sufficiency of man in overbold relief, so that he becomes
not more but less of a man. The sharpness of his separation
from other individuals can be overstressed. Indeed, through
sharp separation from his poem, his microscope, his church, his
political party, he becomes not more human but simply more
lonely and inadequate. It is the movement of men not out of
relation to but as fulfillment of the resources of the world that
constitutes the integration of the three human natures. The fulfillment of human potentialities lies not in separating the man
more cleanly from his world and enriching his implicit nature
by a finer inner differentiation. Rather, it consists in making
that implicit nature come to life through its necessary reciprocity
with that which is coming to life as it makes contact with man.
All transactions change both the parties to the transaction.

• Fulfillment Cannot Be Final

The task, therefore, of writing a serious essay on the fulfillment
of human potentialities consists largely of the capacity to perceive and describe the ways in which human nature transcends
and fulfills itself by moving beyond the specific components
which today constitute it. The fulfillment of all that man latently
is today would not be the fulfillment of human potentialities five
hundred years from now. Such a fulfillment can come only
through the reciprocity of inner and outer potentials working
toward an increasing wealth of climaxes in the production of
biosocial realities not implicit even in the most veiled form in
the stuff of man and his environment today. It will still, however, be fully human, in the same sense in which the life of today
is human; for no life, and least of all a human life, is fulfilled
by the satisfaction or saturation of any tendency in and for itself. Rather, the tendencies, whether cognitive, instinctual, or

impulsive, give rise to new biosocial interactions at higher levels of complexity, with richer and fuller perception, finer discrimination, more majestic imaginative integrations, more balanced control of the structure in which many impulses can without conflict realize a *personal* rather than simply an impulse-determined goal. At its simplest level the writing of a poem or the creation of a statue is a fulfillment in exactly this sense. The feeling of the futility of the poem or the statue as a fulfillment *of the person* is likewise evident. For a poem and a statue can be perfect; but the poet and the sculptor never reach permanent fulfillment. Once he has written the poem, he is a different man: he sees with different eyes.

The universe is, after all, greater than man and calls the tune as it undergoes its own evolution. Man will be stretched forever as he moves toward receptivity to that which the cosmos offers. For the point is that the discovery of the world brings into man's view and therefore into man's mind and heart new realities which become in time parts of the man. Insofar as the world can be known, either through the methods of science or through the methods of poetry, to take note of it, to respond to it, to digest it, to love it are all processes by which the nature of man is *transformed,* and unless science comes to an end by discovering all there is (which seems, to say the least, a grotesquely improbable outcome), we face, as long as we are human, an unlimited procession of discoveries.

• The Creation of New Human Natures

To say that man could be fulfilled by the completion of his own inner nature is to assume a strange out-of-tuneness between man and the stuff of this world. And that conception of science which represents man as genuinely capable of grasping certain aspects of the reality and moving slowly toward grasping ever more and more allows for a sort of deep-staining of the mind of the observer, selectively bringing out that which was hidden before the stain was used. Man's interaction with the things of this world through the methods of the arts and through the methods of science will produce more and more that is new in man as the centuries pass. The very process of interaction with that which was previously unknown produces new content, new stuff, new realities, new things to understand and to love, as well as new instruments of observation, new ways of knowing, new modes of esthetic apprehension. These, too, will change the nature of man, not simply by enriching that which lies under the threshold of his immediate nature but by broadening the doorway through which he passes, so that he may see more of the vista he approaches and may as he does so become always a larger man. It is because of man's capacity for intimate union with the stuff of this world through the methods of the arts and through the methods of science that he may hope to do more than to transcend himself, may hope to become in each new emergent phase of his life a new kind of man.

Lest our thesis should seem to have become obscure, let us say flatly here that we often look for human nature in the wrong place; we merely look inside the living system. We are trying, as it were, to get the golden eggs by killing the goose; or indeed by studying the pedigree of the goose we have hoped to find specifically where those eggs come from. Actually, they are not in the goose; they are not even in the life history of the goose or in the life history of geese on this planet. The golden eggs, or any products whatever which life yields, are in a sense the products of a system of events displayed and deployed through a vast system of forces. Indeed, life can be destroyed and any given avenue can be blocked, but to find the wellsprings of human nature by looking inside the capsule is to miss the field character of the event.

It may seem more effective to look for human nature in the existing societies, or in the present and past societies yielded by man's genius for social organization. This is, indeed, somewhat more effective, but not much. What has been realized at a given time has depended upon a wealth of specific time-determined and culture-determined events of which we know relatively few, and the plan or system of which we hardly understand at all. Even if "system theory" enables us to understand the potentialities within a given set of cultural organizations— such as determining what can and cannot be done by a Stone-Age culture as compared with a pre-Stone Age culture, or determining what can and cannot be done by a process of banking or a process of utilization of nonanimal power—we cannot extrapolate to the kinds of human nature which can and must exist when the present human nature interacting with the present and future forces in the universe have yielded a new human nature.

Regarding the field forces, we make a few discoveries every decade and still go on acting as if we thought there were no discoveries to make. The amazing range of chemical and bioelectric phenomena yielded in the last hundred years, the amazing new information about atomic structure which comes pouring in year by year certainly gives us a new system of environmental forces with which humankind must come to terms. Many of them, as we have already seen, certainly have direct effects upon genes; many others have limiting effects upon both genes and growth; many have an effect upon the extension and the variability of the gene-pool; and many of them, in interaction with cultural factors, specifically the organization of science and of medicine, are bound to determine in a major way within a few decades the evolutionary character, the direction, and the various kinds of sub-directions which human evolution can display. At a less tangible level, the types of social organization and particularly the types of value systems which are bound to respond to this new multidimensional flow of forces will yield kinds of human nature which it is not within the power of even the most prophetic to glimpse today. Our task, rather, is an attempt at a systematic and sober panoramic survey of the *kinds of directions which might be taken within the very large areas marked as unknown on the map.*

From such a way of thinking, the future seems to become even more difficult to divine than from a purely cultural viewpoint. It seems virtually certain that mankind, having created for itself a new environment and having undergone various transformations in the process, will not recognize itself in the mirror of a few thousand years hence. Against this, profound resistances will inevitably be mobilized, because we shall, insofar as we do effective planning, plan ourselves out of existence. It is doubtful, however, whether we shall plan ourselves out of existence any more rapidly than the Commercial and Industrial Revolutions have thrown out of existence the kinds of humanity which existed a few centuries ago or which industrial and technological developments are bound to produce with or without planning. There is no solution for the problem of our insecurities here. We must face them and make the alternatives as clear as we can, taking our chances with those forces in ourselves and in the cosmos about which we shall always remain insufficiently informed. We can only say that the more research we have and the more carefully we sift the evidence from present and future research, the less likely the creation of an internal contradiction, a self-defeating humanity, a humanity cultivating those attributes which we already know to be nonviable or productive of more distress than joy.

We have already asked what can be done about the huge blind spots which man has always created for himself. The problem is especially pressing when we ask what will happen when the "other side of the organism," the side which no culture has ever played upon, begins to be drawn into active play. We try to imagine events which involve the operation of natural laws which we cannot at present glimpse. Each era creates its own system of ideas, and new events which cannot be fitted into the scheme, such as the three-dimensional activities unintelligible to the Flatlanders, require either to be cast aside or to be reduced or forced into the existing scheme. Before the isolation of oxygen, for example, the phlogiston theory held sway,[3] even though decade by decade it became more and more obvious that the theory was unsound. The point was that no radically new way of conceiving the whole issue had been clearly formulated, and chemists would rather go on with a makeshift that was known to be wrong than work without some sort of conception.

We face the increasing probability that the system of science developed from the time of Galileo to that of Einstein will prove more and more inadequate as a fit for human nature, and in particular that the ideas of Darwin and Freud, magnificent and liberating as they are, will have their own hour in court and have to be replaced by radically different conceptions. We shall fight frantically against this, of course. But the entire world system—and man system, so to speak—will have to be refurbished.

[3] J. B. Conant, *op. cit.*

In our search for "science talent" we are not likely to search for those who look for the unusual or the impossible. In our Utopiologies we have small place for those who can go off at right angles from the known. It is not difficult to extrapolate the present changes in culture and to dream up a world of "man and superman"; and it will not be too difficult, on the basis of present biological data, to dream up a new picture of the biology of humankind. What will be difficult, however, will be the imagining of that kind of reciprocity between the new man and the new social order which will certainly be realized within a few centuries.

Is there any reason to end upon an optimistic note, despite the mess which humanity has been making of the world in the last few decades? There are two such reasons which lie in present attitudes toward science. First, we have somehow become less afraid of studying ourselves, looking straight at, through, and into ourselves; and without a great deal more knowledge of ourselves, and of the nature of our dependence upon one another, we can do but little in the realization of human potentialities. Secondly, if curiosity be the soul of science, curiosity is not only a tool in the discovery of needed truths; it is in itself one of those satisfiers that lead on and on to ever fresh delights. The hunger for discovery rather than practical gain was the mother of both science and philosophy, and though science today is often deflected from the satisfactions of curiosity into the production of competitive tools of many sorts, the flame of curiosity, once kindled, cannot be put out. One may feel that out of this era of political interference with science, and frequently of intimidation of scientists, no good can come, but there is another approach. Socrates had to drink the hemlock, and Giordano Bruno to die at the stake, but the stifling of the quest for understanding is a trick that no despot has ever fully mastered. If there is in mankind a potential love of his neighbor that can be nourished through centuries and become more and more a norm, which, however imperfectly, we strive to realize, there is also a potential craving to understand the world which, as fast as it is satisfied, broadens into a greater craving, works into new material, works in a richer and broadening fashion.

Such an approach would mean not simply the fulfillment of

the known biological nature of man or the elaboration of the known potentialities of culture but a constant probing of new emergent qualities and realities given by a system of relationships that can today hardly be glimpsed; a leaping into existence of new realms of experience; *not an extrapolation of the present, but new in kind.*

The realization of human potentialities lies in studying the directions in which human needs may be guided, with equal attention to the learning powers of the individual and the feasible directions of cultural evolution. The last thousand years have created a level of scientific and esthetic satisfaction which has already made human nature different today from what it was in the middle ages; yet this is merely a beginning. Even this much of an evolution has hardly commenced in the area of interpersonal relations, where modern psychology, including psychoanalysis, has shown us more about the roots of conflict and destructiveness among people than about the development of positive social feeling. If we cannot make rapid gains in the control of conflict, there will be no human future. But if we can, the future extension of scientific and esthetic interest, together with the evolution of greater capacity for satisfaction in relations between people, will not constitute a goal or a Utopia, but will define a widening theater for the development of new potentialities.

Bibliography

ALLEN, FREDERICK LEWIS. *The Big Change; America Transforms Itself: 1900-1950*. New York, Harper, 1952.

ARNHEIM, RUDOLF. *Art and Visual Experience: a Psychology of the Creative Eye*. Berkeley and Los Angeles, University of California Press, 1954.

ASHBY, W. R. *Design for a Brain*. New York, Wiley, 1952.

BESTER, ALFRED. *The Demolished Man*. Chicago, Shasta, 1954.

BROAD, C. D. *The Mind and Its Place in Nature*. London, Kegan Paul, and New York, Harcourt, 1925.

BROWN, HARRISON. *The Challenge of Man's Future*. New York, Viking, 1954.

CARINGTON, WHATELY. *Thought Transference*. New York, Creative Age, 1946.

CASSIRER, ERNST. *An Essay on Man: An Introduction to a Philosophy of Human Culture*. New Haven, Yale University Press, 1944.

CONANT, J. B. *On Understanding Science: An Historical Approach*. New Haven, Yale University Press, 1947.

DARWIN, CHARLES. *The Origin of Species*. London, 1859.

DAY, CLARENCE. *This Simian World*. New York, Knopf, 1920.

DIAMOND, SOLOMON. *Personality and Temperament*. New York, Harper, 1957.

DU NOÜY, LECOMTE. *Human Destiny*. New York, Longmans, 1949.

EDDINGTON, A. *The Philosophy of Physical Science*. New York, Macmillan, 1939.

FREUD, SIGMUND. *New Introductory Lectures on Psycho-analysis*. New York, Norton, 1933.

FROMM, ERICH. *Escape from Freedom*. New York, Farrar, 1941.

HOLT, E. B. *Animal Drive and the Learning Process*. New York, Holt, 1931.

HUXLEY, ALDOUS. *Brave New World*. New York, Harper, 1950.

HUXLEY, JULIAN. *Man in the Modern World*. New York, Universal, 1947.

HUXLEY, T. H. *Evolution and Ethics, and other Essays*. London and New York, Macmillan, 1894.

JAMES, WILLIAM. *The Will to Believe and other Essays in Popular Philosophy*. New York, Longmans, 1903.

KALLMAN, F. J. *Heredity in Health and Mental Disorder*. New York, Norton, 1942.

LANGER, SUSANNE. *Philosophy in a New Key*. Cambridge, Mass., Harvard University Press, 1951.

LEARY, LEWIS (Ed.). *The Unity of Knowledge,* Garden City, Doubleday, 1954.

LEWIN, KURT. *A Dynamic Theory of Personality*. New York, McGraw-Hill, 1935.

LOWES, J. L. *The Road to Xanadu*. Boston, Houghton Mifflin, 1927.

MANNHEIM, KARL. *Ideology and Utopia*. New York, Harcourt, 1936.

MEAD, G. H. *Mind, Self, and Society*. Chicago, University of Chicago Press, 1934.

MEAD, MARGARET. *New Worlds for Old*. New York, Morrow, 1956.

MORE, THOMAS. *Utopia*. 1519.

MULLER, H. J. *Out of the Night: A Biologist's View of the Future*. New York, Vanguard, 1935.

MULLER, HERBERT J. *Uses of the Past; Profiles of Former Societies*. New York, Oxford, 1952.

MUMFORD, LEWIS. *The Story of Utopias*. New York, Boni & Liveright, 1922.

NORTHRUP, F. S. C. *Science and First Principles*. New York, Macmillan, 1931.

OSBORN, FREDERICK H. *Preface to Eugenics*. New York, Harper, 1951.

RIESMAN, DAVID. *Individualism Reconsidered*. Glencoe, Illinois, Free Press, 1954.

RIESMAN, DAVID. *The Lonely Crowd*. New Haven, Yale University Press, 1950.

ROSSMAN, J. J. *The Psychology of the Inventor*. Washington, Inventors Publishing Co., 1931.

RUSH, J. H. *The Dawn of Life*. New York, Hanover, 1958.

RUSSELL, BERTRAND. *The Free Man's Worship*. Portland, Maine, Mosher, 1923.

SCHRÖDINGER, ERWIN. *What is Life? The Physical Aspect of the Living Cell*. New York, Macmillan, 1945.

SEIDENBERG, RODERICK. *Posthistoric Man*. Chapel Hill, North Carolina, University of North Carolina Press, 1950.

SIMPSON, G. G. *The Meaning of Evolution: A Study of the History of Life and of its Significance for Man*. New Haven, Yale University Press, 1950.

SOAL, S. G., and BATEMAN, F. *Modern Experiments in Telepathy.* New Haven, Yale University Press, 1954.

STAPLEDON, W. O. *To the End of Time.* New York, Funk & Wagnalls, 1953.

STEFANSSON, V. *Adventures in Error.* New York, McBride, 1936.

THOMSON, SIR GEORGE. *The Foreseeable Future.* Cambridge, Cambridge University Press, 1955.

TOYNBEE, ARNOLD. *A Study of History,* New York, Oxford, 1949.

WARNER, L. W., and LUNT, P. S. *The Social Life of a Modern Community* (Yankee City Series V. 1). New Haven, Yale University Press, 1941.

WEBB, W. P. *The Great Plains.* Boston, Houghton Mifflin, 1936.

WHITE, LYNN, JR. (Ed.). *Frontiers of Knowledge in the Study of Man.* New York, Harper, 1956.

WHYTE, LANCELOT L. *The Next Development in Man.* New York, Holt, 1948.

WHYTE, WILLIAM H., JR. *The Organization Man.* New York, Simon & Schuster, 1956.

WIENER, NORBERT. *The Human Use of Human Beings: Cybernetics and Society.* Garden City, Doubleday, 1951.

Index